Pilgrims Of New England:
A Tale Of The Early American Settlers

by

Mrs. J. B. Webb

Double 9
BOOKS

PILGRIMS OF NEW ENGLAND:
A TALE OF THE EARLY AMERICAN SETTLERS
by MRS. J. B. WEBB

ISBN: 978-93-59326-35-1

Published by

DOUBLE 9 BOOKS
2/13-B, Ansari Road, Daryaganj
New Delhi – 110002
info@double9books.com
www.double9books.com
Tel. 011-40042856

ABOUT THE AUTHOR

Mrs. J. B. Webb has worked on the amazing books with his amazing thoughts, which results in Naomi or the last days of Jerusalem. This collection of ideas is by Mrs. J. B. Webb attempts to compile many of his classic thoughts and offer them at an affordable price, in an attractive volume so that everyone can read them. Many of the books by Mrs. J. B. Webb has been out of print for decades and therefore have not been accessible to the general public. Her novel was well-received by critics at the time of its publication and has since become a classic of historical fiction.

CONTENTS

PREFACE

In the following story, an attempt has been made to illustrate the manners and habits of the earliest Puritan settlers in New England, and the trials and difficulties to which they were subjected during the first years of their residence in their adopted country. All the principal incidents that are woven into the narrative are strictly historical, and are derived from authentic sources, which give an impartial picture both of the virtues and the failings of these remarkable emigrants. Unhappily, some of these incidents prove but too clearly, how soon many of these exiles 'for conscience sake' forgot to practice those principles of religious liberty and toleration, for the preservation and enjoyment of which they had themselves abandoned home and kindred, and the church of their forefathers; and they tend to lessen the feelings of respect and admiration with which their piety, and their disinterested spirit, must necessarily inspire us. We cannot but regret to find how early, in many of the Puritan communities, that piety became tinged with fanaticism, and that free spirit degenerated into bigotry and intolerance in their treatment of others, who had an equal claim with themselves to a freedom of private judgement, and to the adoption or rejection of any peculiar forms or mode of discipline.

It is hoped, that a story founded on the history of these admirable, but sometimes misguided, men, may prove interesting to many who have hitherto been but slightly acquainted with the fate of their self-exiled countrymen; and may tend to remove the prejudice with which, in many minds, they are regarded: for, while we remember their errors and infirmities, we should also remember that their faults were essentially those of the age in which they lived, and the education they had received; while their virtues were derived from the pure faith that they possessed, and which was dearer to them than aught on earth beside.

KINGS PYON HOUSE, HEREFORD

CHAPTER I

The breaking waves dashed high
On a stern and rock-hound coast:
And the woods against a stormy sky,
Their giant branches tost.
And the heavy night hung dark
The hills and waters o'er,
When a hand of exiles moored their bark
On the wild New England shore. HEMANS.

It was, indeed, a stern and rock-bound coast beneath which the gallant little Mayflower furled her tattered sails, and dropped her anchor, on the evening of the eleventh of November, in the year 1620. The shores of New England had been, for several days, dimly descried by her passengers, through the gloomy mists that hung over the dreary and uncultivated tract of land towards which their prow was turned; but the heavy sea that dashed against the rocks, the ignorance of the captain and his crew with regard to the nature of the coast, and the crazy state of the deeply-laden vessel, had hitherto prevented their making the land. At length the ship was safely moored in a small inlet, beyond the reach of the foaming breakers; and the Pilgrim Fathers hastened to leave the vessel in which they had so long been imprisoned, and, with their families, to set foot on the land that was henceforth to be their home. Cold, indeed, was the welcome which they received from their adopted country; and cheerless was the view that met their gaze, as they landed on a massy rock of granite, at the foot of a precipitous cliff, and looked along the barren, inhospitable shore, and over the dark waters which they had so lately crossed.

But hope was strong in the hearts of these exiles; and the faith that had led them to seek these untrodden shores, had not deserted them during their long and tempestuous voyage; and they looked upward through the gloom and dreariness that surrounded them, and fixed their trusting eyes on Him who had guided them in safety over the great deep, and brought them at length to a resting-place. Their first act was to kneel down on the cold rock, and offer up their prayers and praises to that God for whose sake they had given up country, and friends, and home, and to whose service they now dedicated themselves and their children: and strikingly grand must have been that act of worship. The manly voices of the sturdy Pilgrims rose in deep and solemn unison, followed by those of the women and children, and resounded along the silent coast, while the heavy urges of the receding tide kept up a hoarse and monotonous accompaniment. Then arose a hymn of thanksgiving — and the rocks and the neighboring hills re-echoed the exulting strain, that seemed to drown the voices of the wind and the waves, and to rise unmixed to heaven. It was the triumph of faith — the holy and heartfelt expression of undying trust and confidence in God! Surely, at that time, the Pilgrims were meet objects for the admiring gaze of men and angels! But they were not always so.

It was on the shore of Cape Cod Bay that the new settlers had landed, in the inlet now called New Plymouth Harbor: but this was not the place of their original destination. They had intended to steer for the mouth of Hudson's River, and to have fixed their habitation in that less exposed and inhospitable district. But the Dutch had already conceived the project, which they afterwards accomplished, of settling in that part of the new continent; and it is supposed that the captain of the Mayflower was bribed by them to convey the English emigrants further to the north; so that the first American land which they beheld was Cape Cod. They found that the place where they had landed was beyond the precincts of the territory which had been granted to them; and even beyond that of the Company from which they derived their right of colonization; and after exploring hastily the neighboring coast, and finding it dreary and unpromising, they again embarked, and insisted on the captain's conveying them to the district which they had first desired to reach. They sailed to the south, and many days were lost in endeavoring to find a more convenient spot for their settlement: but it was in vain. The shoals and the breakers with which the coast was lined, presented obstacles that were insurmountable at that advanced, and unusually inclement, season; and, weary and disheartened, they returned to the place of their first landing. There they fixed their abode, and there they founded the infant city of New Plymouth. It was a desolate situation, and one that subjected the new settlers to many trials and privations; for the nearest English settlements then established were upwards of five hundred miles distant. Winter having set in with more than common severity, they felt that no more time could be wasted in seeking for a better spot, on which to build their first American habitations. Sickness also had begun to show itself among the little band of men, women, and children who were all unaccustomed to the hardships and confinement of a long voyage; and it was necessary to disembark with all possible speed, and erect huts to shelter them from the daily increasing inclemency of the weather. For this purpose, the forests of oak, pine, juniper, and sassafras, that had grown undisturbed for centuries along the coast, furnished them with abundant materials; and the woods soon echoed to the unaccustomed sound of the hatchet and the saw, at which all the men, of every rank and condition, labored unremittingly, while the women and children gathered up the great muscles, and other shell-fish, which abounded on the shore, and collected dry wood for firing.

But before we follow the settlers in the detail of their sufferings and trials, and of their ultimate success and prosperity, it will be needful to go back a few years, and consider the motives that led these brave men to expose themselves and their families to such severe hardships, and to abandon their home and their kindred. A brief glance at their previous history will suffice for this purpose.

It is well known that the Puritans were greatly dissatisfied with the state of the Church in England at the time when James the First ascended the throne of this country. From him they hoped for protection and encouragement; but in this expectation they were grievously disappointed. The conference at Hampton Court proved how little sympathy he entertained for their party; and the convocation which was held soon after utterly all their hopes. Already a considerable number of these dissenters had joined themselves into what they called a 'Church Estate, pledged to walk in God's ways,' and to renounce the evil passions of the world. They had protested against the episcopal form of church government, and declared their approval of the discipline and the forms adopted by the Church of Geneva, and also of that established in the Netherlands. In order to enjoy the liberty in ecclesiastical matters which they so greatly desired, they made up their minds to retire to Amsterdam, under their excellent and respected pastor, John Robinson; and this project was effected by the greater number of their party; though some were discovered before they could embark, and were detained and imprisoned, and treated with much severity. Ultimately, however, they all escaped, and remained unmolested at Amsterdam and the Hague, until the year 1608, when they removed to Leyden with their pastor, where they resided for eleven years, and were joined by many others who fled from England during the early part of the reign of James.

These men now felt that their only hope of enjoying perfect religious liberty, and of establishing a church according to their own dearly-loved principles, lay in a voluntary exile. Their English prejudices made them shrink from continuing to dwell among the Dutch, who had hitherto given them a hospitable asylum; for they feared that, by frequent intermarriages, they should eventually lose their nationality; and they resolved to seek a new home, where they might found an English colony, and, while they followed that mode of worship which was alone consistent with their views and principles; might still be subjects of the English crown, and keep up an intercourse with the friends they dearly loved, and the land where their forefathers had lived and died.

The recent discovery of the vast continent of America, in several parts of which the British had already begun to form colonies, opened to them a field of enterprise, as well as a quiet refuge from persecution and controversy; and thither the Puritans turned their eyes. Nor were they the first who had taken advantage of the unoccupied wastes of the New World, and sought in them an asylum from intolerant oppression. Already a numerous band of French Huguenots had retired thither, under the conduct of their celebrated Calvinistic leader, De Monts, who was invested with the government of the district lying between Montreal and Philadelphia, by a patent from his sovereign, Henry the Fourth. No traces of this colony now remain, while those planted by the English Puritans have taken root in the American soil, and flourished so greatly, that a few years ago their descendants were found to amount to 4,000,000: so remarkably has the blessing of God, at least in temporal matters, been bestowed on an enterprise which was, doubtless, undertaken in dependence on His protection; and was carried out with that fortitude and resolution which are the results of sincere piety struggling with deep adversity.[*]

[Footnote: For this account of the cause which led to the emigration of the Puritans, and the manner in which they effected it, the authoress is chiefly indebted to Mardens History of the Puritans, and Talvis History of the Colonization of America.]

The idea of retiring to the shores of America was first suggested to his followers by their pastor, John Robinson, whose influence over his flock was almost unexampled. This influence was derived from the purity of his life, and the holy consistency of his conduct. He was possessed of a gentle temper; and the strictness of his religious principles was united with a spirit of toleration towards others, which was too little felt or practiced in those days, and which was not, as is too often the case, changed into bitterness by the sufferings that he had himself experienced. Well had it been for those who professed to be guided by his example and advice, and who left the shores of Europe with the sanction of his counsel and his blessing, if they had carried with them the truly Christian spirit of their respected minister, and had suffered that spirit to guide them in the formation, and during the growth, of their infant church in America! But, as we shall presently see, this was not the case: the mercy and toleration which the Puritan exiles had vainly asked at the hands of their brethren at home, they denied to others who differed from them; and, consequently, while they have so greatly prospered in the things of this world, in religion they have evidently declined.

Emigration being resolved on, the first step that was taken by the Puritans, was an application to King James for an assurance of protection and toleration in the new home which they desired to seek; but this was more than the wary king would guarantee to them. All that they could obtain was a vague promise, that so long as they conducted themselves peaceably, they should not be molested; and, relying on this promise, they immediately commenced a negotiation with the Virginian Company, for the possession of a tract of land within the limits of the patent which had been granted to them for colonizing that part of America. This was easily obtained; for the Society had hitherto only been able to occupy a few isolated spots of their extensive territory, and, therefore, were willing to encourage fresh settlers.

The congregation over which Robinson presided, amounted, at the time of their intended emigration, to upwards of three hundred in number; but their resources were inadequate to the expense of moving all together, and it was therefore arranged that only a part of the flock should sail at first, under the guidance of William Brewster; while the rest should remain at Leyden, under the care of their pastor, and wait for the report of their friends before they followed them to their chosen place of exile.

The names of the vessels which were engaged to convey the Pilgrims from the shores of Europe, were the Mayflower and the Speedwell—names still cherished by heir descendants. When they were ready for sea, the whole congregation assembled themselves together, and observed a solemn fast, which concluded with prayer; and Robinson preached to them from Ezra viii, 21: 'Then I proclaimed a fast there, at the river of Ahava, that we might afflict ourselves before our God, to seek of him a right way for us, and for our little ones, and for all our substance.' He afterwards addressed them in a deeply impressive speech, in which he earnestly deprecated all party spirit and bigotry, and exhorted them to be guided only by the pure doctrines of God's Word.

'I charge you,' said this truly Christian and evangelical minister, 'that you follow me no further than you have seen me follow the Lord Jesus Christ. The Lord has more truth yet to break forth out of his Holy Word. I cannot sufficiently bewail the condition of the reformed churches, which are come to a period in religion, and will go, at present, no further than the instruments of their reformation. Luther and Calvin were great and shining lights in their times, yet they penetrated not into the whole counsel of God. The Lutherans cannot be drawn to go beyond what Luther saw; and the Calvinists, you see, stick fast where they were left by that great man of God.

[*] I beseech you, remember it — 'tis an article of your church covenant — that you shall be ready to receive whatever truth shall be made known to you from the Word of God.

[Footnote: See Remarks on the Dangers of the Church,' by Rev. Edward Bickersteth.]

The congregation then repaired to the house of their pastor, and partook of a farewell repast together; after which they proceeded to Delft Harbor, and there the Pilgrims embarked. Again their minister offered up fervent prayer in behalf of this portion of his flock who were about to encounter the dangers of a long voyage, and to seek a home in an almost unknown land — and then in deep silence they parted. 'No cheers or noisy acclamations resounded along the shore, for such demonstrations were little in accordance with the usual serious habits of the Puritans, and still less so with the feelings of sadness which now oppressed their hearts. But a volley of small shot, and three pieces of ordnance,' writes Winslow, one of the emigrants, 'announced to those on shore the hearty courage and affectionate adieus of those on board; and so, lifting up our hands to one another, and our hearts to the Lord, we departed.'

Thus the Pilgrims set sail, with mingled feelings of hope for the future, and regret for what they left behind; and greatly would their sorrow have been increased, had they known that they would never again behold on earth the countenance of their much-loved pastor. They fully anticipated his following them, with the rest of their brethren, as soon as they should have found a suitable place of settlement for the whole congregation. But poverty and other obstacles detained him in Europe, and he terminated his useful and exemplary life at Leyden.

The emigrants had not proceeded far on their voyage, when it was discovered that the Mayflower, commanded by Captain Jones, was in need of some repairs; and the two vessels put into Dartmouth — not to sail together again. The captain of the Speedwell declared that he was afraid to encounter the voyage; and from this, or some other motive, he positively refused to proceed any further. Several of the passengers also, had already begun to feel disheartened, and they returned with him to London, and abandoned the enterprise altogether. Doubtless, the Pilgrims bad no cause to lament the departure of these faint-hearted comrades; but it occasioned them much present inconvenience, for, not being able to procure another vessel to convey the remainder of the passengers who had embarked in the Speedwell, they were all obliged to be crowded into the Mayflower, which sailed again on the sixth of September, 1620, with considerably upwards of a hundred men, women, and children on her narrow decks, in addition to her own crew of seamen.

After a very tedious and tempestuous voyage, they came in sight of the American shores on the eighth of November; and, as we have already seen, they landed three days afterwards in Cape Cod Bay, and eventually founded the city of New Plymouth at the place of their disembarkation. A portion of the granite rock on which the Pilgrim Fathers first set foot has since been removed from the coast, and placed in front of' The Pilgrim's Hall,' enclosed in an iron railing; and the anniversary of their landing, afterwards called Forefather's-day, has ever since been observed by their descendants as a day of solemn festivity, in remembrance of the mercy of Providence, which led them safely through so many difficulties and dangers; and permitted them to find a new home, and a new country, and to bring their enterprise to such a prosperous issue.

It is with the first period of their establishment on the uncultivated shores of North America that our story commences; and it is connected with the sufferings and privations which were so patiently endured, and the difficulties which were so resolutely overcome, by these devoted men, before they had taken root in their new settlement, or gathered around themselves and their families the comforts which they had abandoned in their own land for conscience sake. Many trials awaited them ere prosperity became their portion, and ere they could feel either rest or security in the wild regions where they had sought a refuge: and these trials will be brought more distinctly to our minds, if we view them in connection with some of the individuals of the expedition, and follow the fortunes of one family more particularly. This family we will call by the name of Maitland, and endeavor in their somewhat imaginary history, to describe the mode of life, and some of the joys and sorrows—the difficulties and successes—of the Pilgrim Fathers.

Owing to the many delays which the emigrants had experienced, a severe winter had set in before they landed, and had fixed a spot for their permanent abode; and they found themselves exposed to the inclemency of a North climate, with no other shelter than a few tents, besides that which the vessel continued to afford. In haste they felled the trees of the neighboring forests; and in haste they constructed the village of log huts which was to be their present abode, and which, ultimately, grew into the flourishing and wealthy city of New Plymouth. In the erection of this hamlet, no head was so fertile in plans and expedients, and no arms were so strong to execute them, as those of Rodolph Maitland, the head of the family in whom we are specially interested. He was a younger member of a very respectable family in the North of England, and had passed his youth and early manhood in the service of his country as a soldier. This profession, however, became distasteful to him when the religious dissensions which troubled the land called on him, at times, to obey his commander in carrying out schemes of oppression which were contrary both to his feelings and his principles. His marriage with Helen Seatown, the daughter of a nonconforming minister, increased his repugnance to bearing arms, which might be turned against the party to which he was now so closely connected; and he threw up his commission, and soon afterwards accompanied his father-in-law to Holland, and joined the congregation of the respected Robinson at Leyden.

Here he continued to reside until the resolution to emigrate was formed by the Puritan refugees, when he was among the first to embrace the proposition of the pastor, and to lend all the aid which his comparative wealth, and the influence of his connections in England, enabled him to offer in furtherance of the enterprise. His father-in- law had died soon after his arrival at Leyden; but his amiable and devoted wife was most willing to follow him in his voluntary exile, and to take her children to the New World, where she hoped to bring them up in the same principles of pure evangelical religion which she had learnt from her own parents, and which were dearer to her than home or friends or aught on earth besides.

At the time when the Pilgrims reached America, the Maitlands family consisted of two sons, Henrich and Ludovico; the elder of whom was sixteen years of age, and the younger about seven; and one little girl between ten and eleven, named Edith. In the thoughtful seriousness of his eldest boy, which was united with great intelligence and spirit, and a manly resolution beyond his years, Rodolph saw his own character again depicted; and Helen proudly hoped that her Henrich would one day manifest all those qualities of mind and person by which his father had first won her admiration and love, and by which he had since gained the esteem and affection of all who were in any way connected with him. Henrich was now old enough to understand, and almost to appreciate, the motives which had induced his parents and their companions to become exiles from home: and his young heart exulted in the resolution that freed him from the cold formality of Dutch manners, and opened to his adventurous spirit a prospect of liberty and enterprise, far better suited to his inclination and character. Religious freedom he desired, because he had been taught that it was his rightful privilege, and that the want of it had occasioned those troubles which first drove his parents and friends from their native land. But personal freedom he yearned for with his whole soul; and the wild shores of New England,

and the depths of the unexplored forests that now met his eager gaze, filled his ardent mind with anticipations of adventurous joys hitherto unknown to him. These anticipations were destined to be fulfilled, ere long, in a manner which he neither foresaw nor desired.

His brother Ludovico was a playful child, too young to share all the feelings of the earnest Henrich, who always acted as his guide and protector during their sports and rambles; but in the gentle little Edith he found a kindred spirit, and a heart that could sympathize in all his joys and sorrows. Young as she was, Edith felt the influence of her brother's character; and she looked up to him with feelings of devoted love and admiring pride. She was his constant companion, and his ever-ready assistant in all his difficulties. This had been very much the case during their residence in Holland; but on their arrival in New England, Edith was left still more to her brother's guidance. Their parents were necessarily too much occupied with the cares end anxieties which their new situation brought upon them, to devote much time to their children; and when the light labors in which Henrich and Edith were able to render any assistance were over, they and Ludovico amused themselves by wandering along the shore in search of shells and seaweed; or else they followed the wood-cutters into the forest, to seek for such flowering plants as still were to be found in the more sheltered spots, and to transplant them to the garden that was to surround and embellish their rude dwelling.

As soon as a tolerable shelter had been obtained, by the erection of a sufficient number of log-huts, to contain the families of the settlers, it was resolved that a party of men should go on an exploring expedition, and endeavor to ascertain the nature and resources of the coast on which they had landed; and, also, whether it was inhabited by any tribes of native Indians. Hitherto they had seen no human beings, and they had remained undisturbed possessors of the soil. But they could hardly expect that this state of things would long continue; and they were anxious, if possible, to discover the native inhabitants and natural possessors of the country, and to establish friendly relations with them.

Sixteen of the Pilgrims volunteered for this expedition, headed by Rodolph Maitland, whose military experience, and superior intelligence, well fitted him to be the leader of the party. The rest of the men remained to protect their families, and to complete the village; which already presented a very respectable appearance, and promised to afford a tolerably comfortable residence to the new settlers, until they should have leisure and means to erect dwellings more in accordance with their previous habits of life.

The government of the little colony was unanimously confided to John Carver, who was elected President for one year; but he did not live long to exercise his authority, or to enjoy the confidence reposed in him by his fellow-settlers. During the short period, however, that he was spared to them, he exerted himself successfully to promote the welfare of the community, and to preserve peace and unanimity among the members of which it was composed; and before the departure of the exploring party, he called on all the Pilgrim Fathers to sign a covenant, which had been drawn up during the voyage, and which contained a statement of the peculiar religious principles of the congregation, and also of the mode of civil government that they proposed to establish in the colony. This government was not to be independent of the mother country, for the Pilgrims regarded themselves as still being the subjects of King James; and the patent which they had procured to enable them to settle in New England was granted by the Company to whom the king had assigned the right of colonizing that part of North America. They, therefore, intended to be governed mainly by English laws, and to keep up a constant and intimate connection with their English brethren. It may be well here to mention that their plan of civil government consisted in the election of a governor or president by general vote, and of seven counselors to assist him; the only privilege granted to the president being that his vote counted double. This state of things continued for eighteen years, after which time the growth of the colony rendered a change expedient, and each new town that was founded sent delegates to a general court. It would, however, be useless here to follow the political changes of these early settlers, as it is only with their first form of government that our story is concerned.

According to the habitual custom of the Pilgrims, the Sabbath which preceded the sending forth this band of spies to search the land, was observed with the utmost solemnity; for no press of occupations—no necessity for haste—ever induced them to neglect this duty. For the liberty of practicing their own mode of worship, they had sought these shores; and, having been permitted safely to reach them, they used that liberty, and were never unmindful of their religious privileges. Every Sabbath was a day of sacred rest; and every undertaking was sanctified by prayer; sometimes even, as we shall have occasion to observe, when the undertaking was such as could hardly be supposed to deserve the blessing of God. Still, there is every reason to believe that their piety, as a body, was sincere; and while we condemn the sternness and severity into which they were too frequently betrayed, we must yield our heartfelt approbation to the self-denying resolution and unflinching faith that were their governing principle and their ever- actuating motive. Well have these principles and motives been described by a late well-known poet, and well may we conclude this introductory chapter with the last verse of that exquisite song, with the first of which we commenced it:

'What sought they thus afar?
Bright jewels of the mine?
The wealth of seas, the spoils of war?
They sought a faith's pure shrine.
Aye—call it holy ground
The soil where first they trod!
They have left unstain'd what there they found
Freedom to worship God!'

CHAPTER II

'In much patience, in afflictions, in necessities, In distresses As having nothing, and yet possessing all things.' —2 COR. vi, 4, 10.

'Is it not much that I may worship Him,
With naught my spirit's breathings to control,
And feel His presence in the vast, and dim,
And whispering woods, where dying thunders roll
From the far cat'racts?' HEMANS.

With some anxiety the settlers saw the exploring party set out on their hazardous enterprise. The season was far advanced, and drifting snowstorms gave warning of the inclement winter that was rapidly setting in. Still it was deemed necessary to make some investigation into the nature of the country, and to endeavor to obtain, if possible, a supply of provisions before the increasing severity of the weather should render it impracticable to do so. But, above all, it was desirable to ascertain what native tribes dwelt in the vicinity of the settlement, and to use every means to establish friendly relations with them; not only because such a course would be most in accordance with the principles of the Gospel which the emigrants professed to hold and to practice, but also because, in the present state of the infant colony, they were altogether unprepared to resist any attack that might be made on them by a large body of Indians.

Maitland led his party inland at first, and for two days they saw no traces or human inhabitants; but on the afternoon of the third day, as they were looking about for a convenient spot on which to encamp for the night, some large and apparently artificial mounds of earth were observed, scattered over an open glade in the forest. At the first glance, they appeared like dwelling places; and, knowing something of the habits of the Indians, Rodolph and two of his companions approached them warily, fearing to surprise and irritate the inhabitants. But after making a circuit, and ascertaining that these supposed huts had no doorways, they went up to them, and found them to be solid mounds, at the foot of which neatly plaited baskets, filled with ears of maize, were placed. These were eagerly seized upon; and a further search being made, several warlike and agricultural implements were discovered buried beneath the surface of the earth. It was evident that these mounds were native graves, and that they had recently been visited by the tribe to which they belonged, who most probably resided in the neighborhood. Therefore, to avoid exciting their displeasure and jealousy, Rodolph caused all the weapons and other tools to be restored to their places; and, in exchange for the corn, which was too much needed to be left behind, he put into the baskets several strings of beads, and other trifles, with which he was provided for the purpose of barter, or as presents to the natives.

It did not appear either safe or desirable to remain near a spot so sacred to the Indians; the party therefore moved further into the depth of the forest, where they erected their tents, which consisted merely of blankets supported on poles; and, lighting large fires, they slept by turns, while half their number kept a vigilant watch. Their rest was, however, undisturbed, either by lurking Indians or by prowling beasts of prey; and at day-break they resumed their march, in the hope of discovering the native camp. But their search was in vain; and Rodolph determined to leave the forest, and return to the settlement along the shore, hoping there to find some traces of the natives. Before he and his comrades left the shelter of the wood, they fired their muskets at the small game which abounded in every direction, partly with a view to supply themselves with food, and partly to attract the notice of any straggling Indians who might be wandering near, and who would conduct them to their wigwams. But the echoes were the only sounds that answered their reports, and it was clear that no native camp was within hearing.

The place where Maitland and his little band reached the coast was nearly twenty leagues from the settlement, towards the north, and has since been known by the name of Angoum. Here they found two empty huts, containing all the curiously-worked utensils used by the Indians of that district—bowls, trays, and dishes, formed of calabashes and carved wood or bark; and beautiful baskets constructed of crabshells, ingeniously wrought together, with well-woven mats of grass and bulrushes, dyed of various brilliant colors. The inhabitants had probably gone on a fishing expedition, and would return in a few days, as they had left behind them a considerable quantity of dried acorns, which, at that period, formed a common article of food with these children of the forest.

Rodolph suffered nothing to be taken from the huts, but proceeded along the coast in a southerly direction and, at length, he perceived two canoes at a considerable distance from the shore, containing several Indians, who took no notice of the signals they made, but rowed rapidly away on an opposite course. Finding it useless to linger any longer in this part of the bay, Maitland led his party back to the settlement at New Plymouth, taking accurate observations of the line of coast, and communicated to President Carver all the information that he had been able to collect. This was not very satisfactory; and the governor resolved to send out a second party, well armed, who should proceed in the shallop to the southern part of Cape Cod Bay. This expedition was placed under the command of Captain Standish, who was regarded as the military chief of the settlers; and Maitland again formed one of the number. On this occasion he obtained permission to take Henrich with him, as he wished the boy to become early inured to the hardships and privations which it would probably be his lot to bear for many years, and also to acquire habits of courage and vigilance that might be of service to him hereafter. Henrich was delighted with this arrangement, which gratified his desire for adventure, and also proved that his father now placed some confidence in him, and no longer regarded him as a mere child. His astonishment was great when first he beheld the whales, those huge and fearful-looking monsters of the ocean, lifting their gigantic heads above the waves, and lashing the surface to foam with their powerful tails; or ejecting vast spouts of water like fountains, from their upraised heads. These, and many other strange objects, attracted his attention as the boat moved down the bay; but all were forgotten in the absorbing interest with which he regarded, for the first time, the wild red men that met his view as the boat neared the shore, at a spot about eight leagues from New Plymouth, called by the Pilgrims *Thievish Harbor*. Several of these savages, in their strange attire of skins, and feathers, and woven grasses, showed themselves among the rocks that stood above the landing-place; but, regardless of the peaceful signs that were made to them by Captain Standish and his crew, they hastily retreated and when the party disembarked, not an Indian was to be seen. With much circumspection, the captain advanced at the head of his resolute band, who all held their muskets ready for action, if self-defense should compel them to use them; but with a positive order from their commander to refrain from any act of hostility so long as it was possible to do so.

This command could not, however, be long obeyed; for as the party proceeded through the rocks and stunted trees that lined the coast, they came in sight of a burial ground, similar to that which had been discovered in the first expedition, except that, in this case, the mounds of earth were enclosed by a strong palisade of upright poles, bound together firmly at the top. Through the interstices of these poles, Standish and his men saw the glittering eyes of the savages watching their approach; and before they could decide whether to advance or retreat, a shower of arrows was discharged, several of which took effect, though not mortally. This wanton aggression roused the spirit of the sturdy Englishmen, and regardless of the efforts which Captain Standish made to restrain them, a volley of musket balls instantly replied to the challenge of the red men; and the wild cries that arose from the cemetery plainly told that they had not sped in vain. Even Rodolph Maitland was surprised out of his usual calm resolution and presence of mind; for he saw his son fall bleeding to the ground, pierced through the leg by an arrow, and almost involuntarily he fired off his musket at an Indian whose body was more exposed than the rest, and whose greater profusion of ornament showed him to be one of their chief warriors. Rodolph saw him fall from the palisades on which he had climbed to take a better aim at the white men; and instantly a gate was opened in the enclosure, and, with a hideous yell, the savages rushed forth, brandishing their spears and battle-axes, and shouting their war-cry, 'Woach! woach! ha, ha, hach, woach!' Their number appeared to be about thirty men; and Standish knew that his party, several of whom were already slightly wounded, could not resist the fury of their attack. He therefore gave the word for an instant retreat to the boat, as the only means of safety. His gallant band would gladly have pressed on, and met the savages in close combat; but they had promised to obey their leader, and reluctantly they followed him to the shore.

The path by which they had emerged on the burial-place was narrow and winding, and they were soon hidden from the sight of the Indians; but they heard their wild whoop among the rocks and bushes, and knew that they were in eager pursuit. Maitland had caught up his wounded boy in his arms, and now bore him rapidly forward; but the weight of his burden, and the roughness of the way, retarded his steps and, powerful as he was, he could not keep up with his comrades, who were unconscious that he had fallen behind them. He thought of his wife—of Henrich's mother—and he pat forth his utmost strength. Still the war cry came nearer and nearer; and Henrich, who had hitherto uttered no sound of pain, or word of complaint exclaimed wildly—

Father! I see them! There—there—they have entered the thicket, and one has climbed the rock, and will soon overtake us. O, father, fly! for his battle-axe is lifted up, and his eyes glare terribly'

Maitland's heart beat furiously. He could not pause, or turn, to look at the coming foe; but his quick and ready mind was active in devising some means of saving the life of his child.

'Load my gun, Henrich!' he exclaimed. 'I cannot long continue this speed. Be steady, and be quick: our lives depend upon it!'

The gallant boy instantly obeyed the difficult command; and the instant it was done, Rodolph dropped on one knee, supported his bleeding son on the other, and taking a deliberate aim at the Indian, who was preparing to leap from the rock into the path behind them, he fired. The upraised arms of the savage fell powerless—the heavy axe dropped from his hand—and, falling forward over the rock, he lay expiring in the narrow pathway. The feathery coronets of several of his comrades were seen above the bushes at some distance: and again the father raised his son, who now hung fainting in his arms, and hurried, with renewed speed, towards the shore. As he neared it, he met two of his companions who, having reached the boat, had missed him and Henrich, and hastened back to secure their retreat. It was a seasonable reinforcement, for Rodolph's strength was failing him. He gave his boy into the arms of one of his friends, and loading his gun, he stood with the other, to defend the passage to the shore. The savages came on; and the white men fired, and retreated, loading as they fell back, and again firing; until their pursuers, either wounded or disheartened, came to a stand still, and contented themselves with yelling their discordant war-cry, and shooting arrows, which happily missed their aim.

The whole party embarked safely, and were soon beyond the reach of the missiles which the Indians continued to discharge; and Maitland had the joy of seeing young Henrich speedily recover his senses, and his spirit too. It was evident that the arrows used by the red men on this occasion were not poisoned, and no great or permanent evil was likely to arise from any of the wounds received; but a spirit of hostility had been established between the settlers and the Nausett tribe, to which their assailants belonged, and Rodolph was a marked man, and an object of determined revenge, to all who had shared in the conflict. The spot where it took place was named *the First Encounter*, in memory of the event, and long retained that name: and the consequences of this first combat proved to be equally calamitous to the savages, and to their more civilized foes, for many subsequent years.

The exploring party returned to their settlement as speedily as possible, being anxious to obtain medical relief for the wounded. Helen Maitland and her children were wandering on the shore when the boat first came in sight; and for several evenings the desolate coast had been her constant haunt, after the necessary labors of the day were completed. It had been with much reluctance that she had consented to her husband's wish of taking Henrich on the hazardous expedition; and his being of the party had greatly increased the anxiety and uneasiness which Rodolph's absence always caused her. As the days passed on, this anxiety became greater; and visions of fatal encounters with the savages beset her naturally timid mind. Daily therefore she left her hut, and wrapped in the mantle of fur with which her husband had provided her before he brought her to brave a North American winter, she paced backwards and forwards on the beach, looking out over the dark waters, and lifting her heart in prayer for the safe and speedy return of the wanderers. Edith and Ludovico accompanied her but they could not share her anxiety. They looked, indeed, with eagerness for the expected boat which was to bring back their much-loved father and brother; but they soon forgot the object of their search, and amused themselves by climbing the rocks, and gathering the shells which the wintry waves now cast up in abundance.

They were thus engaged when Edith happened to glance to the south and saw the long desired coming round a little promontory that concealed it from her mother as she walked below. In an instant the treasure of shells and seaweed was forgotten, and little Edith was bounding down to the beach, followed by Ludovico.

'The boat mother, the boat!' she eagerly exclaimed, as she pointed in the direction in which it was approaching; and in another moment she and her little brother were at Helen's side, and all hastening to the landing-place—that very granite rock on which they had first disembarked on the American shore. The boat came rear; and as soon as the crew perceived Helen and the children on the rock, they raised a hearty cheer to tell her that all was well. She saw her husband standing on the prow, and her heart bounded with joy; but she looked for Henrich, and she did not see him, and fear mingled with her joy. A few more strokes of the oars, and the boat glided up to the rock, and Rodolph leaped on shore, and embraced his wife and children.

'Heaven be praised! you are safe, my Rodolph,' exclaimed Helen. 'But where is Henrich?—where is my boy?

'He also is safe, Helen. His life is preserved; but he is wounded, and unable to come from the boat to meet you. Bear up,' he added, seeing that she trembled violently, while the tears flowed down her blanched cheeks 'you need not fear: the brave boy is maimed, indeed, but I trust not seriously injured. He is weak from loss of blood, and must not be agitated; therefore meet him cheerfully, and then hasten to make the arrangements for his comfort that your scanty means will permit.'

Helen dried her tears, and forced, a smile to greet her wounded child, who was now being lifted from the bottom of the boat, and gently carried on shore by two of the men. His pallid countenance, and blood-stained garments, struck a chill to her heart; but she concealed her grief, and silenced the sobs and exclamations of the warm-hearted little Edith and her terrified brother; and then, having affectionately welcomed the almost fainting boy, she hurried away with the children to prepare for his reception in the comfortless log-hut.

Assisted by Janet—the faithful servant who had nursed her children, and followed her from England to Holland, and from Holland to America—she soon arranged a bed for their patient; and Henrich smiled cheerfully, though languidly, when he found himself again beneath the humble roof that was now his home, and surrounded by all whom he loved. His wound proved to be a severe one—more so than his father had imagined; and the loss of blood had been so considerable that he was reduced to extreme weakness. Now it was that Helen felt the absence of all the comforts, and even luxuries, to which she had been accustomed from childhood, but of whose loss she had hitherto never complained. Henrich's illness proved a very long and painful one; and notwithstanding the kindness of all her friends, and the attentions paid by the rest of the settlers to the young patient—who was a general favorite—it was difficult to procure for him either the food or the medical attendance that his case required: and frequently his parents feared that a foreign grave would soon be all that would remain to them of their dearly-loved child.

To add to their anxiety and distress, an epidemic disease, of which some signs had appeared in the settlement before the exploring party set out, now increased to a fearful degree. The stores which had been brought out in the crowded Mayflower were nearly expended, except such a stock as Captain Jones considered necessary for the voyage back to England: and a great scarcity of bread began to be felt. The animals, which they procured by the gun and the chase, were not sufficient to supply the wants of the settlers, and famine—actual famine—stared them in the face, and increased the violence of the pestilence. Many sank beneath the accumulated evils of hardship, privation, and sickness, and the number of the little settlement was sadly reduced during the inclement months of January and February.

The constant care which was bestowed on Henrich at length proved effectual in healing his wound, and partially restoring his strength; and his parents had, eventually, the happiness of seeing that the a anger was past, and their son was restored to them. They also had cause to acknowledge, with gratitude, that the affliction had been blessed to him as well as to themselves. The elders of the community, who acted as the pastors of the infant colony, were unwearied in their attentions to their weaker and more distressed brethren. They were, indeed, the physicians both of their bodies and souls; and Henrich was not neglected by them. The excellent and venerable William Brewster was the intimate and valued friend of Rodolph Maitland and his wife. He had been both their friend and adviser for many years of comparative peace and prosperity; and now that he shared their troubles and adversities, his ready sympathy, and active kindness, rendered him dearer to them than ever.

Brewster was a man whose character and position in life naturally gave him great influence with the Pilgrim Fathers. He had received a liberal education, and possessed a far greater knowledge of the world than the generality of his companions in exile, having been brought up as a diplomatist under Davison, when he was Secretary of State to Queen Elisabeth. He was devoted to the cause of religious liberty; and it was he who had assisted his friend, John Robinson, in withdrawing his congregation from the persecution that threatened them in England, to a peaceful asylum in Holland. At the time of the emigration to America, he was already in the decline of life; but his energies were in no degree weakened, and his zeal for the glory of God, and the good of his fellow Christians, was unabated.

He desired to spend all his remaining years in promoting the welfare of the colony, and in proclaiming the Gospel to the heathen; and while he was ever mindful of the wants, both spiritual and temporal, of the flock ever whom he was appointed to preside, until their pastor Robinson could join them, he never forgot the grand object of his voluntary exile, or ceased to pray that the Lord would be pleased to open 'a great door and effectual,' before him, and enable him to bring many of the savage and ignorant natives into the fold of Christ. In all these plans he was warmly seconded by Edward Winslow, but hitherto no such opening had appeared and the sickness and distress which prevailed in the settlement gave full occupation to them and to their brother elders. During all the period of Henrich's tedious illness, not a day passed in which Brewster did not visit the suffering boy to cheer him, to soothe him, and, above all, to prepare him for that better world to which he then believed he was surely hastening. To these visits Henrich looked forward with delight; and often, when domestic business called away his mother and Janet, the minister would remain with him for hours, seated on a low stool by of his bed, and read to him, or talk to him, in a strain so holy and yet so cheerful, that Edith would leave her work and softly seat herself on Henrich's couch, that she might catch his every word, while little Ludovico would cease from his noisy sports, and creep up on the good man's knee, and fix his large soft eyes on his sweet and noble countenance.

These hours were not unimproved by Henrich. His character was formed, and his principles were fixed, and his mind and spirit grew strong and ripe beyond his years. Never were these hours of peaceful happiness forgotten; and often amid the strange and stirring scenes which it was his lot in after-life to witness and to share, did he bless the over- ruling providence of God, which had laid him on a bed of pain and weakness, that he might learn lessons of piety and of usefulness, which otherwise he would never have acquired.

It was while they were thus happily engaged one afternoon, when Henrich was slowly recovering his strength, that the elder and his young audience were startled by wild and discordant sounds, mingled with cries of fear, which proceeded from the outskirts of the straggling village, and seemed to be approaching. Henrich raised himself on his bed, and a look of terror overspread his countenance, as he exclaimed: 'It is the war cry of the savages! O! I know it well! Go, Mr. Brewster, fly! save my mother. I will follow you.'

And the brave boy tried to leap from the couch, and reach his father's sword, which hung against the wooden walls of his chamber. But it was in vain; the wounded leg refused to bear his weight, and he was forced to relinquish his design. Brewster, however, snatched the sword, and drawing it, rushed from the hut, leaving Edith and Ludovico clinging with trembling hands around their brother.

Henrich's fears proved but too true. No sooner had the elder traversed the enclosure that surrounded Maitland's dwelling, than he beheld Helen, and several of the other women who had gone out to assist their husbands in the lighter parts of their agricultural labors, flying in terror and confusion to their huts, while the men were engaged in close combat with a party of native Indians. The same war-cry which had rung on their ears in the first encounter told Rodolph and his comrades that these savages were of the same tribe, and probably the same individuals from whom they had escaped with such difficulty on that occasion. They were right; for it was indeed a band of the Nausetts, who, headed by their Chief, had come to seek revenge for the loss they had sustained at their former meeting. The warrior whom Rodolph's musket had laid low was Tekoa, the only son of the Nausett chief; and he was resolved that the white man's blood should flow, to expiate the deed. He knew that the son of the stranger who had slain his young warrior had been wounded, and, as he hoped, mortally; but that did not suffice for his revenge, and he had either suddenly attacked the settlement, in the hope of securing either Rudolph himself or some of his comrades, that he might shed the white man's blood on the grave of his son, and tear off their scalps as trophies of victory.

The settlers who now contended with the savages were but few in number, for many of the men lay sick, and many had died; and they were mostly unarmed, except with their agricultural implements. Rudolph and a few others had short swords, or dirks, attached to their girdles, and with these they dealt blows that told with deadly effect on the half-naked bodies of their foes; and the good broad-sword that Brewster quickly placed in Maitland's hand, was not long in discomfiting several of the Indians, who had singled him out, at the command of their Chief, as the special object of their attack. Meanwhile, many of the women, and such of the invalids as had power to rise, had again left the huts, and borne to their husbands and friends the arms which had been left in their dwellings; and in spite of the arrows and darts of the Indians, by which several of them were wounded, they continued to load the guns for the combatants while the conflict lasted. Happily this was not long. The *fire-breathing* muskets struck terror into the ignorant savages; and when two or three of their number had fallen, they turned to fly; first, however, catching up the bodies of their comrades, which they carried off to ensure their honorable burial, and to save them from the indignities which they supposed the pale-faces would heap on the dead.

In vain their Chief endeavored to rally them, and compel them to return to the conflict. In vain he waved his battle-axe on high, and shouted his war-whoop, Woach! woach! ha, ha, hach, woach!' A panic had seized his followers, and they fled precipitately into the forest from they had issued, so suddenly and so fiercely, to the attack. One warrior stood alone by the Chief. He was young and handsome, but his countenance was dark and sinister and an expression of cunning was strongly marked in his glittering deep-set eyes and overhanging brows. He saw that it was hopeless to contend any longer with the powerful strangers, and, by words and actions, he was evidently persuading the Chief to retire. The settlers had ceased to fire the moment that their enemies fled; and there was a deep silence, while every eye was fixed on the striking figure of the enraged Chief, whose every feature was distorted by excited passions. He stood with his tomahawk uplifted, and his tall and muscular figure in an attitude of command and defiance; while, in a loud and distinct voice, he uttered a vow of vengeance, the words of which were unintelligible to the settlers, though the meaning could easily be guessed from his looks and gestures. Then he hung his battle-axe to his gaudy belt, and pointing his hand at Rodolph, he retired slowly and majestically like a lion discomfited but not subdued, to seek his people and to upbraid them with their cowardice.

This attack of the Indians effectually destroyed all feelings of security in the minds of the settlers. Henceforth they were obliged, like the Jews of old, to go to their labor every man with his sword girded to his side, and continually to hold themselves in readiness for a sudden assault. The pestilence continued to rage, and the scarcity of food increased to such a degree, that for several weeks no bread was to be been in the settlement. The governor, Mr. Carver, exerted himself with zeal and benevolence to lesser the misery of his people; but with so little effect, that when the spring at length set in, and the captain of the Mayflower prepared to return to England, the little band of settlers was found to be reduced to one half the original number; and these were weakened by illness, and by want of proper nourishment.

But great as were their difficulties and sufferings, their faith and resolution never failed; and when the Mayflower again set sail for England, not one of the fifty emigrants who remained expressed a desire to return.

CHAPTER III

What men were they? Of dark-brown color,
With sunny redness; wild of eye; their tinged brows
So smooth, as never yet anxiety
Nor busy thought had made a furrow there.
. . . . Soon the courteous guise
Of men, not purporting nor fearing ill,
Won confidence: their wild distrustful looks
Assumed a milder meaning. MADOC.

We have said that the band of the exiles was reduced to half the number that had, six months before, left the shores of Europe, so full of hope and of holy resolution; and still, in spite of all their outward trials and difficulties, the hope and the resolution of the survivors were as high and as firm as ever. They trusted in the God whom they had served so faithfully; and they knew that, in his own good time, he would give them deliverance. But their days of darkness were not yet over. The inclemency of the winter had indeed passed away, and the face of nature began to smile upon them; yet sickness still prevailed, and the many graves that rose on the spot which they had chosen for a burial ground, daily reminded them of the losses that almost every family had already sustained. The grief that had thus been brought upon them by death was also greatly aggravated by the harassing attacks of the Indians, who Were evidently still lurking in the neighboring woods; and who now frequently came in small parties, and committed depredations of every kind that lay in their power. Their real but concealed object was to capture Rodolph, either alive or dead; for nothing short of his destruction, or at least that of some member of his family, could satisfy the bereaved Chief for the loss of his son. He, therefore, left a party of his bravest and most subtle warriors in an encampment about a day's journey from the Christian village, with orders to make frequent visits to the settlement, and leave no means untried which either force or cunning could suggest, that might lead to the full gratification of his revenge.

The old Chief himself returned to his wigwams, which lay some distance from New Plymouth, near the burial ground where the first encounter 'had taken place. The detachment was left under the command end guidance of Coubitant, the young warrior who had stood by him to the last in the conflict at the village; and who was, since the death of Tisquantum's son, regarded as the most distinguished of the young braves of that part of the tribe over which the Sachem ruled. His cunning, and his ferocious courage, well fitted him for the task assigned to him; and as the young warrior who fell at 'the first encounter' had been his chosen friend and companion in arms, his own desire for vengeance was only second to that of the Chief; and the malignant gaze which he had fixed on Rodolph when he led Tisquantum from the field, well expressed the feelings and the determination of his heart.

That glance had been seen by Janet; who, on that occasion, had displayed a courage and resolution hardly to be expected at her advanced age. She had easily induced her trembling mistress to remain in the house, whither they had both fled at the first attack of the Indians; but she had herself returned to the place of conflict, bearing Rodolph's musket and ammunition, and she bad remained by the side of Brewster, to whose ready hand she transferred it, until all danger was over. Then she had fixed her attention on the Chief and his companion; and the fine form and handsome features of the young Indian warrior appeared like a statue of bronze, while he stood motionless by Tisquantum. But when he turned to follow his Chief, the expression with which he looked at Rodolph transformed his countenance into that of a demoniac. Janet never forgot that look.

The state of continual watchfulness and suspense in which the emigrants were kept by their wary and active foes, was extremely harassing to their weakened force; so much so, that the President resolved to make another attempt to establish a friendly intercourse with some other native tribe, who might, possibly, assist them in driving of' the Nausetts; and whose friendship would also be useful to them in various ways. An opportunity for this attempt soon presented itself; for a party of the settlers, in following the windings of a brook that flowed through their new town into the sea, in pursuit of wild fowl, came upon two large and beautiful lakes, about three miles inland. The shores of these lakes were adorned with clumps of lofty and majestic trees, and the grass was spangled with wild flowers, and studded with graceful shrubs and underwood. Among the bushes they descried several fallow deer, and the surface of the water was animated by flocks of water fowl, among which the brilliant and graceful wood duck was conspicuous.

But the objects that chiefly attracted the notice of the sportsmen, were several wigwams that stood on the further side of the lake, beneath the shade of some overhanging trees. In front of these huts the hall-naked children were playing, while the women were pursuing their domestic occupations.

Some were weaving baskets and mats, and others washing their fishing nets in the lake. But no men were to be seen; and Rodolph, who, as usual, led the hunting party, determined to approach the wigwams. In order to show his peaceful intentions, be gave his musket to one of his companions; and inviting his friend Winslow to do the same, and to accompany him, he proceeded round the lake. As soon as the women perceived them, they uttered wild cries of fear; and, snatching up their children, attempted to escape into the thicket behind their huts. Rodolph and Winslow then started in pursuit, and succeeded in capturing one little copper-colored fellow, who was endeavoring to keep pace with his mother. She could not carry him, for she had already an infant in her arms, and she knew not that he was in the power of their dreaded pursuers until she reached the thicket, and looked back for her boy. He was struggling violently in Maitland's hands, but not a cry escaped his lips; and when he found all his efforts to free himself were vain, he gave up the attempt, and stood motionless, with a look of proud endurance that was highly characteristic of his race. His mother had less fortitude. She uttered a shriek that pierced the heart of Rodolph; and laying her infant on the grass, she almost forgot her own fears, and, in an imploring attitude, crept forward towards her imaginary foes while her eloquent eyes pleaded for her child's release more than any words could have done. Maitland could not resist that appeal. He only detained the boy until he had hung round his neck several strings of gaily-colored beads, with which the hunters were always provided, and then he set him at liberty.

In an instant the child was in his mother's arms; and when her passionate caresses had expressed her joy, she waved with a graceful salutation to the Englishman, and bent to the ground in token of gratitude. Then she looked at the beads, and her white teeth glittered as she smiled a sunny smile of delight and admiration at what seemed to her such priceless treasures. Rodolph drew from the pouch which hung at his leathern belt a string of beads more brilliant still, and held them towards the woman. She gazed at them, and then at the frank and open countenance of the stranger; and fear gave way to the desire of possessing the offered gift. She slowly approached, holding her child by the hand, and suffered Rodolph to suspend the gaudy necklace round her graceful and slender throat. Then she motioned to him to remain, and ran swiftly to the thicket to bring back her companions, who had paused in their flight, and were now watching with eager eyes the actions of the white man.

Her persuasions, and the sight of her newly-acquired ornament, soon overcame the remaining fears of her auditors, and all returned in a body, smiling, and extending their hands, in the hope of receiving similar gifts. Maitland and Winslow, who had now joined him, divided all their store of trinkets among the eager applicants; and then, in return, made signs requesting to be permitted to enter the wigwams. This request was acceded to; and Apannow—for that was the name of the female who had first approached the strangers—led the way to the hut in the center of the village, which was larger and better appointed than any one of the rest. It was evidently the dwelling of the chief of the tribe; and the beautifully carved implements which hung to the walls, and the skulls and scalps that adorned the roof, showed that its possessor was a distinguished warrior.

Apannow brought forth the best refreshment that her hut afforded, and placed it with a native grace before her guests, inviting them to partake of it, and first tasting of each article herself, to show that it was harmless. Her gentle and intelligent manners greatly interested Rudolph and his companion; and by degrees they succeeded in obtaining from her, and the other women who crowded the wigwam, such information as they chiefly desired. By expressive signs and gestures, they were made to understand that all the red men were gone on a fishing expedition to the head of the further lake, and would not return until the morrow. They afterwards learnt, also, that the village had only been occupied for a few days, as it was merely the summer residence of a part of the tribe of the Wampanoge Indians, who, with their chief, annually repaired to that beautiful station for the purpose of fishing in the extensive lakes. The rest of the tribe were located in various places to the west, occupying the district since known as the state of Rhode Island.

Maitland and Winslow took leave of their new friends, intimating that they would return and seek an interview with the Chief in two days, and bearing with them a supply of fish and dried maize, which they received from Apannow as a pledge of amity, and which they knew would be most welcome to the invalids who were still suffering from disease at the settlement. They quickly rejoined the rest of their comrades, who had remained at a distance, for fear of alarming the timid Indian females; and all returned to New Plymouth. The intelligence they brought, and the seasonable refreshment they bore to the sick, were joyfully welcomed by the whole community; and the spirits of the settlers rose at the prospect of securing Indian friends and allies, who might, under their present distressing circumstances, afford them such essential help and security. The necessity for such aid had lately become more urgent than ever, for a party of their untiring enemies, the Nausetts, had very recently invaded the enclosure within which lay the loved remains of all who bad perished since their arrival in America. The graves were sadly numerous; and the sorrowing survivors had reverently decked the mounds that covered them with shrubs, and green boughs from the evergreens that abounded in the neighboring woods, as emblems of their abiding grief, and also of their immortal hopes. These marks of affectionate regard the savages had rudely torn away; and not content with this, they had even, in some instances, removed the fresh-laid turf, and dug up the earth, so as to expose the coffins that lay beneath. No other injury or outrage could have so deeply wounded the feelings, or aroused the indignation, of the emigrants, as this desecration of the homes of the dead and they earnestly desired to form some alliance with another tribe, which might enable them to punish and to prevent such gross and wanton indignities. In the meantime, in the hope of avoiding a recurrence of so distressing a calamity, the colonists ploughed over the whole surface of their cemetery, and sowed it with corn; thus concealing what was to them so sacred from the eyes of their wild and ruthless foes.

The day after Maitland's visit to the wigwams, the emigrants were astonished at the appearance of a fine athletic Indian, armed with a bow and arrows, who walked up to the common hall, near the center of the village, and saluted the Governor and those who were with him, in the words 'Welcome Englishmen!' In reply to their eager inquiries, he informed them that his name was Samoset, and that he was 'a Sagamore of a northern tribe of Indians dwelling near the coast of Maine, where he had acquired a slight knowledge of the English language from the fishermen who frequented the island of Monhiggon near that shore. He had been for several months residing among the Wampanoges; and on the return of the Chief and his followers to the wigwams, he had heard from the Squaw-Sachem, that two strangers, who, from her account, he concluded to be Englishmen, had visited the encampment, and proposed to do so again in two days. He had, therefore, by desire of the Chief, Mooanam, come over to the British settlement, to assure the emigrants of a friendly reception, and to conduct the embassy to the presence of the Sagamore. His kind offices were gratefully and joyfully accepted by the Governor; and Samoset remained that day as his guest. Although the Indian's knowledge of English was very limited, the Pilgrim Fathers learnt from him the name, and something of the history, of their inveterate foes, the Nausetts; and also, that the commencement of their enmity to the settlers arose not merely from their being intruders on their domains, but from the remembrance of an injury which they had received, some years previously, from an English captain of the name of Hunt, who, when cruising on these shores, had allured a number of natives on board his ship, and had then treacherously carried them off, and sold the greater part of them at Malaga, as slaves. Two he took with him to England, and they at length got back to Cape Cod Bay, in a vessel belonging to the Plymouth Company. This scandalous action had filled the Nausetts and Pokanokits,[*] who were the injured tribes, with bitter hatred against the white men; and five years afterwards, they would have sacrificed the life of Captain Dermer, when he was skirting these shores, had he not been saved by Squanto, one of the kidnapped Pokanokits, whom he had brought back in his vessel, and who had become attached to the English.

[Footnote: The Pokanokit, dwelt on the peninsula which forms the Bay of Cape Cod, and on a small pert or Rhode Island; the rest being occupied by the Wampanoge; of whom Masasoyt was Grand Sagamore.]

The feeling of animosity thus engendered had been aggravated by the slaughter of Tisquantum's only son; and little hope could be entertained of establishing a friendly intercourse with a tribe who felt that they had so much to revenge against the white race.

In two days, according to the intimation of Rodolph to the Indian women, a deputation of the settlers, headed by Captain Standish, and accompanied by Maitland, repaired to the Indian village under the guidance of Samoset. They were expected by the inhabitants; and, as soon as they were perceived approaching round the margin of the lake, two young men came forth to meet them, and accompany them to the tent of the Chief. Mooanam was prepared for their reception, and attired in his gala costume of furs and feathers, with his most elaborately worked battle-axe hung to his side, and a long and slender spear, tipped with bone, in his hand. He rose from his seat on the ground at the entrance of the strangers, and greeted them courteously; while his wife, the Squaw-Sachem Apannow, and his lively little son Nepea, stood by his side, and smiled a welcome to Rodolph, pointing at the same time significantly to the beads which adorned their necks and arms.

Standish had now an interpreter, though a very imperfect one; and by his means a sort of friendly compact was formed, and gifts were exchanged as the pledges of its sincerity. An invitation was then given to the young Chief and to his brother Quadequina—who was one of those who had conducted the white men to their presence—to return the visit of the settlers, by coming the following day to their town. The invitation was accepted, and the deputation returned to their homes, escorted a great part of the by many of their Indian allies.

Great preparations were made at New Plymouth for the reception of the red Chief and his attendants, in such a manner as to impress them with the wealth and power of emigrants. The large wooden building which was intended as a sort of council chamber and public hall, was hung inside with cloth and linen of various colors, and ornamented with swords, and muskets, and pistols that the colony could produce. An elevated seat was placed for the Governor at the upper end of the apartment, and tables composed of long planks were laid down on each side, on which were arranged such viands as the settlers could produce. The repast was humble; but Helen and her female friends arranged it with taste, and the children gathered the bright wild flowers that so early enliven the groves and meadows when an American winter has passed away, to deck the tables, and form garlands along the walls. A strange contrast did these buds and blossoms of spring form to the implements of war and death with which they were mingled: but the effect of the whole was gay, and appeared very imposing to the simple children of the wilderness, as they entered the wide portal, and passed up the hall to meet the Puritan Governor.

John Carver and his attendants were clad in the dark-colored and sober garments which were usually adopted by their sect; and their long beards and grave countenances struck a feeling of awe and reverence into their savage guests. But the red men betrayed no embarrassment or timidity. They advanced with a step at once bold and graceful, and even controlled their natural feeling of curiosity so far as to cast no wandering glances at the novelties that surrounded them. They kept their eyes steadily fixed on the Governor, and returned his salutation with a courteous dignity that did credit to their native breeding; and then the Chief and Quadequina seated themselves on the high-backed chairs that were placed for them on each side of the seat of the President. Such a mode of sitting was certainly altogether new to these sons of the forest, and they found it both awkward and disagreeable; yet they showed no discomposure or restraint, and not a smile betrayed their surprise, either at this or any other of the strange customs of their hosts.

After a few rather amusing efforts to carry on a communication with his guests, through the intervention of Samoset, Carver invited them to table, and again had occasion to admire the readiness and the natural grace with which they accommodated themselves to customs so new and so wonderful as those of the white men. When the repast was concluded, the President led Mooanam and his party round the village, and showed them everything that was worthy of attention; and so intelligent did he find them, that he had no difficulty in making them comprehend the use of many European implements, and many of the inventions and contrivances of civilized life. With much satisfaction the good pastor, Brewster, marked the sparkling eyes and speaking countenances of these gentle savages; for he there hoped he saw encouragement to his ardent hope of ere long bringing them to a knowledge of the simple and saving truths of the gospel.

With the Governor's permission, he led them to the plain and unadorned edifice which was the emigrants' place of worship, and easily made them understand that it was dedicated to the service of the one Great Spirit who reigns over all; and from thence they were conducted to the cemetery, and shown, by expressive signs, the insult that had been offered to the dead by men of their own race. Some war- like implements that had been picked up after one of the recent skirmishes were shown to Mooanam and his brother, when they instantly exclaimed, Nausett!' and knitting their brows, and putting themselves into an attitude of defiance, they plainly intimated that the tribe was one with which they were at enmity.

They pointed in the direction where the Nausetts dwelt, and seemed to invite the settlers to join them in assaulting their encampment; but ignorance of their language, and of their habits prevented the President from assenting to what appeared to be their earnest wish.

As the sickness that had so long raged in the colony had now nearly disappeared, and the advance of the season promised soon to open sources of plentiful provision in the and the fields and streams, Brewster felt that he could be spared for a time from the settlement; and he proposed to Mr. Carver that he should return with Mooanam to his village, and endeavor to acquire such a knowledge of the native language, as should enable hint to act as an interpreter, and also give him the means of imparting to the red men the spiritual knowledge that he so ardently desired to bestow. The Governor willingly consented to this proposal; and when it was explained to the Indian Chief, he gave the most cordial and ready assent. The mild yet dignified countenance of the elder had won his respect and confidence; and he hoped to gain as great advantages from a more intimate connection with the white men, as they expected from his alliance and support.

Henrich was now able to leave his couch, and again to join Edith and his young companions out of doors; but he still looked delicate, and his former strength and activity had not fully returned. He was, however, able to walk with the assistance of a crutch that his father had made for him; and he formed one of the group that followed the Indians in their procession through the village, and also escorted them as far as the confines of the wood in whose depths their village lay. The Chief remarked the boy, and showed sympathy for his lameness, which he was given to understand was owing to an aggression of the Nausetts; and his eyes flashed, and his nostrils dilated, and his whole countenance was changed from its habitual expression of gentle dignity, to one of fierce hostility. It was evident that, in these Wampanoges, the settlers had secured allies who would be zealous and persevering in protecting them from the attacks of their harassing enemies, the Nausetts; and who would, when the proper time should arrive, assist them in fleeing the district of such troublesome inhabitants.

The Indians returned to their wigwams, and the elder accompanied them, and became an inmate of Mooanam's lodge. He soon began to acquire some knowledge of the language of his host, and also to instruct him and his wife in many English words and phrases, in which their aptitude to learn astonished him. A constant communication was kept up between the Indian village and that of the settlers, and a real regard and esteem sprang up between them. As the spring advanced, Henrich was able to throw aside his crutch, and to accompany his father and mother in their frequent visits to the wigwams, and much of his leisure time was passed in the company of the young Indians of his own age, whose activity and address in all their sports and games he admired and emulated. The presence of his friend Brewster in the Wampanoge village, also gave it increased attractions in the eyes of Henrich. The good man was still his friend and preceptor; and with his assistance, he made considerable progress in the acquirement of the native language, as well as in every other kind of knowledge that Brewster was able to impart. But all the elder's instructions were made subservient to that best of all knowledge – the knowledge of God, and of his revealed Word; and in this his pupil advanced and grew in a manner that both surprised and delighted him. The boy's naturally thoughtful character had become matured during his long and painful illness; and he had learnt to feel the value of heavenly things, and the comparative littleness of all 'those things which are seen, and are temporal.' He entered warmly into all the elder's benevolent desires and intentions for the conversion of the dark heathen among whom their lot was cast; and he already looked forward to being his assistant in the holy work. Brewster regarded him as destined to become both a pastor and a zealous and successful missionary, when he should arrive at a proper age; and he frequently spoke of him as his own appointed successor in the spiritual direction of the congregation.

This sacred office Henrich anticipated with pride and satisfaction; for where could he find a more fitting exercise for his adventurous and enterprising spirit, and also for his love of the truth, than in seeking the wild men amid their forests and wildernesses, and winning them to peace, and happiness, and civilization, by the knowledge of the all-powerful doctrines of the gospel?

With the Indians he soon became a great favorite; and the readiness with which he acquired the use of the bow, and learnt to cast the dart, and wield the light tomahawks that were used by the Indian boys to practice their young hands, excited their warmest admiration, and made them prophesy that he would one day become a distinguished Brave. His skill in hunting and fishing also became considerable; and he learnt from his copper-colored friends many of their songs and dances, with which he delighted Edith and Ludovico at home. His new companions did not draw away his affections from his sister. She was still the object of his warmest love; and to give her pleasure was the strongest desire of his heart. In his long rambles with his Indian play-fellows he never forgot his Edith; and many a stream was crossed, and many a rock was climbed, to procure flowering plants to deck her garden, and creepers to clothe the bower which he had formed for her beneath a venerable walnut-tree that stood within their father's little domain, and at no great distance from their dwelling.

An attempt had been made, at first, by the colonists to follow the example of the primitive church at Jerusalem; and to hold the land of which they had taken possession in common, to be worked by the whole community, and the produce to be equally divided amongst their families in due proportion. But this plan was soon abandoned, as quite unsuited to the habits and manners of these men of Britain; and every family had a small portion, consisting of an acre each, assigned to it for the special use and maintenance of its members. The fields in every allotment had been sown chiefly with grain procured from the friendly Wampanoges; and for some time past the Nausetts had left them unmolested.

The knowledge which Brewster soon acquired of the soft and musical language of the natives enabled him, with the assistance of Samoset, who still resided among them, to transact all business between them and his countrymen; and also to become acquainted with the history and circumstances of these useful allies. He learnt that Mooanam was not the great Sachem or Sagamore of the whole tribe, but that he was the eldest son of Masasoyt, the king or chief of the Wampanoges, who resided at Packanokick, their principal village, which was situated in the state of Rhode Island, near a mountain called Montaup, at a considerable distance from Patupet, the native name for New Plymouth.

The means of a still more extended intercourse was about this time opened to the settlers, by the arrival at New Plymouth of another Indian, who was already acquainted with the English, and who was also a much greater proficient in their language than their friend Samoset. This was no other than Squanto, the man who had been taken prisoner by Captain Hunt some years previous, and conveyed to England. During his residence there, he had learnt to make himself understood in the white man's tongue, and he had also learnt to admire and respect the white man's character. When, therefore, he had found his way hack to his native land in a fishing vessel, and was informed by the Wampanoge Sagamore—whom he visited in his journey to rejoin his own tribe—that an English settlement had been formed on the shores of Cape Cod Bay, he determined to visit it. Masasoyt encouraged him in this intention, and sent him to his son Mooanam, to be introduced to the strangers, and to assist in forming a permanent alliance with them.

These overtures were joyfully received by the Governor, Mr. Carver, and he determined to take immediate advantage of this opportunity of adding to the strength and security of the infant colony. The intended departure of Samoset also made it very desirable to secure the friendship and the services of the newcomer Squanto; as, notwithstanding the progress which Winslow and some others were making in the Wampanoge language, a native interpreter must long be required, in order to carry on a mutual intercourse.

An embassy to the great Sagamore was therefore resolved on, with a view to confirm and strengthen the alliance that had been formed with his sons: and again Rodolph was selected to accompany Captain Standish as his aide-de-camp, while Samoset and Squanto were to act as interpreters. The journey was long, and Maitland was obliged reluctantly to refuse Henrich's request to attend him. He feared the fatigue of so many days' travelling on foot would be too much for his son's strength, and Helen strongly opposed his going. He therefore gave up the much desired expedition, and endeavored to chase away his feeling of disappointment by renewed exertions in ornamenting the garden, and putting the grounds into a state of perfect order, to please his father on his return.

The expedition was accompanied by the Sagamore's younger son, Quadequina, who was anxious to introduce the new allies of his tribe to his father, and to ensure their friendly reception. They reached Packanokick after a pleasant journey of about forty miles, and were kindly welcomed by Masasoyt, to whom a messenger had been sent beforehand to prepare him for their arrival.

The Sagamore was a noble-looking old man, and was treated by his son, and by all his subjects, with the most profound respect; nor did his strange costume in any way destroy his kingly appearance. His limbs were naked, and were curiously painted and oiled, and his neck and arms were decorated with strings of large white beads composed of polished bone; while a richly embroidered bag or pouch, containing tobacco, was suspended at the back of his neck. His coronet of feathers was lofty, and of the most brilliant colors, and the rest of his dress consisted of a tunic and moccasins of dressed deer skin, exquisitely worked with colored grass and porcupine's quills. He willingly and fully ratified the treaty which had been made by his sons with the white strangers, whose appearance and manners seemed to prepossess him much in their favor; and after detaining them for some days in his lodge, and entertaining him with the greatest hospitality and kindness, he dismissed them with presents of native manufacture, in return for the European arms and ornaments which they had offered to his acceptance. Samoset here left the settlers, and Squanto became henceforth their faithful friend and useful interpreter.

CHAPTER IV

In your patience possess ye your souls. LUKE, xxi 19.

One evening, about the time that Helen began to expect the return of the embassy from Packanokick, Henrich was unusually busy in the garden, arranging the flower-beds, and beautifying Edith's bower, in which he and his sister had planned a little fête to welcome their father home. Their mother had learnt to feel, that while they were thus employed, and within the precincts of their own domain, they were safe from every danger. The Nausetts had not attempted any depredations for an unusual length of time; and a feeling of security and peace had taken the place of that constant watchfulness and anxiety, which had long proved so harassing to the settlers. They began to flatter themselves that their foes had retired from the neighborhood, and would no more return to molest them, now that they knew the emigrants to be on such friendly terms with their powerful rivals, the Wampanoges. But false was this appearance of security; and vain was every hope that the Nausetts would forego their designs of vengeance, or cease to devise schemes of mischief against those by whom they thought themselves injured! They did not, indeed, continue to attack the settlement openly, for they had been taught to dread the British fire-arms and the British courage; but they still continued to lurk in the neighboring forest, and to keep a vigilant watch over all that took place at the settlement. Often were the keen eyes of Coubitant and his most trusty followers fixed, with a malignant gaze, on the dwelling of Rodolph and often were his movements, and those of his family, carefully noted by these sagacious savages, when no suspicion of their presence existed in the minds of the settlers. They would climb by night to the summit of some lofty tree that overlooked the village, and there remain all day unseen, to obtain a knowledge of the habits and proceedings of their hated enemies, and to devise plans for turning this knowledge to account.

The departure of the embassy to Packanokick was, consequently, well known to Coubitant, and he resolved to take advantage of the absence of so considerable a part of the British force, to execute, if possible, his schemes of vengeance. What they were, and how he attempted their accomplishment, will be presently seen.

Edith's bower looked gay with its spring blossoms and luxuriant creepers, but Henrich was not quite satisfied with its appearance, and he wished to place at its entrance a graceful climbing plant which he had observed during his last walk to the Wampanoge village, and had neglected to secure it on his return. It had been the desire of his parents that he should not go into the forest which bordered their grounds, except in the company of his father or some of his friends; but the apparent departure of the Nausetts had caused this injunction to be neglected of late, and he, and even his younger brother and sister, had frequently strayed, unmolested, a short distance into the wood, in search of flowers and fruits; and even Helen had ceased to feel alarm.

'Edith,' said Henrich, on the evening of which we are speaking; 'I think my father will return tonight, or tomorrow at the farthest; and I must complete my task before he arrives. Your bower still requires a few plants to adorn the entrance, and the seats of moss are scarcely finished. Let us go into the wood, and procure what we want before the sun sets, and our mother comes out to see what progress we have made.'

No, Henrich,' replied his sister; 'do not go this evening. I know not why, but the wood looks dark and gloomy; there is no sunlight on the path, and the shadows are so deep, that I could fancy every low bush was a crouching Indian. I cannot go into the wood tonight.'

'You are timid, dear Edith. You never feared to go with me before; and why should you fear this evening? See, the sun is still high in the horizon, and the darkness is all in your own fancy. Come and see that lovely creeper I told you of; and when you have admired it hanging from the decayed trunk of the old tree that supports it, you shall help me to remove it to your bower, where it will be the fairest flower that grows, except the little fairy queen herself.'

Henrich caught his sister's hand, and kissing her playfully, attempted to draw her from the bower. But she looked sad and anxious, and replied —

'O, Henrich! do not ask me; my bower is fair enough, and I would not go as far as that old tree tonight, for all the flowers that grow in the forest. Stay with me, Henrich, dear. Our mother will join us soon, and she will be alarmed if you are not here.'

The boy looked at his sister's pensive face with an affectionate smile: but he was not to be diverted from his scheme.

Stay here, then, Edith,' he replied; 'and tell my mother that I shall return in little more than ten minutes. Come, Ludovico,' he added, calling his little brother, who was always ready to follow where Henrich led. 'Come, Ludovico, you are not afraid of the shadows. Bring your basket, and you shall gather moss while I dig up my creeper. When Edith sees its drooping white flowers, she will forgive me for laughing at her unusual fears.'

Edith said no more. She was sure that Henrich knew best; and she silently watched him leave the garden, and enter the shade of the thick forest, accompanied by her joyous little brother. Were her fears, indeed, the mere creation of her own young fancy I or were they occasioned by one of those strange and unaccountable presentiments which have been felt so frequently as to justify the old proverb,

'Coming events cast their shadow, before them.'

Edith sat on the mossy seat that Henrich had formed in her bower. It looked towards the wood, and the commanding situation which it occupied, on a rising ground towards the center of the garden, enabled her to overlook the green fence that enclosed the grounds, and to watch the receding forms of her brothers, until they were hidden from her sight by the winding of the path through the underwood. Still she gazed, and her heart grew sad; and tears, which she could not check, rolled down her cheeks. Did she again fancy? and did her tearful eyes now convert the bushes into the figures of two dark Indians, in the costume of the dreaded Nausetts? Surely those were human forms that moved so swiftly and so silently from the dark stem of a gigantic oak, and crossing the forest path, were instantly again concealed. Edith wiped her glistening eyes. She held her breath, and feared to move; but the beating of her young heart was audible. No sound met her listening ear—no movement again was detected by her straining eye—and she began to think that her own fears had conjured up those terrible forms.

But what was that distant cry that sounded from the wood in the direction in which her brothers had gone? And why does she now behold Ludovico running wildly, and alone, down the path, with terror depicted in his countenance?

Edith flew to meet him; but ere she reached him, the dreadful truth was made known to her by his agonized cry.

'O, my brother! my brother! they have taken him, Edith; they are dragging him away! They will kill him!' he shrieked aloud, as he threw himself into Edith's arms, almost choked with the violence of his feelings, and the speed with which he had fled.

What could Edith do? She dared not leave him, to be carried off, perhaps, by some other prowling savage, who might still be lingering near; and she could not carry him home. Slowly she drew him on, while every moment seemed an hour, that delayed her from giving the alarm, and sending friends to the rescue of her darling brother.

O! why did he leave me?' she murmured. 'Why did he go, when I knew that danger was near?'

As soon as she had brought the panting and terrified Ludovico within the precincts of the garden, she left him, and ran towards the house, calling loudly on her mother, who rushed out on hearing her voice of terror, and was instantly made acquainted with the appalling fact that had occurred. Who shall tell the agony of her feelings, or describe the sufferings of that mother's heart, when she knew that her child was in the power of the savage and relentless enemies of the white men? She was, indeed, ignorant of the peculiar vengeance that they desired to wreak on her husband and all his race; but the malevolent character of the Nausetts had been sufficiently manifested in their repeated and destructive attacks on the settlement, and their willful desecration of the graves of the exiles, to awaken the most poignant fears in her breast. Rodolph, too, was absent, and Brewster was still at the Wampanoge village; and where should she seek for succor or for counsel!

Hastily calling Janet, who was the only domestic at home, she committed Ludovico to her care; and taking Edith by the hand, she hurried from the garden, scarcely knowing whither she bent her steps, but in the vague hope of meeting some of the settlers returning from their labors in the fields, and inducing them to go to the rescue of her boy.

Onward she fled along the skirts of the forest, towards the fields of her husband's friend Winslow, who, she well knew, would aid her with all his power: but she found him not, and no human being appeared in sight to listen to her appeal for succor. The sun was setting, and all had returned to the village. What then could Helen do? To retrace her steps, and seek her friends and neighbors in their homes, would be to lose precious moments, on which the life and liberty of her Henrich might depend. To strike into the depths of the forest, and cross the belt of wood that divided the settlement from Mooanam's encampment would be the quickest plan, and probably the most effectual, as her Wampanoge friends would know far better than the settlers how to follow in the train of the fugitives, and how either to persuade or to compel them to release their prisoners. Helen had never dared to enter the wood, except under the protection of her husband, even in the broad light of day; and now the gloom of evening was gathering around her, and the path that led into the wood was obscured by the shadows of the thick foliage above. Bat where were all her fears and apprehensions? She was unconscious of such feelings now. The timid woman's heart was nerved to the occasion, and no danger could now make her shrink.

She turned rapidly into the narrow path, and pursued her way with a firmness and decision, of which, at any other time, when she was trusting to the arm and guidance of Rodolph, she would have believed herself incapable. She knew the direction in which the Indian village lay, and the slanting rays of the declining sun occasionally penetrated the thick wood, and cast bright streaks of light on the mossy ground, and the boles of the giant trees around; but soon they faded away, and a deep gloom overspread her path.

'Mother,' said the trembling little Edith, as she clung to Helens hand, and exerted her utmost strength to keep up with her rapid steps; 'Mother, do you not fear to pass through this forest now? Shall we not meet more of those dreadful savages who have taken away my brother? Oh, Henrich! Henrich!' she cried – while tears burst afresh from her eyes at the recollection of her brother's fate – 'why did you venture into this wood to seek plants for my bower?' and the child sobbed convulsively, from mingled grief and fear.

Cease, Edith, cease!' replied the deeply distressed, but now firm and courageous Helen: 'I fear nothing while I am seeking aid for Henrich. God will protect us, my child! she added: and she raised her glistening eyes to heaven, and gazed, hopefully and trustingly, on one bright star that shone upon her between the summits of the lofty trees. Her heart was strengthened by her pious confidence in her heavenly Father. She remembered also that Edith looked to her for protection; and all personal fears were absorbed by that generous and elevating feeling of self-devotion, which is shared even by the lower and weaker animals when their offspring are in danger. So Helen forgot herself, and felt strong to guard her child, and strong to seek and obtain aid for him whose peril was more real and urgent.

Onward she pressed in silence but her soul was pleading eloquently with God. Soon Edith checked her suddenly, and exclaimed, as she stumbled over something in the pathway, 'Oh mother, here are Henrich's tools; and there I see Ludovico's basket full of moss! This is the spot to which my brothers were coming; and yonder is the old tree, with the white flowers hanging on it, that Henrich wished to plant by my bower. It must have been here that the Indians seized him while he was at work.'

That part of the wood was more light and open than the rest of their way had been; and Helen hastily surveyed it, that she might be able to guide the Wampanoges thither, and point out to them where to commence the pursuit. Again she resumed her way; and, regardless of fatigue, she never paused again until she reached the border of the quiet and lonely lake, on which the rising moon was now shining in all her silvery splendor. The huts of the friendly natives stood out, clear and dark, on the level shore of the lake, and Helen and her weary child soon reached them, and hastened to

Mooanams lodge. There they found the Chief, and his interesting young wife and children, sitting on the matted floor, listening with deep attention to the words of life and salvation which Brewster was reading and interpreting to them from the Holy Scriptures. The hurried entrance of Helen startled and alarmed them; for her countenance plainly told them, that some calamity had occasioned her unlooked-for appearance at such an unwonted time.

With breathless haste she told her sad errand, and Brewster quickly explained her words to the Chief, Mooanam seized his arms, and rushed from the lodge, calling, in a loud and commanding voice, on his people to arm themselves and accompany him in the pursuit of the cruel and vindictive Nausetts. All was hurry and excitement throughout the village, and every swarthy warrior pressed forward, and desired to share in the expedition to save their young English favorite. It was necessary, however, to leave a strong party at the village, to guard it from any act of treachery or violence on the part of their malicious rivals, who, it was now evident, were still lurking in the neighborhood; and, while Mooanam was selecting his party, and arranging his plans, a clear shrill voice was heard from the margin of the lake, crying, 'The canoes! the canoes! Quadequina is returning.'

'The canoes, the canoes!' resounded through the crowd; and Helen's heart hounded with joy and gratitude. Rodolph was near; and all would yet be well.

Little Nepea had led Edith to the shore while the warriors were discussing their plans; and in a strange mixture of English and Indian words, the children were conversing on the recent sad event. The quick ear of the young savage had detected the splash of oars at the farther side of the lake, and he instantly discovered the three canoes that were leaving the opposite coast, and emerging from the deep shadow of the overhanging trees. He had raised that joyful cry; and now all the inhabitants of the village rushed down to the shore to welcome their brethren, and to tell the startling news.

Nearest to the brink stood Helen and her little girl, closely attended by Mooanam and the Squaw-Sachem Apannow, who shared her impatient anxiety for the return of the embassy, that they might have the benefit of Maitland's counsel, and also obtain an addition to their forces. The elder, Brewster, was deeply moved at the misfortune that had befallen his young friend, Henrich. But he knew that not a moment was to be lost! and, while all others were crowding down to the lake side, he busied him self in arranging the volunteers for the pursuit, and seeing that his own musket was in a proper state for active service.

The canoes sped swiftly across the moonlit waters; and as they neared the shore, Rodolph perceived the forms of his wife and daughter, surrounded by the dark Indians, and ready to receive him. But he felt only pleasure at this unexpected and welcome meeting. No feeling of alarm crossed his breast, until he drew near enough to distinguish Helen's countenance; and then he knew that she had come with evil tidings. He sprang from the canoe, eager to hear the truth: but all the firmness and courage which had so wonderfully sustained his wife while she was obliged to act for herself, forsook her the moment she felt herself supported by her Rodolph's arm; and faintly exclaiming, 'O my son, my son!' she fainted; while little Edith burst into tears, and sobbed out her brother's name.

'Tell me, in the name of heaven, what all this means!' exclaimed Maitland, turning a look of eager inquiry on Mooanam, who stood with characteristic silence and apparent composure, waiting the proper moment to speak. 'Tell me,' cried the distracted father again, 'what dire calamity has befallen my boy?'

'My heart is dark for you,' replied the Sachem, in a voice of perfect calmness, though a tear glistened in his coal black eye, and his brow was clouded by anxiety. 'My heart is very dark for you, and for your young warrior—for, boy as he was, he was a brave at heart.'

Mooanam spoke in his native tongue, intermixed with English words and phrases, which he had learned from Brewster and the other settlers; but the father's heart comprehended all he said, and needed no interpreter.

'Is my son dead, then?' he exclaimed. 'Has accident or violence quenched his young spirit?'

'Worse than dead,' slowly replied the Sachem; and he looked pityingly at Helen, who now began to recover her senses. 'Leave your wife to the care of the squaws,' he added, 'and come with me to the wise man yonder, and he will tell you all.'

He led Rodolph to where Brewster was occupied in making preparations, and soon the afflicted father was made acquainted with the fate of his son. He felt indeed that death—a calm and peaceful death beneath his own accustomed roof, and with those he dearly loved around him—would have been a far happier lot for Henrich than that to which he now feared he might be doomed—than that which, possibly, his darling boy was at that moment enduring at the hands of his cruel and malignant enemies.

The thought was maddening. But there was still a hope of saving him by speed and resolution; and he urged the Sachem to depart instantly. One moment he gave to visit and endeavor to cheer his wife, who now lay powerless and weeping in Apannow's lodge; and then he joined the Chief, who, with Brewster and a band of picked men, were ready to accompany him. The pastor had already learnt from Edith all that she could tell relative to the spot where her brother had been captured; and to that spot the pursuing party hurried, and soon discovered the basket and the tools that told where the boys had been so rudely interrupted in their work. Quickly the trodden grass, and the broken branches of the thick underwood, showed in what direction the boy had been dragged by his captors; and on the track the Wampanoge warriors followed, like hounds in the chase. But, alas! the Nausetts had had a fearful start of them; and little hope existed in the breast of Mooanam that they could overtake them, in time to avert the dreadful fate that he had feared for Henrich.

The Sachem was himself an Indian, and he well knew the Indian desire for retaliation and vengeance. He was, indeed, a man of a mild and generous nature, and he belonged to a tribe less distinguished by cruelty than the Nausetts. But still he felt that, according to the savage code of the natives, blood must atone for blood, and he believed that already the life of Henrich had probably been sacrificed in expiation of his father's having slain the son of the Nausett Chief. Still he led his warriors on, and neither paused nor spoke until the party emerged from the thick wood, upon a little opening that was lighted up brilliantly by the moon-beams. Here, where it was evident a small temporary encampment had existed, and had only been very recently and hastily removed, he stopped, and looked earnestly around. The poles still stood erect which lied supported the tents of the Nausetts; the fires were still burning; and many articles of domestic use lay scattered about, which the hasty departure of the inhabitants had probably prevented their removing.

Rudolph hurried through the camp in search of some sign of his son; and his eager eye fell on the well-known tunic that Henrich was accustomed to wear. He snatched it up hastily; and then, with a deep groan, let it fall again upon the ground. The breast of the tunic was pierced through in several places, and the whole dress was stained with blood—blood that was newly shed.

Maitland pointed to this evidence of his son's death! and when the Sachem had examined it, he set his teeth together, and drew in his breath with an oppressed, hissing sound, as of severe pain.

'It is over, my friend,' he said, in a low deep voice to Rodolph—'it is over; and we are too late. Naught now remains but to take revenge— full, ample revenge. Let us follow the miscreants.'

Rudolph turned, and looked at him. He fixed on him such a searching gaze—a gaze so full of gentle reproof and of deep settled grief-that the warm-hearted Chief stood silent, and almost abashed before his Christian friend.

'Is it thus you have learned of Brewster?' said the sorrowing father. 'Is it thus that you are taught in that book which the Great Spirit has dictated? The Father of us all has declared, "vengeance is mine; I will repay "; and since we are too late to save my son, we will not commit deeds of blood which his now happy and ransomed spirit would abhor.'

Mooanam was silenced, but not convinced. Inwardly he vowed vengeance against those who had dealt so cruelly with the unoffending boy; though, under similar circumstances, he would probably have acted with the same spirit. But the Chief bad allied himself with the white men. He loved and reverenced them; and he was resolved to avenge the wrongs of Maitland, as if they had been his own.

Sadly and silently the party returned to the Indian village, where they arrived at the break of day. We will not attempt to describe the mother's anguish when she was made acquainted with the dreaded fate of her son; but Helen was a Christian, and while her heart was bowed down with crushing grief, her spirit strove to hush its rebellious questionings, and to submit itself to the will of God.

'It is the Lord,' she meekly exclaimed: let Him do what seemeth Him good!'

That morning she returned with her husband and Edith to the settlement; and they were accompanied by Brewster, whose pious exhortations and sympathizing kindness were invaluable to the bereaved and afflicted parents. The grief of Edith was less capable of being suppressed; and it broke out afresh when little Ludovico came to meet them, and inquired for his brother. From the child they learnt, that while he and Henrich were busily engaged in their several occupations in the wood, two Indians had suddenly rushed from the thick brushwood, and seized on his brother before he had time to fly. Ludovico was gathering moss at some distance, but he saw what passed, and uttered a cry that attracted the attention of the savages; and one of them east a spear at him with such violence, that, missing its intended mark, it stuck firmly in a tree close behind him. Seeing this, his noble and courageous brother called out to him to hide among the bushes, and make his way home as quickly as possible; and the Indians, eager to secure the prize they had so long been watching for, hurried away through the forest, dragging Henrich with them.

The murderous attempt made by these savages against the life of Ludovico proved but too clearly that the destruction of Rodolph's children was their object, and banished every hope that lingered in Helen's breast; and this conviction of their cruel intentions was still further confirmed by Janet's account of the look and gesture of the warrior who attended his Chief when the Nausetts first assailed the settlement. Rodolph had seen, and understood the action; and as he had also learnt through his Wampanoge friends that Tekoa, the son of the Nausett Chief, had fallen in the first encounter, he knew enough of Indian customs to be aware that he, as the slayer, was a marked object of their vengeance. He had, however, always concealed his suspicions from Helen; and the only effect they had produced on him was causing him, at that time, to prohibit his children from venturing unguarded into the wood, more strictly than he would otherwise have done.

CHAPTER V

'Surely the wrath of man shall praise thee: the remainder of wrath shalt thou restrain.' PSA. lxxvi,10.

We will now, for a time, leave the settlement—where the sad news of the capture and supposed death of Henrich had spread a general gloom and consternation—and follow the subject of their pitying grief, from the time that he was seized and made a prisoner in the hands of the savages. They did not slay him; for the Lord had work and service in store for the young missionary, and he suffered not a hair of his head to be hurt.

Coubitant—for he was one of those whose patient vigilance had, at length, been crowned by success—and his companion had hurried him at their greatest speed through the wood, to the spot where their temporary camp was pitched, and where several others of their tribe awaited their return. A few minutes sufficed to remove the matting that formed their tents, and to collect their arms and utensils; but Coubitant well knew that the child who had escaped his cruelty would soon alarm the settlers, and that an instant pursuit would follow. He therefore, devised plan to deceive, and, perhaps altogether to check the white men, at least for a time, by making them believe that the death of the captive had already taken place. He would have instantly gratified the feelings of his cruel and revengeful heart, and have shed the innocent blood of Rodolph's son to atone for the death of his friend, but that he feared to disappoint his Chief, who so earnestly desired to imbrue his own hands in the blood of the slayer. He, therefore, resolved on the stratagem we have described. He stripped off the captive's tunic, and, after piercing it several times with his dagger, he opened a vein in his own arm with the same weapon, and let the hot blood flow freely over the torn vesture.

This done, he smiled a demon's smile, as he cast the tunic on the ground, and thought with malignant pleasure of the anguish that its discovery would occasion to his hated foe.

Henrich gazed in trembling wonder at this act; and when Coubitant again approached him to bind his hands, he believed that he was about to plunge that blood-stained knife into his beating heart. He was young, and life was new and precious to him; and for a moment he shrank back, while the blood curdled in his veins. But, young as he was, he was also a child of God; and he knew that all events are governed by His Almighty power, and over-ruled by His wisdom and love. So he was enabled to lift up his eyes and his trusting heart to heaven, and to await his expected fate with calmness. Coubitant saw his firmness, and he wondered and admired. He placed the dagger in his belt and hastily tying the captive's hands behind his back, he motioned to his companions to follow, and struck into a narrow and almost undistinguishable path.

Forcing Henrich to go before him, while he held the rope of twisted grass that bound his hands he followed close behind, and placed his foot in each print that the prisoner made, so as to destroy the impression of the boy's European shoe. The other Indians did the same; as exactly did they tread in one another's steps, that, when all had passed, it seemed as if only one solitary traveler had left his track on the soft ground.

Thus, 'in Indian file,' they traversed a belt of wood, till they came out on a dry and sun-burnt plain, where their steps left no impression. Coubitant then advanced to the side of his prisoner, and, taking his arm in his powerful grasp, he compelled him to advance, at an almost breathless speed, across the plain. In the wood, on the other side, he allowed a short pause, and gave Henrich some water from a bottle made of a dried gourd, which hung about his neck; and thus they traveled on, with slight refreshment and little rest, until the sun arose in all his splendor, and displayed to Henrich's admiring gaze the wild and magnificent woodland scenery through which he was travelling. Under other circumstances, he would keenly have enjoyed the novelty and the beauty of the objects that met his eyes, so different from the luxuriant, but flat and monotonous fields, and gardens, and canals, that he so well remembered in Holland. Here all was wild and varied; and all was on a scale of grandeur that inspired him with a feeling of awe and solemnity, heightened, no doubt, by the fearful uncertainty of his fate, and the thought that, perhaps, this was the last time that he should look upon these glorious hills, and ancient forests, and wide rushing rivers—the handiworks, and the visible teachers of God's power. Something of American scenery he had become acquainted with in his rambles round the Indian village, but only enough to make him long to see more; and had he now been travelling by the side of his father, or his friend Brewster, the elastic morning air, and the splendid and ever-varying views, would have made his young heart bound with joy and health.

As it was, the silent beauty of nature was not without its influence on the captive boy. He seemed to feel more strongly the presence and the goodness of his heavenly Father; and his young spirit was cheered to endure his present desolate situation, and strengthened to meet whatever future trials might await him. He had learnt from Brewster to make himself understood in the Wampanoge language, and he resolved to try whether his Nausett guide would reply to his questions in that tongue. He therefore besought him to tell him whither he was leading him, and for what purpose. But Coubitant deigned him no reply. He understood him—for the Nausett language was but another dialect of the Wampanoge—but he did not choose to inform the boy of his destination at present, and he preserved a profound silence, and an expression of sullen gravity.

It was not until the evening of the fourth day that the party reached the Nausett village, which, as we have already observed, was situate near the site of the 'first encounter'; and to which Tisquantum, and the greater part of his warriors had returned, when Coubitant and a few picked associates were left to carry out his schemes of vengeance. Henrich was instantly conducted to the lodge of the old Chief; and brightly did Tisquantum's dark eyes glitter when he beheld the son of his enemy in his power. He praised the skill and the perseverance by which Coubitant had thus procured him the means of revenge; and, taking off his own brilliant coronet of feathers, he placed it on the head of the proud and successful warrior, as a distinguished mark of his approbation.

Coubitant was highly gratified; but his desire for vengeance was stronger than his vanity, and forgetting the honor that had been conferred upon him, he entreated the Chief to allow him instantly to drive his spear into the boy's heart, or else with his own weapon to take the life of the slayer's child.

'Not yet!' replied Tisquantum—and Henrich comprehended the full purport of his words—'not today, Coubitant. I would pour out the blood of the white youth with pomp and ceremony, as an offering to the spirit of my murdered son. Let the boy be fed and refreshed: tomorrow, at break of day, he shall die. Go. I have said it.'

'And will the Sachem give him into my charge until the morning dawns?' inquired Coubitant.

Tisquantum fixed his piercing eye on the savage, and read his malevolent feelings; and he calmly answered, 'No: the victim shall bleed because his father's blood flows in his veins. But he shall not be tortured; for his was not the hand that deprived me of my son. The boy shall remain in my own lodge, and sleep securely for this night beneath the same roof that shelters my last remaining child—my lovely Oriana.'

Had the Chief observed Henrich's changing countenance, he would have perceived that all he said was understood by the intended sufferer. But he marked him not, and the boy commanded himself, and kept silence, determined to await Coubitant's departure before he made one effort to move the Chief to pity. He had, however, no opportunity of trying the effect of his earnest appeal; for Tisquantum ordered one of his attendants to remove him at once to the inner division of the lodge, and to secure him there for the night: and then, motioning Coubitant to retire, and resuming his pipe, he proceeded to 'drink smoke,' as composedly as if his evening repose had not been interrupted.

But, notwithstanding his outward composure, the Nausett chief was not unmoved by the event that had just occurred. The sight of the son of him whose hand had slain his young Tekoa brought back the image of his brave young warrior, as he stood beside him at the fatal burial-ground, full of youthful ardor, to combat the invaders of his land, and the supposed enemies of his race. He recalled his daring look as he mounted the palisade, and placed in his unerring bow the arrow that wounded the English boy. And then he seemed to hear again the sharp report of the white man's musket, and to behold once more the sudden fall of his son, bleeding and expiring, to the ground.

Tisquantum thought on that hour of anguish, when his duties as a chief and a warrior had forbidden all expression of his grief; and he thought of his return to his lodge, where only Oriana remained to welcome him— for the mother of his children, whom he had loved with unusual affection, was dead—and tears gathered in the Sachem's eyes. Oriana had deeply mourned her brother's death; for since she had lost her mother, she had been permitted to enjoy much more of his society than had previously been allowed her; and her father, also, had seemed to transfer to her much of the love that be had borne towards his wife. Now his daughter was his only domestic tie; and his chief object in life was to give her in marriage to a warrior as brave as her young brother, and who would supply to him the place of his departed son.

At present, this prospect was not immediate, for Oriana was only in her fourteenth year; but the Sachem was resolved that she should be worthy of the hand of the greatest warriors of her tribe, and he took pains to have her instructed in every art that was considered valuable or ornamental to an Indian female. Already she could perform the most elaborate patterns in native embroidery on her father's pouches and moccasins; and her own garments were also delicately and fancifully adorned in the same manner, with feathers, and shells, and colored grasses. Besides this accomplishment, her skill in Indian cookery was very great; and she could also use a bow and arrows, or cast a light javelin, or swim across a rapid river, with a grace and activity that delighted her proud father.

Oriana, too, was gentle—as gentle as her mother, and her influence over Tisquantum bade fair to equal that which his much-cherished and deeply regretted wife had exercised over him. That influence had ever been employed in the cause of mercy! and many an enemy, and many a subject, had lived to bless the name of the Squaw-Sachem Oriana, when she had quelled the wrath of the offended Chief, and turned aside his intended vengeance.

It was to the inner apartment of his spacious lodge, where his daughter and her attendants were busily engaged in their domestic occupations, that Henrich bad been led. His arms were still tied behind his back, and the end of the rope that bound them was secured to a post in the wall. The Indian who, at his chief's command, conducted him thither, briefly informed Oriana that he was a prisoner, and desired her women to look to his security: and then he left the captive to his strange and inquisitive jailers.

When Tisquantum had emptied his long pipe, he bethought himself of the young captive's position, and proceeded to his daughter's apartment to give orders for his hospitable entertainment that evening, and his safe lodgment for the night—that night which he was resolved should be his last. As he approached the thick curtain of deer-skins that hung over the aperture between the two apartments, he thought he heard a strange sweet voice speaking the Indian language with a foreign accent; and hastily drawing aside the heavy drapery, he was astonished to see his prisoner, and intended victim, liberated from the cord that had bound him, and reclining on the furs and cushions that formed Oriana's usual resting-place; while his gentle Indian child knelt beside him, and offered him the food of which he was so much in need. Henrich was gratefully thanking her; and as the Sachem entered, he heard him exclaim in mournful accents—

But why do you thus so kindly treat me? It were better to let me die of hunger and fatigue; for I know that to-morrow my blood is to be shed: the cold knife is to pierce my heart.'

'It shall not be,' replied Oriana, fervently. 'I have said that I will save you.' And then she raised her sparkling eyes as she heard her father's entrance; and springing on her feet, she darted forward, and caught his arm.

'Father!' she cried—and now she spoke so rapidly and energetically, that Henrich could only guess the purport of her words, and read it in her sweet expressive countenance—'Father! do not slay the white boy. He says that he is doomed to die because his father caused my brother's death. But surely Tekoa's generous spirit does not ask the blood of a child. My brother is now happy in the great hunting grounds where our fathers dwell. He feels no wrath against his slayer's son: he never would have sought revenge against an innocent boy. Give me the captive, O my father! and let him grow up in our lodge, and be to me a playfellow and a brother.'

Tisquantum gazed at his child in wonder, and his countenance softened. She saw that he was moved and hastily turning from him, she approached Henrich, who had risen from the couch, and now stood an earnest spectator of the scene, on the issue of which his life or death, humanly speaking, depended. She took his band, and led him to her father, and again pleaded earnestly and passionately for his life; while the touching expression of his own deep blue eyes, and the beauty of his fair young face, added greatly to the power of her appeal.

I have a little sister at home,' said Henrich—and the soft Indian language sounded sweetly from his foreign lips—'and she will weep for me as Oriana has wept for her brother. Let me return to Patupet, and she and my parents will bless you.'

At the mention of his parents, Tisquantum's brow grew dark again. He thought of Rodolph as the destroyer of his son; and he turned away from the two youthful suppliants, whose silent eloquence he felt he could not long resist.

'Your father killed my young Tekoa,' he replied. 'His fire weapon quenched the light of my lodge, and took from me the support of my old age. Should I have pity on his son?'

'But let him dwell in our lodge, and fill my brother's vacant place!' exclaimed Oriana. 'Do not send him back to the white men; and his father, and his mother, and his little sister will still weep for him, and believe him dead.'

The same idea had crossed Tisquantum's breast. He looked again at the boy, and thought how much Oriana's life would be cheered by such a companion. His desire of revenge on Rodolph would also be gratified by detaining his child, and bringing him up as an Indian, so long as his parents believed that he had met with a bloody death; and, possibly, he felt a time might come when the possession of an English captive might prove advantageous to himself and his tribe. All fear of the boy's escaping to his friends was removed from his mind; for he was about to retire from that part of the country to a wild district far to the west, and to join his allies, the Pequodees, in a hunting expedition to some distant prairies. The portion of his tribe over which he was Sachem, or chief, was willing to accompany him; and he had no intention of returning again to the neighborhood of the English intruders, who, he clearly foresaw, would ere long make themselves masters of the soil; and who had already secured to themselves such powerful allies in the Wampanoges—the enemies and rivals of the Nausetts.

Tisquantum weighed all these considerations in his mind; and he resolved to spare the life of his young captive. But he would not at once announce that he had relented from his bloody purpose, and yielded to his child's solicitations. He therefore maintained the severe gravity that usually marked his countenance, and replied—

'But what can the white boy do, that he should fill the place of an Indian chieftain's son? Can he cast the spear, or draw the bow, or wrestle with our brave youths?

Reviving hope had filled the heart of Henrich with courage, and he looked boldly up into the Sachem's face, and merely answered, 'Try me.'

The brevity and the calmness of the reply pleased the red Chief, and he determined to take him at his word.

'I will,' he said. 'To-morrow you shall show what skill you possess, and your fate shall depend on your success. But how have you learned anything of Indian sports, or of the Indian tongue?'

'I have been much in Mooanam's lodge, and have played with the youths of his village,' replied Henrich; 'and the Sachem was well pleased to see me use a bow and arrow in his woods. And from him, and my young companions, I learnt to speak their tongue.'

'It is good,' said the old Chief, thoughtfully. Then, fixing his penetrating eyes on Henrich again, he hastily inquired: 'And can you use the fire-breathing weapons of your countrymen? and can you teach me to make them?

'I can use them,' answered the boy; 'but I cannot make them. They come from my father's land, beyond the great sea. But,' he added—while a stronger hope of life and liberty beamed in his bright blue eye and flushing face—'send me back to my countrymen, and they will give you muskets for my ransom.'

'No, no!' said the Sachem: and the dark cloud again passed over his countenance. 'Never will I restore you to your father, till he can give me back my son. You shall live, if you can use our Indian weapons; but you shall live and die as an Indian.'

He turned and left the apartment; and the heart of Henrich sank within him. Was he then taken for ever from his parents, and his brother, and sister? Should he behold his friends, and his teacher, no more? And must he dwell with savages, and lead a savage life? Death, he thought, would be preferable to such a lot; and he half resolved to conceal his skill and dexterity in Indian exercises, that Tisquantum might cast him off and slay him, as unfit to dwell among his tribe. But hope soon revived; and his trust in the providential mercy of God restored his spirits, and enabled him even to look upon a lengthened captivity among the red men with composure. Plans for escaping out of their hands, and making his way back to the settlement, filled his mind; and a short residence among the wild men even appeared to offer some attraction to his enterprising spirit. So he turned to Oriana, who stood gazing on his changing and expressive countenance with the deepest interest, and again resumed the conversation which had been interrupted by the entrance of the Chief.

Many questions did those young strangers ask each other relative to their respective homes, and native customs; and Henrich learnt, with much dismay, that the Nausetts under Tisquantum's rule were so soon to change their place of residence. His hopes of escape became less strong, but they were not destroyed: and when he was summoned to pass the night in the Sachem's apartment, he was able to lift up his heart to God in prayer, and to lie down to sleep on the rude couch prepared for him, with a calm trust in His Almighty power and goodness, and a hope that He would see fit to shorten his trials, and restore him to his friends.

The Chief watched him as he knelt in prayer; and when he rose, and prepared to lie down to sleep, he abruptly asked him why he had thus remained on his knees so long?

'I was praying to my God to protect me,' answered Henrich; and a tear rose to his eye, as he remembered how he had knelt every evening with his own beloved family; and thought how his absence, and their probable belief in his death, would sadden the act of worship that would that night be performed in his father's house.

'Do you pray to the Great Spirit?' asked Tisquantum.

'I do!' replied the young Christian. 'I pray to the Great Spirit, who is the God and Father of all men; and I pray to his Son Jesus Christ, who is the friend and Savior of all who love him.'

'It is good!' said the Chief. 'We know the Great Spirit; but we know nothing of the other gods of the white men. Sleep now; for your strength and activity will be tried to-morrow.' And Henrich lay down, and slept long and peacefully.

He was awakened the next morning by the gentle voice of Oriana, who stood beside him, and said, 'You must rise now, and eat with me, before you go out to try your strength and skill. Come to my apartment.'

Henrich opened his eyes, and gazed around him in wonder. But quickly the whole sad reality of his situation came over him, and he felt that he must nerve himself for the coming trial. Soon he followed Oriana to her inner room, where a slight Indian repast of maize and fruits had been prepared by the young Squaw-Sachem and her attendants. Tisquantum had left the lodge, and was now occupied in preparing a spot for the exercise of the white boy's skill. At his side stood Coubitant, silent and gloomy. His indignation at the Chief's merciful intentions towards the intended victim was great; and strongly had he urged him to the immediate slaughter of the captive. But Tisquantum was not to be lightly moved, either to good or evil. He had said that the boy should live, if he proved himself worthy to bear Indian arms, and all the cruel suggestions and arguments that Coubitant could bring forward only made him more resolved to keep his word.

The young savage then forbore to speak, for he saw that it was useless, and he feared to displease his Chief, whose favor was the highest object of his ambition. Since the untimely death of his son, Coubitant had been constantly his companion and attendant, until he had been left near the English settlement to carry out his schemes of revenge. His success in this enterprise a raised him still higher in Tisquantum's estimation; and visions of becoming the son-in-law of the Chief, and eventually succeeding him in his office, already floated in the brain of Coubitant. In a few years, Oriana's hand would be given to some fortunate warrior; and who could have so strong a claim to it as the man who had risked his own life to procure vengeance for her brother's death? Therefore Coubitant held his peace, and checked the expression of his deadly and malignant feelings towards the young prisoner.

Soon Henrich was summoned to the ground where his fate was to be decided, and he was directed to try his powers with several Indian boys of his own age. In shooting with the bow and arrow, he could not, by any means, rival their skill and accuracy of aim; but in casting the spear, and wielding the tomahawk, he showed himself their equal; and when he was made to wrestle with his swarthy and half-naked competitors, the superior height and muscular powers of the British lad enabled him to gain the victory in almost every instance.

Tisquantum was satisfied. He pronounced him worthy to live; and, notwithstanding the opposition of Coubitant, which was once more cautiously manifested, he presented Henrich with the arms that he knew so well how to use, and informed him that he should henceforth dwell in his lodge among his braves, and should no more inhabit the apartments of the women. To a young and generous mind success and approbation are always grateful; and Henrich's eye kindled, and his cheek burned, as he listened to the praises of the Chief, and felt that he owed his life, under Providence, to his own efforts. And when his little friend Oriana came bounding up to him, with joy and exultation in her intelligent countenance, and playfully flung a wreath of flowers across his shoulders in token of victory, he felt that even among these children of the wilderness—these dreaded Nausett Indians— he could find something to love.

In Coubitant, he instinctively felt that he had also something to dread; but the savage tried to conceal his feeling and even to please the Chief and Oriana, by pretending an interest in their young favorite, which for a long time deceived them as to his real sentiments. The bustle of preparation for the intended removal of the encampment began that day—for Tisquantum was now more eager than ever to get beyond the reach of the settlers—and before sunset all was ready. The next morning the march commenced at daybreak, and continued for many days uninterruptedly, until the Chief and his followers reached the residence of his Pequodee allies, when he considered himself safe from pursuit, even if the settlers should attempt it. He therefore halted his party, and took up his abode among his friends, to wait until they were prepared to set out on their hunting expedition to the western prairies. A period of repose was also very needful for the women and children, for the march had been a most fatiguing one. Not only had the Sachem dreaded the pursuit of the injured settlers, and therefore hurried his party to their utmost speed; but the country through which they had traveled was inhabited by the Narragansett tribe, the ancient and hereditary foes of the Pequodees. It was, consequently, desirable for the Nausetts, as allies of the latter, to spend as little time as possible in the territories of their enemies; and little rest ad been permitted to the travelers until they had passed the boundary of the friendly Pequodees.

CHAPTER VI

The woodsoh! solemn are the boundless woods;
Of the great western world, when day declines,
And louder sounds the roll of distant floods,
More deep the rustling of the ancient pines;
When dimness gathers on the stilly air,
And mystery seems o'er every leaf to brood,
Awful is it for human heart to bear
The might and burden of the solitude!' HEMANS.

Many weeks elapsed after the Nausett party had joined the friendly Pequodees, ere any preparations were made for journeying to the west; and these days were chiefly employed by Henrich in improving his knowledge of the Indian language, and especially of the Nausett dialect, by conversing with Oriana and her young companions, both male and female. He also endeavored to learn as much as possible of the habit and the ideas of the simple people among whom his lot was now cast; for he hoped, at some future time, when he had succeeded in returning to his own countrymen, that such a knowledge might prove useful both to himself and them.

He was treated with much kindness by Tisquantum; and his favor with the Chief ensured the respect and attention of all his dependants and followers. From the day that the white boy had been spared from a cruel and violent death, and established as a regular inmate of Tisquantum's dwelling, it seemed as if he had regarded him as a son, and had adopted him to fill the place of him whose death he so deeply deplored; and Oriana already looked on him as a brother, and took the greatest delight in his society. No apprehensions were now felt of his escaping to the settlement; for the distance which they had traveled through woods, and over hills and plains, to reach the Pequodee encampment, was so great, that it was utterly impossible for any one but an Indian, well accustomed to the country, to traverse it alone. Henrich was, therefore, allowed to enjoy perfect liberty, and to ramble unmolested around the camp; and it was his greatest pleasure to climb to the summit of a neighboring hill, which was crowned by a few ancient and majestic pines, and there to look in wonder and admiration at the scenery around him. To the west, a vast and trackless forest spread as far as the eye could reach, unbroken save by some distant lakes, that shone like clear mirrors in their dark green setting. Trees of gigantic growth rose high above their brethren of the wood, but wild luxuriant creepers, many of them bearing clusters of bright blossoms, had climbed ambitiously to their summits, seeking the light of day, and the warmth of the sunbeams, which could not penetrate the thick underwood that was their birth-place. It was a sea of varied and undulating foliage, beautiful and striking, but almost oppressive to the spirit; and Henrich gazed sadly over the interminable forest, and thought of the weeks, and months—and, possibly, the years that this wilderness was to be his home. Escape, under present circumstances, he felt to be impossible; and he endeavored to reconcile himself to his fate, and to look forward with hope to a dim and uncertain future. Could his parents and Edith but have been assured of his safety, he thought he could have borne his captivity more cheerfully; but to feel that they were mourning him as dead, and that, perhaps, they would never know that his blood had not been cruelly shed by his captors, was hard for the affectionate boy to endure.

To Oriana, alone, could he tell his feelings, and pour out his griefs and anxieties; and Edith herself could not have listened to him with more attention and sympathy than was shown by the young Indian girl. When her domestic duties were accomplished, she would accompany her new friend to his favorite retreat on the hill-top; and there, seated by his side beneath the tall pines, she would hold his hand, and gaze into his sorrowful countenance, and listen to his fond regrets for his distant home, and all its dearly-loved inmates, till tears would gather in her soft black eyes, and she almost wished that she could restore him to his countrymen. But this she was powerless to do, even if she could have made up her mind to the sacrifice of her 'white brother,' as she called him. She had, indeed, wrought upon her father so far as to save his life, and have him adopted into their tribe and family; but she well knew that nothing would ever induce him to give up his possession of Rodolph's son, or suffer his parents to know that he lived.

All this she told to Henrich; and his spirit, sanguine as it was, sickened at the prospect of a lengthened captivity among uncivilized and heathen beings. He gazed mournfully to the east; he looked over the wide expanse of country that he had lately traversed, and his eye seemed to pierce the rising hills, and lofty forests, that lay between him and his cherished home; and in the words of the Psalmist he cried, 'Oh that I had wings as a dove, for then would I flee away and be at rest!'

Would you leave me, my brother?' said Oriana, in reply to this unconscious utterance of his feelings; 'would you leave me again alone, to mourn the brother I have lost?' The Sachem loves you, and I love you, too; and you may be happy in our lodge, and become a brave like our young men.'

Yes, Oriana, you and your father are kind to me; and I had never known any other mode of life, I might be happy in your lodge. But I cannot forget my parents, and me dear Edith who loved me so fondly, and my little brother also. And then I had a friend — a kind friend, and full of wisdom and goodness — who used to teach me all kinds of knowledge; and, above all, the knowledge of the way to heaven. How can I think that I may, perhaps, never see all these again, and not be sad?' And Henrich buried his face in his hands and wept without restraint.

Oriana gazed at him affectionately, and tears of sympathy filled her large eyes also. But she drew away Henrichs hand, and kissed it, and tried to cheer him in the best way that her simple mind could suggest.

'My brother must not weep,' she said; 'for he is not a child, and our Indian youths are ashamed of tears. Henrich will be a brave some day, and he will delight in hunting, and in war, as our red warriors do; and he will, I know, excel them all in strength and courage. What can he desire more than to be a Nausett warrior?'

'Oh, Oriana,' replied the boy — as he wiped away his tears, and almost smiled at her attempts to console him by such a future prospect — ' I desire to return to my home, and my friends, and the worship of my God. Among your people none know anything of the true God, and none believe in His Son. I have no one to speak to me as my parents, and my venerable teacher, used to do; and no one to kneel with me in prayer to the Almighty.'

'Do not you worship the Great Mahneto — the Mighty Spirit from whom every good gift comes?' asked Oriana, with surprise. 'He is the one true God, and all the red men know and worship him.'

'Yes, Oriana, I do worship the one Great Spirit; the God and Father of all men of every color and of every clime. But the Christian's God is far more wise, and good, and merciful than the Indian's Mahneto: and He has told his servants what He is, and how they ought to serve Him.'

'Does your Mahneto speak to you?' asked the Indian girl. 'Could I hear him speak?'

'He has spoken to our fathers long ages ago, replied Henrich; 'and we have His words written in a book. Oh, that I had that blessed book with me! How it would comfort me to read it now!'

'And you would read it to me, my brother? But tell me some of your Mahneto's words; and tell me why you say He is greater and better than the Good Spirit who protects the red men.'

'I will gladly tell you all I know of the God whom I have been taught to love and worship ever since I was a little child. I wish I could make you love Him too, Oriana, and teach you to pray to Him, and to believe in His Son as your friend and Savior.'

'I will believe all you tell me, dear Henrich,' answered the ingenuous girl; 'for I am sure you would never say the thing that is not.[*] But what do you mean by a Savior? Is it some one who will save you from the power of the evil spirit Hobbamock—the enemy of the red men?'

[Footnote: The Indian expression for speaking a falsehood.]

Then Henrich told her of Jesus the Merciful—Him who came to save a world that was lost and ruined through sin; and to die for those who deserve nothing but wrath and condemnation. Long the youthful teacher and his attentive pupil conversed; and many and strange were the questions that Oriana asked, and that Henrich was enabled, by the help of the Spirit, to answer. The dark searching eyes of the intelligent young Indian were fixed on his, and her glossy black hair was thrown back over her shoulders, while she listened in wonder and admiration to every word that fell from the lips of her 'white brother.'

That evening, a new and awakening source of interest was opened to the young captive, and the dreariness of his life seemed almost to have passed away. The affection of Oriana had hitherto been his only solace and comfort, and now the hope of repaying that affection by becoming the humble means of leading her out of the darkness of heathenism, and pointing out to her the way of eternal salvation, raised his spirits, and almost reconciled him to his present banishment from home, and all its cherished joys and comforts.

More deeply than ever did he now regret that he was deprived of all access to the Word of Life, from which he might have read and translated the story of mercy to his young disciple, and have taught her the gracious promises of God. But Henrich had been well taught at home; his truly pious parents had early stored his mind with numerous passages of Scripture; and the effort he now made to recall to his memory all the most interesting stories, and most striking texts, that he had learnt from the Word of God, was the means of fixing them indelibly on his own heart. He never in after life forgot what he now taught to Oriana. The instruction was, as is generally the case, quite as much blessed to the teacher as to the learner; and Henrich was himself surprised to find how readily he could call to mind the very passage he wanted; and how easily he could convey its import to Oriana in her own melodious language.

Frequently were these interesting conversations renewed, and never without Henrich's perceiving, with thankfulness, that Oriana was making progress in spiritual knowledge, and also in quickness of understanding and general intelligence; for it may truly be said, that no kind of learning awakens the dormant powers of the intellect, or quickens the growth of the mind so effectually, as the knowledge of the one true God, who created the spirit, and of his Son who died to redeem it from the ignominious and degrading bondage, of sin and Satan. Henrich had, at first, imagined that it would be utterly impossible for him to find an intelligent companion among the savage race into whose hands he bad fallen and he had deeply felt that sense of loneliness which a cultivated mind, however young, must experience in the society of those whose ideas and feelings are altogether beneath its own, and who can in no way sympathize with any of its hopes, and fears, and aspirations. But now the well-informed English boy began to perceive that the superiority of the white men over the dark aborigines of America might, possibly, arise much more from difference of education, than from difference of race and color. He remembered, also, how ardently he had desired to share with the pious Brewster and Winslow, in their projected plans for the conversion of the natives; and he hoped that, young and comparatively ignorant as he knew himself to be, it might, perhaps, please God to make him the instrument of bestowing spiritual blessings on some, at least, of the heathen among whom he dwelt. He, therefore, resolved to employ all 'his powers of argument and persuasion to convince the mind, and touch the heart of the young Squaw-Sachem; not only for the sake of her own immortal soul, but also in the hope that her influence, if she became a sincere Christian, might greatly tend to the conversion of her father and his tribe.

Since the night when Tisquantum had seen his young captive kneel in prayer, and had questioned him as to the object of his worship, he had never spoken to him on the subject of his religion; and, Henrich had feared to address the stern old Chief, or to introduce a theme which, though constantly present to his own mind, and the source of all his consolation, would, probably, he rejected with scorn and contempt by the Sachem.

The more the Christian boy became acquainted with the character of Tisquantum, the stronger became this fear, and the more he despaired of any influence proving sufficiently strong to break the chains of error and superstition that bound him to heathenism. The Chief was a distinguished Powow, or conjuror; and was regarded by his own people, and even by many other tribes, as possessing great super natural powers. His pretensions were great, and fully accredited by his subjects, who believed that he could control the power of the subordinate evil spirits, and even exercise a certain influence on Hobbamock himself. He was called a Mahneto, or priest; as being the servant or deputy of the Great Mahneto, and permitted by him to cure diseases by a word or a charm, to bring down rain on the thirsty land, and to foretell the issue of events, such as the results of wars or negotiations. The influence which these acknowledged powers gave him over other tribes besides his own was very gratifying to his pride and ambition; and could Henrich hope that he, a young and inexperienced boy, could have wisdom or eloquence sufficient to 'bring down the high thoughts' that exalted him, and to persuade him to 'become a disciple of the meek and lowly Jesus? No; he knew that such a hope was, humanly speaking, vain: but he knew, also, that 'with God all things are possible'; and he ceased not to pray that the Spirit of light and truth might enter the soul of the heathen Chief, and banish the spirit of evil that now reigned so triumphantly there.

Henrich's desire to see the Sachem become a Christian was increased in the same measure that his hope of its accomplishment became less; for the more intimately he became acquainted with him, the more he found in his natural character that was interesting, and even estimable. Tisquantum was brave; and he was also generous and sincere, far beyond the generality of his race. We have said that the influence of his wife, whom he had, loved to an unusual degree for an Indian, had tended to soften his temper and disposition; and his regret for her loss, and his anxiety that his only daughter should resemble her, had made him more domestic in his habits than most of his brother chiefs. He was kind, also, when not roused to harshness and cruelty by either revenge or superstition; and he was capable of strong attachments where he had once taken a prepossession in favor of any individual.

Such a prepossession he had formed for his English captive on the evening when his child had pleaded for his life, and when his own ingenuous and beautiful countenance had joined so eloquently in her supplications. No insidious efforts of the wily Coubitant had availed to change the Sachem's sentiments; and he continued to treat Henrich as an adopted son, and to allow him all the privileges and indulgences that had once been bestowed on his beloved Tekoa. The white boy was permitted to enjoy full and unrestricted liberty, now that he was beyond all possible reach of his countrymen. He was encouraged to hunt, and sport, and practice all athletic games and exercises with the Nausett and Pequodee youths; and he was presented with such of the arms and ornaments of the lost Tekoa as were deemed suitable to his use, and his unusually tall and muscular figure.

Often when adorned with these strange and curious specimens of Indian art and ingenuity, did Haunch smile to think how Edith and Ludovico would wonder and admire if they could see him thus attired: and then he would sigh as he remembered that months and years must probably elapse—and possibly even his life might come to an end—ere he could hope to see their loved countenances, or to excite their surprise and interest by a relation of all his perils and adventures. To Oriana, alone, could he unburden his mind on such subjects; and from her he always met with deep attention and heartfelt sympathy; but every day she felt his presence to be more necessary to her happiness, and her dread of his escaping to his own people to become greater. Not only did she shrink from the idea of parting with her 'white brother '—her newly-found and delightful friend and companion—but daily, as she grew in the knowledge of Henrich's religion, and learnt to know and love the Christian's God and Savior more sincerely, did she fear the possibility of losing her zealous young teacher, and being deprived of all intercourse with the only civilized and enlightened being whom she had ever known.

She therefore rejoiced when the time arrived for leaving the Pequodee village, and pursuing the intended route to the west; for in spite of the distance and the many difficulties and obstacles that divided Henrich from the British settlement, she had lived in continual fear and expectation of either seeing a band of the mighty strangers come to demand his restitution, or revenge his supposed death; or else of his escaping from the camp, and braving every danger, in the attempt to return to his happy Christian home. Henrich often assured her with sincerity that he had no idea of venturing on so hopeless an attempt; but whenever the Indian girl saw his eyes fixed sadly on the eastern horizon, and dimmed, as they often were, by tears of sad remembrance, she felt her fears again arise, and longed more earnestly to leave the spot, and plunge into the trackless forest that lay between the Pequodee encampment and she proposed hunting grounds.

The summer had passed away and autumn was beginning to tinge the varied foliage of the forest with all its gaudy hues of yellow, and scarlet, and purple, when the Nausetts, and such of their Pequodee friends as desired to share in their hunting expedition, set forth from the village. Many women and girls accompanied the caravan, the greater part on foot, and bearing on their shoulders either the younger children, or a large pack of baggage; while their husbands, and fathers, and brothers, marched before them, encumbered only with their arms and hunting accoutrements. Such was, and still is, the custom among the uncivilized tribes of America, where women have ever been regarded as being very little more exulted than the beasts that perish, and have been accustomed to meet with scarcely more attention and respect. But there are exceptions to this, as to every other rule; and where women have possessed unusual strength of mind, or powers of influence, their condition has been proportionately better. Such had been the ease with Tisquantum's wife: and he had ever treated her with gentleness and respect, and had never imposed on her any of those servile duties that commonly fall to the lot of Indian squaws, even though they may be the wives and daughters of the most exalted chiefs. To his daughter the Sachem was equally considerate, and none but the lightest toils of domestic Indian life were ever required from her; nor was any burden more weighty than her own bow and quiver ever laid upon her slender and graceful shoulders, when she followed her father in his frequent wanderings.

On the present occasion, as the journey promised to be unusually long and uninterrupted, Tisquantum obtained for her a small and active horse of the wild breed, that abounds in the western woods and plains; and of which valuable animals the Pequodees possessed a moderate number, which they had procured by barter from the neighboring Cree Indians. The purchase of this steed gave Henrich the first opportunity of remarking the Indian mode of buying and selling, and the article that formed their medium of commerce, and was employed as money. This consisted of square and highly-polished pieces of a peculiar kind of a peculiar muscle-shell, called quahock, in each of which a hole was bored, to enable it to be strung on a slender cord. The general name for this native money was wampum, or white, from the color of those shells most esteemed; but a dark-colored species was called luki, or black; and both were used, of various forms and sizes, as ornaments by the warriors, and their copper-colored wives and children.

Several strings of wampum, both white and purple, were silently offered by the Sachem for the horse which he selected as most suitable for his daughter's use, and, after a pause, were as silently rejected by the possessor. Another pause ensued; and Tisquantum added a fresh string of the precious shell to the small heap that lay before him; and the same scene was repeated, until the owner of the horse was satisfied, when he placed the halter in the hands of the purchaser, gathered up his treasure, and, with a look of mournful affection at the faithful creature whom he was resigning to the power of another master, hurried away to his wigwam.

The next day the march began; and proud and happy was Oriana as she closely followed her father's steps, mounted on her new palfrey, and led by her adopted brother; while by her side bounded a favorite young dog, of the celebrated breed now called Newfoundland, which had been given to her brother as a puppy just before his melancholy death, and had been her only playfellow and loved companion, until Henrich had arrived to rival the faithful creature in her affections. At his request, the dog received the name of Rodolph, in memory of his father; and Henrich was never tired of caressing him, and teaching him to fetch and carry, and to plunge into his favorite element, and bring from the foamy torrent, or the placid lake, any object which he directed him to seize. He was a noble fellow, and returned the care and kindness of his new friend with all the ardor and faithfulness of his nature. It was his duty to accompany Henrich in all his expeditions in pursuit of game, and to bring to his feet every bird, or small animal, that his increasing skill in archery enabled him to pierce with his light and bone-pointed arrows.

During his residence in the Pequodee village, he had generally gone on such expeditions in company with several other men and boys; and Oriana had, consequently, enjoyed little opportunity of perceiving how much he had improved in dexterity since he had made his first trial before his captors. But now, as they traversed the woods together, he frequently aimed, at her desire, at some brilliant bird, or bounding squirrel; and the young maiden exulted at his success, and at the sagacity and obedience of Rodolph in bringing her the game.

The constant occupation, and the change of scene that Henrich enjoyed during this journey, tended greatly to raise his spirits, and even to reconcile him to his new mode of life. He did not forget his friends and his home—he did not even cease to think of them with the same regret and affection; but it was with softened feelings, and with a settled hope of eventually returning to them after a certain period of wandering and adventure. The kind of life which he had often longed to try was now his lot, and he enjoyed it under, peculiarly favorable circumstances; for he partook of its wildness and excitement, without enduring any of its hardships. No wonder, then, that a high-spirited and active-minded youth of Henrich's age, should often forget that his wanderings were compulsory; and should feel cheerful, and even exhilarated, as he roamed through the boundless primeval forests, or crossed the summits of the ranges of lofty hills that occasionally lifted their barren crags above the otherwise unbroken sea of foliage.

Pitching the camp for the night was always a season of excitement and pleasure to the young traveler, and his lively companion, Oriana. The selection of an open glade, and the procuring wood and water, and erecting temporary huts, were all delightful from their novelty. And, then, when all was done, and fires were kindled, and the frugal evening meal was finished, it was pleasant to sit with Oriana beneath the lofty trees, whose smooth straight trunks rose like stately columns, and to watch the glancing beams of the setting sun as they shone on the varied foliage now tinted with all the hues of autumn, and listen to the sighing of the evening breeze, that made solemn music while it swept through the forest. These were happy and tranquil hours; for then Henrich would resume the interesting topics to which his dusky pupil was never weary of listening. He would tell her—but no longer with tears—of his home, and all its occupations and joys; he would repeat the holy instructions that he had himself received; and, when far removed from the observation of other eyes and ears, he would teach her to kneel by his side, as Edith used to do, and to join him in supplications to 'the High and Lofty One that inhabiteth eternity'; but who yet listens to the humblest prayers that are addressed to Him in sincerity, and hears every petition that is offered up in the name of His beloved Son.

The heart of Oriana was touched; and with a beautiful child-like simplicity, she received all the blessed truths that her 'white brother' taught her. Her affections were strongly drawn towards the character of Jesus the Merciful, as she always called the Savior; and she became sensitively alive to the guilt of every sin, as showing ingratitude to the Benefactor who had laid down His life for His creatures. Oriana was, in fact, a Christian—a young and a weak one, it is true: but she possessed that faith which alone can constitute any one 'a branch in the true vine; and Henrich now felt that lie had found a sister indeed.

As the young Indian grew in grace, she grew also in sweetness of manner and refinement of taste and behavior. She was no longer a savage, either in mind or in conduct; and Henrich often looked at her in wonder and admiration, when she had made her simple toilette by the side of a clear stream, and had decked her glossy raven hair with one of the magnificent water lilies that be had gathered for her on its brink: and he wished that his mother and his fair young sister could behold his little Indian beauty, for he knew that they would love her, and would forget that she had a dusky skin, and was born of a savage and heathen race.

CHAPTER VII

'We saw thee, O stranger, and wept!
We looked for the youth of the sunny glance,
Whose step was the fleetest in chase or dance!
The light of his eye was a joy to see;
The path of his arrows a storm to flee!
But there came a voice from a distant shore;
He was call'dhe his found 'midst his tribe no more!
He is not in his place when the night fire, burn;
But we look for him still—he will yet return!
His brother sat with a drooping brow,
In the gloom of the shadowing cypress bough.
We roused him—we bade him no longer pine;
For we heard a step—but that step was thine.' HEMANS.

'What was that cry of joy, Oriana?' exclaimed Henrich, as one evening during their journey, he and his companion had strayed a little from their party, who were seeking a resting-place for the night. 'What was that cry of joy: and who is this Indian youth who has sprung from the ground so eagerly, and is now hurrying towards us from that group of overhanging trees? Is he a friend of yours?'

I know him not! replied Oriana. 'I never passed through this forest before: but I have heard that it is inhabited by the Crees. They are friendly to our allies, the Pequodees, so we need not fear to meet them.'

As she spoke, the young stranger rapidly approached them, with an expression of hope and expectation on his animated countenance; but this changed as quickly to a look of deep despondence and grief, when he had advanced within a few paces, and fixed his searching eyes en Henrich's face.

'No!' he murmured, in a low and mournful voice, and clasping his hands in bitterness of disappointment.'No; it is not Uncas. It is not my brother of the fleet foot, and the steady hand. Why does he yet tarry so long? Four moons have come, and have waned away again, since he began his journey to the land of spirits; and I have sat by his grave, and supplied him with food and water, and watched and wept for his return; and yet he does not come. O, Uncas, my brother! when shall I hear thy step, and see thy bright glancing eye? I will go back, and wait, and hope again.'

And the young Indian turned away, too much absorbed in his own feelings to take any further notice of Henrich and Oriana, who, both surprised and affected at his words and manner, followed him silently. Several other Indians of the Cree tribe now made their appearance among the trees, and hastened towards the travelers. But a look of disappointment was visible on every countenance: and the young travelers wondered greatly.[1 and 2]

[Footnote 1: 'J'ai passé moi-même chez une peuplade Indienne, qui se prenaît a pleurer à la vue d'un voyageur, parce qu'il lui rappelait des amis partis pour la contrée des Ames, et depuis long-temps en voyage. − CHATEAUBRIAND.]

[Footnote 2: 'They fancy their deceased friends and relatives to be only gone on a journey; and, being in constant expectation of their return, look for them vainly amongst foreign travelers. − PICART.]

But, though evidently grieved at not meeting the being they looked for so earnestly, the elder Crees did not forget the duties of hospitality. With simple courtesy they invited Henrich and his companion to accompany them to their wigwams, which were situated in a beautiful glade close by, and were only concealed by the luxuriant growth of underwood, that formed a sort of verdant and flowering screen around them. The invitation was gratefully accepted; for the countenances of the Crees inspired confidence, and Oriana knew that her father intended to visit a settlement of these friendly people, in the district they were now traversing. She also felt her curiosity strongly excited by what had just occurred, and she longed for an explanation of the conduct of the interesting young savage who had first accosted them.

She therefore requested one of their new acquaintances to go in search of the main body of their party, and to inform the Sachem that she and Henrich had preceded them to the wigwams; and then−with a dignity and composure that were astonishing in one so young and accustomed to so wild a life−she guided her palfrey into the narrow path that wound through the undergrowth of evergreens, while Henrich walked by her side, and Rodolph bounded before her.

They came to the spot where the young Indian sat by a grave; and tears were falling from his eyes as he gazed at the grass-covered mound, around which wore arranged several highly-carved and ornamented weapons, and articles of attire; and also a small quantity of firewood, and food, and tobacco, intended for the use of the departed on his long journey to the land of spirits. This is a well-known custom of most of the North American tribes; but the Crees have several superstitions peculiar to themselves, especially that melancholy one to which we have just alluded, and which subjects them to such lengthened sorrow and disappointment; for they watch and look for the return of their lost and lamented friends, who can never come again to gladden their eyes on earth. O that they were taught to place their hopes of a blessed reunion with those they love on the only sure foundation for such hopes — even on Him who is 'the Resurrection and the Life! Then they need never be disappointed.

It was this strange expectation of the reappearance, in human form, of the lately dead, that occasioned the incident we have just related. An epidemic disease had been prevalent in the Cree village; and, among those who had fallen victims to it, Uncas, the eldest orphan son of the principal man of the village, was the most deeply regretted, and his return was the most anxiously desired.

Especially was this vain hope cherished by his younger brother Jyanough, to whom he had been an object of the fondest love and most unbounded admiration; and who daily, as the evening closed, took fresh food and water to the grave, and sat there till night closed in, calling on Uncas, and listening for his coming footsteps. Then he retired sadly to his wigwam, to lament his brother's continued absence, and to hope for better success the following evening. During each night the dogs of the village, or the wild animals of the forest, devoured the food designed for Uncas; but Jyanough believed it had been used by his brother's spirit, and continued still to renew the store, and to hope that, at length, the departed would show himself, and would return to dwell in his wigwam.

When Haunch approached the grave, leading Oriana's pony, the mourner looked up, and gazed in his face again with that sad and inquiring look. But now it did not change to disappointment, for he knew that the stranger was not Uncas. There was even pleasure in his countenance as the clear glance of the English boy's deep blue eye met his own; and he rose from his seat at the head of the grave, and, going up to Henrich, gently took his hand, and said —

'Will the white stranger be Jyanough's brother? His step is free, and his eyes are bright, and his glance goes deep into Jyanough's heart. Will the pale-face be the friend of him who has now no friend; for four moons are guile and Uncas does not answer to my call?'

Henrich and Jyanough were strangers: they were altogether different in race, in education, and in their mode of thinking and feeling. Yet there was one ground of sympathy between them, of which the young Indian seemed instinctively conscious. Both had recently known deep sorrow; and both had felt that sickening sense of loneliness that falls on the young heart when suddenly divided from all it most dearly loves, by death or other circumstances. Jyanough and his elder brother Uncas had been deprived of both their parents, not many months before the fatal disease broke out which had carried off so many victims amongst the Crees. The orphan youths had then become all-in-all to each other, and their mutual attachment had excited the respect and admiration of the whole village, of which, at his father's death, Uncas became the leading man. Had he lived his brother would have assisted him in the government and direction of that portion of the tribe but when he fell before the desolating pestilence, Jyanough was too young and inexperienced to be made Sachem, and the title was conferred on a warrior who was deemed more capable of supporting the dignity of the community. Thenceforth the youth was alone in his wigwam. He had no sister to under take its domestic duties, and no friend with whom it pleased him to dwell. He saw something in Henrich's countenance that promised sympathy, and he frankly demanded his friendship; and the open-hearted English boy did not refuse to bestow it on the young Indian.

He spoke to him in his own tongue; and Jyanough's black eyes sparkled with joy as he heard words of kindness from the lips of the pale-faced stranger. Henrich's height and manly figure made him appear much older than he really was; and as he and his new friend walked together towards the village, he seemed to be Jyanough's equal in age and strength, although the young savage was several years his senior. As they entered the glade that was surrounded by lofty trees, and studded with wigwams, Tisquantum and the rest of the party approached by a path on the other side, and they all met in the center of the open space, and were welcomed by the friendly Crees. Wigwams were appointed to the Sachem and his daughter, and the most distinguished of the Nausetts and their Pequodee allies; while the inferior Indians of both tribes were directed to form huts for themselves beneath the neigh boring trees and all were invited to partake freely of the hospitality of their hosts, and to rest at the Cree settlement for several days, before they resumed their journey.

Jyanough conducted his English friend to his own wigwam, which was neatly furnished, and adorned with native tools and weapons. He bade him repose his tired limbs on Uncas' deserted couch; and while Henrich lay on the bed of soft grass covered with deer skins, that occupied one corner of the hut, the Indian youth busied himself in preparing an evening repast for his guest. The chief article of this simple supper consisted of *nokake,* a kind of meal made of parched maize or Indian corn, which Jyanough mixed with water in a calabash bowl, and, having well kneaded it, made it into small cakes, and baked them on the embers of his wood-fire. The nokake, in its raw state, constitutes the only food of many Indian tribes when on a journey. They carry it in a bag, or a hollow leathern girdle; and when they reach a brook or pond, they take a spoonful of the dry meal, and then one of water, to prevent its choking them. Three or four spoonfuls are sufficient for a meal for these hardy and abstemious people; and, with a few dried shellfish, or a morsel of deer's flesh, they will subsist on it for months.

Such viands, with the addition of some wild fruits from the forest, were all that Jyanough had to offer to his guest; but Henrich had known privation at home, and he had become accustomed to Indian fare. The kindness, also, and the courtesy of the untutored savage, as he warmly expressed his pleasure at receiving him into has wigwam, were so engaging, that the young traveler would cheerfully have put up with worse accommodation.

From Jyanough he now heard the story of his sorrows, which deeply interested him; and, in return, he told his host all that he could remember of his own past life, from his residence in Holland, and his removal to America, even till the moment when he and Oriana had approached the Cree village that evening The red man listened with profound attention, and constantly interrupted the narrator with intelligent questions on every subject that was interesting to him. But especially was his curiosity awakened when Henrich, in speaking of his grief at being torn from all his friends and relations, and his horror when he had anticipated a sudden and violent death, alluded to his trust in God as the only thing that had then supported him under his trials and sufferings, and still enabled him to hope for the future. The young Christian was not slow in answering all his inquiries as to the nature of the white man's Mahneto, and explaining to him why the true believer can endure, even with cheerfulness, afflictions and bereavements that are most trying to flesh and blood, in the confident hope that God will over-rule every event to his people's good, and will eventually restore all that they have lost.

'Then if I worship your *Keechee-Mahneto*[*] eagerly asked Jyanough, will he give back to me my brother Uncas? I have called on my Mahneto for four long moons in vain. I have offered him the best of my weapons, and the chief of my prey in hunting; and I have promised to pour on Uncas' grave the blood of the first prisoner I capture in war, or the first of our enemies that I can take by subtlety. Still Mahneto does not hear me. Tell me, then, pale-face, would your God hear me?

[Footnote: *Keechee-Mahneto* or Great Master of Life, is the name given by the Crees to their notion of the Supreme Being. Maatche-Mahneto is the Great Spirit of Evil.]

Henrich was much moved at the impassioned eagerness of the Indian, whose naturally mild and pensive expression was now changed for one of bitter disappointment, and even of ferocity, and then again animated with a look of anxious hope and inquiry.

'Yes, Jyanough,' he replied, with earnest solemnity; 'my God will hear you; but he will not give you back your brother in this world. If you learn to believe in Him; and to serve Him, and to pray to Him in sincerity, He will guide you to that blessed land where, after death, all His people meet together, and where there is neither sorrow nor separation.'

'But is Uncas there?' cried the young savage. 'Is my brother there? For I will serve no Mahneto who will not restore me to him!'

Our young theologian was disconcerted, for a moment, at this puzzling question, which has excited doubts and difficulties in wiser heads than his, end to which Scripture gives no direct reply. He paused awhile; and then he remembered that passage in the second chapter of the Epistle to the Romans, where the Apostle is speaking of the requirements of the law, and goes on to say, 'When the Gentiles which have not the law, do by nature the things contained in the law, these, having not the law, are a law unto themselves: which show the work of the law written in their hearts, their conscience also bearing witness, and their thoughts the mean while accusing or else excusing one another.' 'If St. Paul could say this of the severe and uncompromising law, surely,' thought Henrich 'the Gospel of love and mercy must hold out equal hope for those heathen who perish in involuntary ignorance, but who have acted up to that law of conscience which was their only guide.' He also recollected that Jesus himself, when on earth, declared, that 'He that *knew not,* and did commit things worthy of stripes, shall be beaten with few stripes': and, therefore, he felt justified in permitting the young Indian to hope that, hereafter, he might again behold that brother whose virtues and whose affection were the object of his pride and his regret.

'I believe,' he replied, 'that your brother—who you say was always kind, and just, and upright while he lived on earth—is now, through the mercy of God, in a state of happiness: and I believe that, if you also act up to what you know to be right, you will join him there, and dwell with him for ever. But I can tell you how to attain a more perfect happiness, and to share the highest joys of heaven in the kingdom that God has prepared for His own son. I can tell you what He has declared to be His will with regard to all His human creatures; even that they should love that Son, and look to Him as their Savior and their King. O, Jyanough, ask Oriana if she is not happier since she learnt to love and worship the God of the Christians!—the only God who can be just, and yet most merciful!'

In the vehemence of his feelings, Henrich bad rather outstripped his companion's powers of following and comprehending him. He saw this in Jyanough's wandering and incredulous eyes; and he carefully and patiently proceeded to explain to him the first rudiments of religion, as he had done to Oriana: and to reply to all his doubts and questions according to the ability that God gave him. A willing learner is generally a quick one; and Henrich was well pleased with his second pupil. If he was not ready to relinquish his old ideas and superstitions, he was, at least, well inclined to listen to the doctrines of his new friend, and even to receive them in connection with many of his heathen opinions. Time, and the grace of God, Henrich knew, could only cause these to give place to a purer belief, and entirely banish the *unclean birds* that dwelt in the cage' of the young Indian's mind. But the fallow ground had already been, in a manner, broken up, and some good seed scattered on the surface: and Henrich lay down to rest with a fervent prayer that the dew of the Spirit might fall upon it, and cause it to grow, and to bring forth fruit.

From the time of Henrich's captivity, he bad endeavored to keep up in his own mind a remembrance of the Sabbath, or the Lord's Day (as it was always called by the Puritans); and, as far as it was in his power to do so, he observed it as a day of rest from common occupations and amusements. On that day, he invariably declined joining any hunting or fishing parties; and he also selected it as the time for his longest spiritual conversations with Oriana; as he desired that she, also, should learn to attach a peculiar feeling of reverence to a day that must be sacred to every Christian, but which was always observed with remarkable strictness by the sect to which Henrich belonged.

In this, as in all other customs that the young pale-face wished to follow, he was unopposed by Tisquantum; who seemed entirely indifferent as to the religious feelings or social habits of his adopted son, so long as he acquired a skill in the arts of war and hunting: and, in these respects, Henrich's progress fully answered his expectations. He was, like most youths of his age, extremely fond of every kind of sport; and his strength and activity—which had greatly increased since he had adopted the wild life of the Indians—rendered every active exercise easy and delightful to him. He consequently grew rapidly in the Sachem's favor, and in that of all his companions, who learnt to love his kind and courteous manners, as much as they admired his courage and address. One only of the red men envied him the esteem that he gained, and hated him for it. This was Coubitant—the aspirant for the chief place in Tisquantum's favor, and for the honor of one day becoming his son-in-law. From the moment that the captor's life had been spared by the Sachem, and he had been disappointed of his expected vengeance for the death of his friend Tekoa, the savage had harbored in his breast a feeling of hatred towards the son of the slayer, and had burned with a malicious desire for Henrich s destruction. This feeling he was compelled, as we have observed, to conceal from Tisquantum; but it only gained strength by the restraint imposed on its outward expression, and many were the schemes that he devised for its gratification. At present, however, he found it impossible to execute any of them; and the object of his hate and jealousy was happily unconscious that he had so deadly an enemy continually near him. An instinctive feeling had, indeed, caused Henrich to shun the fierce young Indian, and to be less at ease in his company than in that of the other red warriors; but his own generous and forgiving nature forbade his suspecting the real sentiments entertained towards him by Coubitant, or even supposing that his expressions of approval and encouragement were all feigned to suit his own evil purposes.

Oriana had never liked him; and time only strengthened the prejudice she felt against him. She knew that he hoped eventually to make her his wife—or rather his slave—for Coubitant was not a man to relax from any of the domestic tyranny of his race; and the more she saw of her 'white brother,' and the more she heard from him of the habits and manners of his countrymen, and of their treatment of their women, the more she felt the usual life of an Indian squaw to be intolerable. Even the companionship of the young females of her own race became distasteful to her; for their ignorance, and utter want of civilization, struck painfully on her now partially cultivated and awakened mind, and made her feel ashamed of the coarseness of taste and manners occasionally displayed by her former friends and associates. In the Christian captive alone had she found, since her mother's death, a companion who could sympathize in her tastes and feelings, which had ever been above the standard of any others with whom she was acquainted. And Henrich could do more than sympathize in her aspirations—he could instruct her how they might be fully realized in the attainment of divine knowledge, and the experience of Christian love. No wonder, then, that Henrich held already the first place in her heart and imagination, and was endowed by her lively fancy with every quality and every perfection, both of mind and body, that she could conceive to herself.

The simple-minded girl made no concealment of her preference for the young stranger, whom she regarded as a brother—but a brother in every way immeasurably her superior—and her father never checked her growing attachment. The youth of both parties, the position that Henrich occupied in his family as his adopted son, and the difference of race and color, prevented him from even anticipating that a warmer sentiment than fraternal affection could arise between them; and he fully regarded his daughter as the future inmate and mistress of an Indian warrior's lodge — whether that of Coubitant or of some other brave, would, he considered, entirely depend on the comparative prowess in war and hunting, and the value of the presents that would be the offering of those who claimed her hand. That she should exercise any choice in the matter never occurred to him; and, probably, had he foreseen that such would be the case, and that the choice would fill on the son of a stranger — on the pale-faced captive whose father had slain her only brother — he would have removed her from such dangerous influence. But he thought not of such consequences resulting from the intimacy of Henrich and Oriana: he only saw that his child was happy, and that she daily improved in grace and intelligence, and in the skilful and punctual performance of all her domestic duties; and he was well satisfied that he had not shed the blood of the Christian youth on the grave of his lost Tekoa. His own esteem and affection for his adopted son also continued to increase; and, young as Henrich was, the influence of his superior cultivation of mind, and rectitude of principle, was felt even by the aged Chief, and caused him to treat him, at times, with a degree of respect that added bitterness to Coubitant's malicious feelings.

He saw how fondly Oriana regarded her adopted brother, and personal jealousy made him more clear-sighted as to the possibility of her affection ripening into love than her father had as yet become; and gladly would the rival of the unsuspecting Henrich have blackened him in the eyes of the Chieftain, and caused him to be banished from the lodge, had he been able to find any accusation against him. But in this he invariably failed; for the pale-face was brave, honest, and truthful, to a degree that baffled the ingenuity of his wily foe: and Coubitant found that, instead of lowering Henrich in the regard of the Sachem, he only excited him to take his part still more, and also ran a great risk of losing all the favor which he had himself attained in Tisquantum's eyes.

The sudden friendship that the young Jyanough had conceived for the white stranger, and the consequent favor with which he was looked upon by Oriana, tended still more to irritate the malignant savage; and when, a few days after the arrival of Tisquantum's party at the Cree village, he saw the three young friends seated amicably together beneath a shadowing tree, and evidently engaged in earnest conversation, he could not resist stealing silently behind them, and lurking in the underwood that formed a thick background to their position, in order to listen to the subject of their discourse. How astonished and how indignant was he to find that Henrich was reasoning eloquently against the cruel and ridiculous superstitions of the Indian tribes, and pointing out to his attentive hearers the infinite superiority of the Christian's belief and the Christian's practice! The acquiescence that Oriana expressed to the simple but forcible arguments of the pale-face added to his exasperation; and he was also angry, as well as astonished, to perceive that the young Cree, although he was yet unconvinced, was still a willing listener, and an anxious inquirer as to the creed of his white friend.

Maddened with rage, and excited also by the hope of at length arousing the anger of the Sachem against the Christian youth, he forgot his former caution, and hurried away, with quick and noiseless step, to the wigwam occupied by Tisquantum, and broke unceremoniously upon his repose as he sat, in a half-dreaming state, on the soft mat that covered the floor, and 'drank smoke' from his long, clay pipe.

With vehement gestures, Coubitant explained to the Sachem the cause of his sudden interruption, and implored him to listen to the counsel of his most faithful friend and subject, and to lose no time in banishing from his favor and presence one who showed himself unworthy of all the benefits he had heaped upon him, and who employed the life that had been so unduly spared in perverting the mind of his benefactor's only child. In vain his eloquence—in vain his wrath. Tisquantum regarded him calmly until he had exhausted his torrent of passionate expostulations, and then, quietly removing the pipe from his lips, he replied, with his and decision—

'My brother is angry. His zeal for the honor of Mahneto has made him forget his respect for the Sachem and the Sachem's adopted son. The life of the white stranger was spared that he might bring joy to the mournful eyes of Oriana. He has done so. My daughter smiles again, and it is well. Coubitant may go.

He then resumed his pipe, and, closing his eyes again, gave himself up to the drowsy contemplations, which the entrance of Coubitant had interrupted; and the disappointed warrior retired with a scowl on his dark brow, and aggravated malice in his still darker heart.

CHAPTER VIII

They proceed from evil to evil, and they know not me, saith the Lord
JER. IX, 3.

The indifference of Tisquantum on the subject of the religious opinions that his daughter might imbibe from her Christian companion, may seem strange. But the Sachem, though a heathen, was, in fact, no fanatic. He believed—or professed to believe—that he was himself in the possession of supernatural powers; and so long as these pretensions were acknowledged, and he continued to enjoy the confidence and veneration of his ignorant countrymen, he was perfectly satisfied. Henrich had also, on their first acquaintance, distinctly professed his faith in the existence and the power of the Great Mahneto, or *Master of Life;* and this was all the *religion*—properly so called—of which Tisquantum had any idea. He did not, therefore, give himself any concern as to the other objects of his adopted son's belief or worship; neither did he care to prevent Oriana from listening to the doctrines of the pale-face, so long as she continued obedient and gentle, and neglected none of the duties of an Indian squaw.

The feelings of Coubitant were different. Not only did he burn with an eager desire to deprive his rival of the Sachem's love and esteem, but he also entertained a strong abhorrence of the religion of the white men, as he had seen it practiced, and knew it was disseminated, by the Spanish settlers in Mexico, whither he had traveled in his early youth. In his eyes, these Christians were base idolaters; for such was the impression made on him by the images and crucifixes that he beheld, and the marks of veneration that were paid to these idols of wood and stone, by the superstitious and degenerate Spaniards of that district. When, therefore, he heard Henrich endeavoring to inculcate the worship of Jesus, as the Son of God, on Oriana and Jyanough, he not unnaturally regarded him as a believer in all the deities whose images he had seen associated with that of Jesus, and receiving equal homage.

Such, unhappily, has too often been the impression made on the minds of the heathen, in every quarter of the globe, by the vain and superstitious observances of the Roman Church, when her ministers have proposed to their acceptance so corrupt a form of Christianity, instead of the pure and holy doctrines of unadulterated Scripture. To those nations already given over to idolatry it has appeared that their civilized teachers were only offering them another kind of image- worship; but to the Indians of North America—who make use of no images of their deity, and generally acknowledge but one Great Spirit of universal power and beneficence, and one Spirit of evil—the carved and painted figures of the Spanish invaders naturally gave the idea of a multitude of gods; and, in some of them, excited unbounded indignation and hatred. This was the case with Coubitant; who, though totally uninfluenced by any love or fear of the Great Mahneto whom he professed to worship, was yet—like many other bigots of various countries and creeds—keenly jealous of any innovations in the religion of his nation; and ready to oppose, and even to exterminate, all who attempted to subvert it.

He now regarded Henrich as such an aggressor on the national faith and practice; and he consequently hated him with a redoubled hatred, and ceased not to plot in secret his ultimate destruction.

Meanwhile, his intended victim was passing his time in considerable enjoyment, and with a sense of perfect security, among the Crees. This tribe was at that time remarkable for hospitality, and likewise for courage and integrity. These good qualities have sadly degenerated since their intercourse with Europeans has enabled them to gratify the passion of all savages for intoxicating liquors: but at the period of which we are speaking, they were a singularly fine race of Indians, and their renown as warriors enabled them to extend protection to such of the neighboring tribes as entered into alliance with them. Disease had, indeed, recently reduced their numbers in many of the villages that were situated in the dense forest, and were thus deprived of a free circulation of air; and the wigwams at which Tisquantum's party had arrived were among those that had suffered most severely. Several of the lodges had been altogether deserted, in consequence of the death of the proprietors; in which case the Indians frequently strip off the thick mats which form the outer covering of the wigwam, and leave the bare poles a perishing monument of desolation! This is only done when the head of the family dies. The property of which he has not otherwise disposed during his life, is then buried with him; and his friends continue, for a long period, to revisit the grave, and make offerings of food, arms, and cooking utensils. These articles are deemed sacred to the spirit of the departed, and no Indian would think of taking them away unless he replaced them with something of equal value. This is permitted; and the custom must often afford relief to the hungry traveler through the forests, who comes unexpectedly upon the burial grounds of some of his race, and finds the graves amply supplied with maize and tobacco—more useful to the living than to the dead.

Many such graves, besides that of Uncas, were to be seen in the vicinity of the Cree village: and it seemed likely that their numbers would be still augmented; for the disease which had already proved so fatal, had not left the wigwams, although its violence had considerably abated. Old Terah, the uncle of Jyanough, and the chief of the present Sachem's council, lay dangerously ill; and all the charms, and all the barbarous remedies usually resorted to in such cases, had been employed by the Cree Powows in vain. Terah was one of the Pinces, or Pnieses—a dignity conferred only on men of approved courage and wisdom—and many a successful incursion had he led into the great plains of Saskatchawan, where dwelt the Stone Indians, with whom the Crees had long been at enmity—and many a prisoner had he brought back to his village, and slain as an offering to Maatche-Mahneto, while he hung the scalp that he had torn from the quivering victim on the walls of his lodge, as its proudest ornament.

Terah was also as wise in counsel as he was valiant in war; and, although his age prevented his assuming the office of Sachem, or ruler of the village,[*] on the death of his brother, yet his wisdom and experience gave him great influence with Chingook, the present Chief, and caused his life to be regarded as of peculiar value by the whole community.

[Footnote: Almost every considerable village has its Sachem, or Chief, who is subordinate to the great Sachem or Sagamore, of the whole tribe.]

The arrival of so celebrated a Powow as Tisquantum during a time of sickness-and especially when the death of so important a personage as Terah was apprehended—was hailed with great joy by the whole village; and presents of food, clothing, and arms poured into the lodge that formed his temporary abode, from such of the Crees as desired to secure his medical and supernatural aid for the relief of their suffering relatives. All day he was occupied in visiting the wigwams of the sick, and employing charms or incantations to drive away the evil spirits from his patients; sometimes also administering violent emetics, and other drugs from his *obee-bag*, or medicine-pouch; which contained a multitude of heterogeneous articles, such as herbs, bones, shells, serpents' teeth, and pebbles—all necessary to the arts and practices of a Powow. On the venerable Terah his skill and patience were principally exercised, and many were the torments that he inflicted on the dying old savage, and which were borne by the Pince with all the calm endurance that became his dignity and reputation. Terah, like all others of his exalted rank, had attained to the honor of being a Pince by serving a hard apprenticeship to suffering and privation in his early youth. He had passed through the ordeal triumphantly—and he who had run barefoot through sharp and tearing thorns—who had endured to have his shins beaten with a hard and heavy mallet, and his flesh burned with red hot spearsand had not even betrayed a sense of pain— in order to attain the rank of a great counselor, and the privilege of attending the Sachem as one of his guard of honor—did not shrink when his barbarous physician burned a blister on his chest with red-hot ashes, and scarified the horny soles of his feet till the blood flowed plentifully. Those, and strong emetic herbs, which he forced his patient to repeat until he fainted away, constituted the medical treatment of Tisquantum: but much greater benefit was expected— and, such is the power of imagination in these ignorant savages, that it was often attained—from the practice of his charms and conjurations.

As soon as Tisquantum saw his noble patient reduced to a state of unconsciousness by his physical treatment, he commenced a course of spiritual incantations. In a fierce and unnatural voice, he called on Hobbamock, or Satan, who he declared was visible to him in one of his many forms of an eagle, a deer, a fawn, and sometimes a gigantic human being. He then adjured the evil spirit, and commanded him to remove the disease; promising, in return, to offer to him skins, and hatchets, and even the scalps of his foes. If any signs of returning consciousness appeared, the Powow speedily banished them by a repetition of his wild howling, which he continued for hours, at the same time throwing himself about with wild and unnatural gestures, and striking his hands violently on his legs, until he became as much exhausted as his unlucky patient.

It was during one of these awful exhibitions of heathen cruelty and superstition, that Henrich one evening drew nigh to the lodge of Terah, accompanied by Oriana; and paused at the open entrance, in amazement and horror at the scene he beheld. The dying man lay stretched on the ground, in the center of the outer room of the hut, where he had been placed that he might enjoy the full benefit of the great Powow's skill. His eyes were closed and his gray hairs hung matted end disordered on the ground, while his emaciated features appeared to be fixed in death. A frightful wound was on his breast, and blood was trickling from his lacerated feet; while the involuntary contractions of his limbs alone denoted that he was yet alive, and sensible to suffering, which he was now unable to make any effort to conceal. Around the walls of the hut stood many of his relatives and dependants, whose countenances expressed anxiety and hope, mingled with fear of the priestly Sachem.

Among the bystanders, Henrich instantly recognized his friend Jyanough; and he shuddered to see the ingenious and inquiring youth assisting at such satanic rites. But the figure that chiefly attracted his attention, and to which his eyes became riveted, was that of Tisquantum — the father of his gentle and beloved Oriana! There stood the Sachem: he whose countenance he had seldom seen disturbed from his usual expression of gravity and composure, and whose dignity of manner had hitherto always commanded his respect. There he now stood — a victim to satanic influence! His tall figure was dilated to its utmost height by excitement and violent muscular effort, as he stood by the side of the sick man. His eyes were fixed with a fearful and unmeaning glare on the darkest corner of the hut, and seemed to be starting from their sockets; while his hands, stiff and motionless, were extended over the body of Terah, as if to guard him from the assault of some demons visible to the conjuror alone. In this statue-like posture he remained for some moments, while his breast heaved convulsively, and foam gathered on his parted lips. Then, suddenly, he uttered a yell — so loud and so unearthly that Henrich started with surprise and terror: and Oriana caught his hand, and tried to draw him away from a scene that now filled her soul with shame and sorrow.

But Henrich did not move: he did not heed the beseeching voice, and the gentle violence of his companion, whose wishes were generally commands to her white brother.

That yell had recalled the patient to partial consciousness, and he rolled his blood-shot eyes around him, as if endeavoring to collect his wandering senses; and then his haggard countenance again resumed the expression of imperturbable composure and firm endurance that an Indian warrior thinks it a disgrace to lose, even in the extremity of suffering. Then Tisquantum sank on one knee beside him, and burst forth into a passionate address to his deities — the powers of good and evil — whom he regarded as almost equally mighty to decide the fate of the patient.

'O, Mahneto!' he exclaimed, in a hoarse and howling voice; 'O, Richtan-Mahneto,[1] who created the first man and woman out of a stone, and placed them in these forests to be the parents of thy red children; is it thy will that Terah shall leave his brethren to mourn his departed goodness and wisdom, and go on that long and toilsome journey that leads to the hunting-grounds of our forefathers? Surely when his spirit *knocks at the door,* it will be opened to him, and the warriors of our tribe will welcome him, while his foes will be driven away with the awful sentence, *Quachet!*[2] Yes, Terah, the wise in counsel, and the fearless in war, shall surely dwell in the fields of happiness, and again strike the prey with the renewed strength and skill of his youth. But not yet, Mahneto! O, not yet! I see Hobbamock lurking there in the gloom! I see his fiery eagle eyes, and I hear the flap of his heavy wing; and I know that he hovers here to suck the blood of Terah, with all his murderous Weettakos around him![3] But Tisquantum's charms are too strong for him: he cannot approach the sick man now. Ha! Maatche- Mahneto!' he cried — and again he fixed his glaring eyes on the dark space in the far corner of the hut, from which the spectators had shrunk trembling away — ' Ha! spirit of evil! I behold thee — and I defy thee! Terah is not thine; and my power has compelled thee to send the *Ashkook*,[4] with his healing tongue, to lick my brother's wounds; and *Wobsacuck*, with eagle beak, to devour the venom that clogs his veins, and makes his breath come short and thick. I feel them on my shoulders, as they sit there, and stretch out their necks to do my bidding! Terah shall live!'

[Footnote 1: *Richtan,* supposed to signify old — Ancient of Days — the Maker]

[Footnote 2: *Quachet,* begone, or *march off;* supposed to be the sentence of condemnation uttered against the souls of the wicked, when they present themselves, and *knock at the door'* that leads to the Indian Paradise.]

[Footnote 3: *Weettako,* a kind of vampire or devil, into which the Crees and other tribes suppose all who have ever fed on human flesh to be transformed after death.]

[Footnote 4: *Ashkooke,* a demon in the form of a snake, who, with his brother-fiend, *Wobsacuck,* are supposed to be sent by Hobbamock to heal the sick, when forced, by the potent spells of the great Powow, to work good instead of evil.]

Tisquantum closed his wild oration with another loud and prolonged yell, to which all the spectators, who crowded the sides of the hut, replied by a short and yelping cry: and the Powow sank on the ground by the side of his patient, faint and exhausted by the violent and sustained exertions to which both his mind and body had been subjected for several hours without intermission. The attendants, among whom Jyanough was foremost, hastened to his assistance, and administered to him some needful refreshment; and Henrich turned away, grieved and disgusted, and fall of sympathy for his once heathen companion, who, he now remembered, was standing by his side, and witnessing the wild and degrading extravagances of a father whom she both loved and respected.

He looked into her deep expressive eyes, and saw that they were filled with tears of humiliation and mental agony. How could it be otherwise? How could she — who had learned to love a God of mercy, and to believe in a meek and lowly Savior—bear to see her father thus the slave of Satan, and the minister of cruel and heathen superstition? Especially, how could she bear that so degrading a scene should he witnessed by him from whom she had derived all she knew of the gospel of joy and peace, and whose esteem was more precious to her than the opinion of all the world beside?

Silently she walked by Henrich's side for neither of them were inclined to speak the thoughts that filled their minds. And silently they would have proceeded to Oriana's dwelling, where her white brother proposed to leave her with her attendants, and then to return and seek his deluded friend Jyanough; but ere they reached Tisquantum's lodge, they were overtaken by the Indian youth.

Jyanough had been too much engrossed by the exciting scene that took place in Terah's dwelling—and too eagerly watching for some favorable appearances that might encourage him to hope for the life of his only surviving relative—to observe that Henrich was also a spectator of these heathen rites, until all was concluded, and the patient and his physician were alike overpowered by heat and exhaustion. Then he had glanced towards the door, and had seen the saddened expression that clouded the open features of the Christian youth, and the look of anguish that Oriana cast on her degraded father; and then all the truths that Henrich had endeavored so simply and so patiently to impress upon his mind—all the arguments that his white friend had employed to win him from heathen darkness, and guide him into Divine truth—rushed at once upon his memory. He felt ashamed of the remaining superstition that had led him to take part in such vain ceremonies, and to deem that they could conduce to his uncle's recovery, after he had heard, and even assented to, the holy belief of the Christians in the universal power of Almighty God, and the victory of His Son Jesus Christ over the devil and all his angels. And he was grieved, also, that his kind and anxious young teacher should regard him as an ungrateful, and, possibly, even as a deceitful hearer.

He, therefore, hastened after Henrich and Oriana, and overtook them as they approached the lodge appropriated to the Nausett Sachem.

'Are you angry with your red brother?' he inquired earnestly, as he laid his hand on Henrich's shoulder, and looked sadly in his face. 'Do you think that Jyanough is a deceiver, and that he has listened to the teaching of the white stranger only to gain his friendship, and then to forsake him, and betray him, and return to the religion of his own people? O, no! Jyanough's heart is open and clear before the eyes of his friend; and he will gladly listen again to all the good things that Henrich tells him, for his heart says that they are true. But his soul is still very dark; and when he saw Terah ready to die, and felt that, when he was gone, there would be none to love him among all his tribe, the cloud grew thicker and thicker; and Maatche-Mahneto seemed to look out of the midst of the deep gloom with wrathful eyes of fire, and beckon him to follow to Terah's lodge, and join in the worship which the great Powow was about to offer. Will your Mahneto forgive him, Henrich?

The heart of the Christian boy was penetrated with joy and thankfulness at this frank confession of the young Indian. He clearly saw that the struggle—the universal and enduring struggle—between the powers of good and evil, had already commenced in the soul of the red man; and he had full confidence in the blessed declaration, that 'He who hath begun a good work of grace in the immortal spirit, will surely perfect it unto the end.' Therefore, he replied without hesitation, 'He will certainly forgive you, Jyanough; and if you desire His help to make your soul light, and strong, and joyful, and ask for that help in sincerity and truth, He will most assuredly give it to you. Let us enter the lodge, and there unite our prayers to the Great Spirit, who is the God and Father of all his creatures, that He will graciously shed His light and His truth into all our hearts; and, especially, that He will remove all the doubts and fears that still lie sadly and heavily on our brother's spirit.'

The three young friends did so: and in the deserted chamber of the great heathen Powow, Tisquantum, the voice of Christian supplication ascended to the throne of a prayer-answering God. Could it ascend unheeded? or fail to bring down, in His own good time, an answer of peace?

CHAPTER IX

The dark places of the earth are full of the habitations of cruelty.
PSA. lxxiv, 20

The night that followed this conversation, Jyanough passed in Terah's lodge, and he nursed his suffering relative with gentle patience. But he saw no signs of recovery, although the women and the Cree Powows assured him that the fatal disease was driven away by Tisquantum's powerful incantations, and that, when the sun rose, he would see the spirit of Terah revive. So had the conjuror declared; and so these misguided heathens believed. But when the first beams of opening day entered the door of the lodge, which was set open to receive them, and fell on the dark and pallid features of the aged sufferer, Jyanough could no longer be deceived into hope. He saw that his revered uncle was dying, and he hastened to inform Henrich of the fact, and to entreat him to return with him to Terah's wigwam, and to prey to the Great Spirit in his behalf.

Henrich readily complied: and he, too, was convinced, by the first glance at the dying Indian, that no human aid, however skilful, could long retain that once powerful spirit in its worn and wasted tenement of clay. He knelt down by the side of Terah's couch, and Jyanough knelt with him; and, regardless of the wondering gaze of the ignorant attendants, he offered up a short and simple prayer to God for the soul of the departing warrior.

The Cree Powows who had watched the sick man during the night, had left the lodge as soon as daylight set in, to collect materials for a great burnt offering they deigned to make, as a last resource, in front of the Pince's dwelling. As Henrich and Jyanough rose from their knees, the heathen priest entered, bearing strings of wampum, articles of furniture, of clothing, food, tobacco, and everything of any value that they had been able to obtain from the friends of Terah. All these various articles were displayed before the dim eyes of the invalid, for whose benefit they were to be reduced to a heap of useless ashes; and a faint smile of satisfaction passed over Terah's countenance: but he spoke not. Jyanough then bent down, and pressed his lips to the cold brow of his almost unconscious uncle, and hurried with Henrich from the lodge; for he could not bear again to witness any repetition of the heathen ceremonies that had caused him so much shame the preceding day: neither could he endure to see his last relative leave the world, surrounded by a spiritual darkness which it was not in his power to dispel.

The young friends took their way into the forest, that they might be beyond the sight and the sound of those rites that were about to be performed for the recovery of one who had already begun to travel through the valley of the shadow of death. They had not, however, gone far in a westerly direction, before they chanced their intention, and resolved to return to the village. The cause of this change of purpose was their meeting with a band of Cree warriors, who had gone out, some weeks previously, on an expedition against a settlement of their enemies, the Stone Indians; and were now returning from the plains of the Saskatchawan, laden with spoils. Many of the Crees bore scalps suspended from their belts, as bloody trophies of victory; and all had arms, and skins, and ornaments that they had carried away from the pillaged wigwams of their foes.

Henrich could not help gazing with admiration at the party of warriors as they approached. The greater part of them were mounted on beautiful and spirited horses of the wild breed of the western prairies, which they rode with an ease and grace that astonished the young Englishman. They wore no covering on their heads, and their black hair was cut short, except one long scalp-lock hanging behind; so that their fine countenances, which were rather of the Roman cast, were fully exposed to view. Their dress consisted of a large blanket, wrapped gracefully round the waist, and confined by a belt, so as to leave the bust and arms bare; and so perfect and muscular were their figures, that they had the appearance of noble bronze statues. Their native weapons, consisting of spears and bows, with highly ornamented quivers suspended from their shoulders, and battle-axes hung to their belts, added much to their martial and picturesque effect. Behind the horsemen followed a band on foot, who carried the stolen treasures of the wasted village; and Henrich looked with curiosity at the various and beautifully decorated articles of dress, and hunting equipments, that had formed the pride and the wealth of the defeated Stone Indians.

But the part of the spoil that interested and distressed both Henrich and his companion more than all the rest, was a young Indian warrior, who, with his wife and her infant, had been brought away as prisoners to add to the triumph, and, probably, to glut the vengeance, of their conquerors. There was an unextinguished fire in the eye of the captive, and an expression of fearless indignation in the proud bearing with which he strode by the side of his captors, that clearly told how bravely he would sell his life but for the cords that tightly bound his wrists behind him, and were held by a powerful

Cree on each side. Behind him walked his wife, with downcast features and faltering steps, and at her back hung her little infant, suspended in a bag or pouch of deer skin, half filled with the soft bog-moss, so much used by Indian squaws to form the bed—and, indeed, the only covering—of their children during the first year of their existence. The eyes of the captive young mother were fixed tearfully on the majestic form of her husband, who was too proud—perhaps, also, too sad—to turn and meet her gaze, while the eyes of his foes were upon him to detect his slightest weakness. Even the low wailing cry of her child was unheeded by this broken hearted wife in that sad hour; for she well knew the customs of Indian warfare, and she had no hope for the life of her warrior, even if her own should be spared.

Henrich gazed on the little group in pity; for be instinctively read their story, and their coming fate, in their countenances, and in the cruel glances that fell on them from their guards. He looked at Jyanough; and in his expressive features he saw a fell confirmation of his worst fears.

'They will sacrifice them to Maatche-Mahneto in the vain hope of lengthening Terah's life,' he softly whispered in Henrich's ear. 'Let us go back and seek Oriana. Perhaps, for her sake, Tisquantum may ask the lives of the squaw and her young child; and, as Chingook's honored guest, they would be granted to him; but there is no hope for the warrior. His blood will surely be shed to appease Maatche-Mahneto, and to atone for the death of several of the Cree braves who have fallen this year by the hands of the Stone tribe.'

Hastily Henrich turned; and, followed by Jyanough, took a by-path well known to them, and entered the village before the arrival of the warriors and their unhappy prisoners. A brief explanation was sufficient to enlist all the kindly feelings, and all the Christian spirit, of Oriana in favor of their project; and she lost no time in seeking her father, who had again repaired to Terah's hut, to superintend the costly sacrifice that was being offered in his behalf. She found him exulting in a partial improvement in his patient, whose senses had again returned with a brief and deceitful brilliance, and attributing what he called the aged Pince's recovery to the potency of his own spells.

This was no time for Oriana to argue with the elated Powow on the fallacy of his pretensions. She therefore listened patiently to his boastings; and then, with much feeling and natural eloquence, told him the cause of her interrupting him at such a moment, and besought him to exert all his great influence with the Crees, to induce them to spare the lives of the Stone captives.

Tisquantum listened with attention to her story and her petition, for he was always gentle to Oriana; but he gave her little hope of that fell success which her warm young heart desired, and anticipated.

'My child,' he said, 'I will do what you ask, so far as to request that the woman and child may be placed at your disposal. But the warrior's life I cannot demand, for it would be an insult to the brave Crees to suppose that they would suffer an enemy to escape, and tell his tribe that they were woman-hearted. No, he must die; and, if the soul of his ancestors dwells in him, he will exult in the opportunity of showing how even a Stone Indian can meet death.'

Oriana was repulsed, but not defeated, by this reply. 'Nay, my father,' she again began, 'either save all, or let all perish. Do not take the brave young warrior from his wife and child, and leave them in poverty and sorrow; but plead for mercy to be shown to him also — and so may mercy be shown to his conquerors, and to you, his deliverer, when — '

'Peace, child,' interrupted the Sachem, with more asperity than he usually showed to Oriana. 'These are the notions you have learned from your white brother, and I desire not to hear them. Tisquantum knows his duty. I will demand the lives of the woman and child of whom you speak; but the warrior must abide his fate. And think you that he would not scorn to live when honor is gone I Go' — he added more gently, as he saw the sorrow that dimmed her eye — 'go, and tell Jyanough to meet me at the Sachem's lodge. Terah may yet be saved — this victim comes at s happy moment, and surely Mahneto demands his life as at offering for that of the venerable Pince.'

Oriana shuddered at what she saw to be her father's meaning. Once she would have felt as he did and have believed that their god could be propitiated by blood and agony. But now she knew that all such cruel sacrifices were worse than vain; and deeply she regretted her own inability to bring her countrymen, and especially her own beloved father, to a knowledge of the Gospel of mercy and peace; and thus save them from imbruing their hands in the blood of their fellow men, and thinking that they did good service to the Great Spirit.

She hurried back to her companions, and, weeping, told them of her partial success. It was all, and more than all, that Jyanough expected; and he immediately went to meet Tisquantum at the lodge of the Cree Sachem, Chingook, where he found the war party and their prisoners assembled. After a few words to Jyanough, Tisquantum commenced a long speech to his brother Sachem, in which he dilated on the friendship that subsisted between them, and the joy that he had felt in exercising his skill for the benefit of the brave and hospitable Crees. He then spoke of Terah's perilous condition, and his fears that even his powers had been baffled by the spirit of evil; and that the Pince would yet be taken from them, unless some offering could be found more precious than all that were now piled before his dwelling, and only waited for the auspicious moment to be wrapped inflame, us a sacrifice to the offended deity who had brought the pestilence. 'And have we not such an offering here?' he added, pointing to the captive warrior, who stood, with head erect, awaiting the sentence that he knew would be pronounced. 'Have we not here a victim, sent by Mahneto himself, at the very moment when Terah's life seems hanging on a breath? Lead him, then, to the sacred pile; and as his soul goes forth, the soul of Terah shall revive.

This speech was received with acclamations by the Crees; and already the warriors were hurrying away their captive, while his wife followed, as if mechanically, to share her husband's fate. Bat here Tisquantum interposed, and, in his daughter's name, requested the life of the woman and her child. His request was readily granted by Chingook; for of what value was a squaw in the eyes of these Indian braves?

The daughter of our friend and benefactor shall be denied nothing that she asks,' replied the Cree Chief. 'Take the woman to Oriana's lodge, and let her be her slave.'

Jyanough approached to lead away the unhappy woman but she turned on him a look of despairing misery, and, laying her band on her husband's arm, said quickly, 'I will see my Lincoya die, and then I will follow you where you will, for Mailah has no home.'

Jyanough did not oppose her, for his heart was touched by her sorrow and her fortitude; and the captive warrior turned his head, and bent on her sad countenance one look of tenderness and approbation, that told how deeply he was sensible of her devotion.

He did not speak—perchance he could not trust his voice in that trying moment—but he followed his guards, and his eye was again steadfast, and his step was firm.

Henrich and Oriana waited anxiously for the return of Jyanough: but he came not; and they almost feared that Tisquantum's request had been too coldly urged to prove successful. It was a calm autumnal day; and as the sun rose high in the heavens, his beams were shrouded by heavy thunder clouds, while a low and distant murmur foretold an approaching storm, and added to the gloom that weighed heavily on Oriana's spirit. All the sin and degradation of the faith of her countrymen seemed to strike upon her mind with a force hitherto unknown, and to bow her down in shame and sadness. Even to Henrich—to her loved Christian friend and teacher—she could not now utter her feelings; and when, to divert her thoughts, and remove her from the village where he knew so cruel a scene would soon be enacted, he led her towards the forest, she followed him silently. They seated themselves beneath an overshadowing tree; and, for some time, no sound broke the oppressive silence save the soft rustling of the leaves, that seemed to be moved by the spirits of the air-for no wind was stirring.

Presently a shriek—one single cry of agony—arose from the village: and all was still again.

'It was a woman's voice!' exclaimed Oriana, in a tone of deep suffering. 'O, Henrich! they murder the helpless and the innocent; and my father consents to the deed!'

Henrich did not reply; he had no comfort to offer. But they both gazed towards the village, as if hoping to discover, through the impervious wood that surrounded it, some indications of what was going on in those 'habitations of cruelty.

Soon a dense cloud of smoke rose high in the still at; and flames shot up above the intervening trees. And then burst forth a mingled din of wild unearthly sounds, that told of sated vengeance, and malignant joy, and demoniac worship. Fiercely the war cry of the Crees rang in the air, while above it rose the shrill sound of clashing spears and tomahawks; and Oriana knew that the savages were dancing round a death- fire, and calling on Mahneto to accept their bloody offering.

But now the threatening storm broke suddenly on that dark place of the earth; and it seemed to Oriana's troubled spirit that the wrath of heaven was poured upon her benighted race. Peal after peal resounded in quick succession, and reverberated from the distant kills; while flashes of forked lightning followed one another rapidly, and dispelled, for a moment, the unnatural darkness. The young Indian clung trembling and terrified to her companion, and hid her face on his shoulder, to shut out the fearful scene, while Henrich spoke to her words of comfort and encouragement, and at length succeeded in calming her agitation. The rain poured down in torrents but so dense was the foliage that hung over Oriana and her companion that it could not penetrate their place of refuge; and they remained awaiting its cessation, and watching the curling smoke, that seemed to die away as the falling torrent extinguished the fire. But as it disappeared, another cloud arose near the same spot; and wider and fiercer flames sprang up, that defied the rain, and continued to burn with more and more strength. Whence could they arise? Surely the wigwams were on fire!

Henrich communicated this fear to Oriana, and they arose and hurried together towards the village, where an appalling scene met their eyes. In front of Terah's dwelling were the smoldering remains of the sacrificial fire, on which — still upheld by the stake to which he had been bound — the burnt and, blackened form of a man was visible; while close by the ashes lay a woman, so motionless that she seemed as totally deprived of life as the wretched victim himself, and a child was reclining on her shoulder, whose faint wailing cry showed that it yet lived and suffered.

None heeded the melancholy group; for the warriors, whose wild songs and frantic dances had been interrupted by the sudden violence of the storm, were all now engaged in fruitless efforts to extinguish the flames that were rapidly consuming the lodge of Terah. The lightning had struck it, and ignited its roof of reeds; and so rapidly had the whole dwelling become a prey to the dreadful element, that even the removal of the dying sage had been despaired of. But Jyanough, who had been a silent spectator of all the previous scene of cruelty, was not to be daunted by the smoke and flame that burst through the entrance, and drove from the chamber of death all the attendants of the sufferer. Boldly he rushed into Terah's dwelling; and, just as Henrich and Oriana entered the open space in front of it, they beheld him issuing forth, blackened with smoke and scorched with fire, and bending beneath the weight of his uncle's corpse.

Yes; Terah was already a corpse! All the charms and incantations of the Powows bad failed to banish the disease that was sent to summon him away. All the treasure that had been destroyed, and the precious life- blood that had been spilled to propitiate false deities, could not for one moment arrest the fiat of the true 'Master of life,' or detain the spirit which was recalled by Him who gave it' That spirit had passed away amidst the noise of the tempest; and when Henrich sprang forward, and assisted his friend to lay the body gently on the earth, they saw that the spark of life had fled!

All further attempts at extinguishing the fire were now abandoned; and the Crees gathered round their departed friend to condole with Jyanough, who was his nearest relative, and to commence that dismal howling by which they express their grief on such occasions. All the property of the dead man was already consumed; but the best mats and skins that Jyanoughs wigwam contained were brought to wrap the corpse in; and when the site of his former dwelling could be cleared of ashes and rubbish, a grave was speedily dug in the center of it, and the, body laid by the simple sepulchre, around which the friends of the venerated Pince seated themselves, and howled, and wept, and detailed the virtues and the wisdom of the dead.

Jyanough was expected to act the part of chief mourner in these ceremonies; and the real affection he had entertained for his uncle induced him to comply, and to remain all that day, and all the following night, at the grate. But he refused to cover his face with soot—as is customary on such occasions of domestic sorrow—or to join the Powows in their frantic cries and exorcisms, to drive off the Weettakos from sucking the dead man's blood. The presence of Henrich seemed to annoy and irritate these priests of Satan; and he was glad to retire from a scene so repugnant to his better feelings, and to return to Oriana, by whose care and direction the unhappy Mailah and her infant had been promptly removed from the place of death and desolation, and conveyed to her own apartment in Tisquantums lodge.

Her kind efforts had restored the poor young widow to consciousness; and she now sat on the floor, with her child on her knee, listening with a calmness that almost seemed apathy, to the words of comfort that were uttered by the gentle Squaw-Sachem.

Mailah was very young. Scarcely sixteen summers had passed over her head; and yet—such is Indian life—she had already been a wife and a mother; and now, alas! she was a widow. Her grief had been passionate at the last, and had burst forth in that one wild cry that had startled Orianas ear in the forest. But that was over now, and she seemed resigned to her hard fate, and willing to endure it. Perhaps this was for her infant's sake; and, perhaps, her sensibilities were blunted by the life she had led, in common with the rest of her race and sex—a life in which the best feelings and sympathies of our nature are almost unknown. It was not until Oriana led her to speak of her past life, and the home of her youth—now desolate and in ruins—that tears of natural grief flowed from her eyes. Then she seemed roused to a full sense of all she had lost, end broke out into mournful lamentations for her murdered Lincoya, whose noble qualities and high lineage she eloquently extolled; while she sadly contrasted her present lonely and desolate position with her happiness as the squaw of so distinguished a warrior, and so successful a hunter.

Oriana said all she could to console her; and assured her of her protection and friendship, and of a home in her lodge when they returned to their own country, where she should live as her sister, and bring up her little Lincoya to emulate his father's courage and virtues: and, ere long, the simple young savage again grew calm, said lifted up her soft black eyes, and smiled gratefully at her new friend and benefactor. She said she bad no wish to return to her own tribe, for all her family and friends had been destroyed in the recent massacre; and the village where she had spent such happy days was reduced to ashes. She, therefore, was well content to remain with the youthful Squaw-Sachem, to whose intercession she knew she owed her own life and that of her child, and in whose service she professed her willingness to live and die.

Her manner and appearance greatly interested Henrich, for they were marked by much greater refinement than he had seen in any of the Indian females, except Oriana. This was to be accounted for by her noble birth; for in those days the Indian chieftains prided themselves on the purity and nobility of their lineage; and no member of a Sachem's family was allowed to marry one of an inferior race. A certain air of dignity generally distinguished the privileged class, even among the females; although their lives were not exempt from much of hardship and servitude, and they were regarded as altogether the inferiors of their lords and masters.

To Oriana the arrival of the young mother and her playful child was a source of much pleasure and comfort; for she had begun to feel the want of female society, and the women who accompanied Tisquantum's party, and assisted her in the domestic duties of the family, were no companions to her. In Mailah she saw that she could find a friend; and her kindness and sympathy soon attached the lonely young squaw to her, and even restored her to cheerfulness and activity. It was only when she visited the grave in which Henrich and Jyanough had laid the murdered Lincoya, and decked it with flowers and green boughs, that the widow seemed to feel the greatness of her affliction. Then she would weep bitterly, and, with passionate gestures, lament her brave warrior. But, at other times, she was fully occupied with the care of her little Lincoya, or in assisting Oriana in the light household duties that devolved upon her. And her sweet voice was often heard singing to the child, which generally hung at her back, nestled in its soft bed of moss.

CHAPTER X

The noble courser broke away.
  And bounded o'er the plain?
The desert echoed to his tread,
  As high he toss'd his graceful head,
And shook his flowing name.

  King of the Western deserts! Thou
  Art still untam'd and free!
Ne'er shall that crest he forced to bow
Beneath the yoke of drudgery low:
But still in freedom shalt thou roam
The boundless fields that form thy home
  Thy native Prairie!' ANON.

The camp of the Indian hunters looked cheerful and picturesque, as Oriana and Mailah approached it one evening on their return from a ramble in the forest, where they had been to seek the wild fruits that now abounded there, and paused at the skirt of the wood, to admire the scene before them. The proposed hunting-ground had been reached the preceding day, and already the temporary huts were completed, and the tents of the Sachem pitched beneath a grove of lofty oaks and walnuts, free from underwood, and on the border of a clear and rippling stream. The Nausett and Pequodee hunters had purchased a considerable number of horses from their Cree friends; and, therefore, the journey from Chingook's village to the prairie, in which the encampment now stood, had been performed with much ease and expedition; and the hardy animals were so little fatigued by their march through the forest, that several of the younger Indians had mounted again the morning after their arrival, and gone off on a reconnoitering expedition, to discover what prospect there was of finding much game in that neighborhood.

Henrich—proud and happy in the possession of a spirited horse, with which Tisquantum had presented him—insisted on being one of the party; end he was accompanied, also, by Jyanough, who had left his native village, now rendered sad and gloomy in his eyes, to follow his white friend, and share his society at least for a time. This arrangement gave Henrich the greatest satisfaction for the young Cree was the only Indian of his own sex in whom he had been able to find a companion, or who had peculiarly attached himself to the stranger: and the more he saw of Jyanough the more he found in him to win his esteem and friendship.

Oriana and Mailah seated themselves on the luxuriant grass to rest; and the young Indian mother removed her child from the strange cradle in which she always carried it, and laid it on her knees; and then, after gazing at it for a few moments, she began to sing a wild, sweet song, to hush it to sleep. In a soft, monotonous cadence, she sang the sad story of its little life—its birth—its captivity—and the death of its murdered father, whom she exhorted it to imitate, and live to equal in courage and in skill. And thus she sang:

'Child of the slain Lincoya, sleep In peace! Thy mother wakes to guard thee. But where is he whose smile once fell on thee as sunshine—thy father, Lincoya? He is gone to the far distant hunting-grounds and there, again, he casts the spear; and there he draws the unerring bow; and there he quaffs the cup of immortality, with the spirits of the good and brave. O Lincoya! thy voice was to me as a sweet song, or as the summer breeze among the tall cypress trees—why didst thou leave me? Thy step was swift and graceful as the roe upon the mountains—why didst thou leave me? But I will follow thee, my warrior, The death-bird has called me, and I come to thee! Thy child shall live; for Mahneto has given him friends and a home. He shall grow up like thee, and Oriana shill be o mother to him when I am gone: and the blue-eyed stranger, whom she loves as I loved thee, shall guide his hand in war, and in the chase. Lincoya! I come to thee!'

Oriana listened to the mournful chant of the young widow with much interest and sympathy; but when she spoke of her love for her white brother, in terms so new and strange, she almost felt offended. She did not, however, remark on her friend's allusion to herself, but turned the discourse to Mailah's sad prophecy of her own early death, which she knew could only be grounded on one of the wild superstitions of her race.

'Why do you talk of dying, Mailah?' she asked. 'You are young and strong; and you may again be happy. Why do you say you will leave your child, and go to the land of spirits?'

'The death-bird[*] called to me last night, as I sat at the open door of the hut, and looked at the moon, and thought how its soft light was guiding my Lincoya on long, long, journey, to the everlasting hunting fields of his fathers. Cheepai-Peethees called me twice from the tree that hung over the lodge; but when I called to it again, and whistled clearly, it made no answer. I heard it the day before the Crees destroyed our village. It called my husband then, and would not answer him; and in two days he was slain. The death-bird is never mistaken.

[Footnote: A small owl called *Cheepai-Peethees,* or the *death-bird,* which the Indians attach the superstition here alluded to, and believe, if it does not answer to their whistle, it denotes their speedy death.]

O, Mailah!' replied the young Christian squaw, 'say not so. Surely it is not thus that the great Mahneto calls His children to come to Him. Once I believed all these Indian stories; but now I know that they are false and vain. I know that our lives, and all things that befall us, are in the hands of the wise and good God—the Mahneto of the Christians and of the red men too. And now I have no fear of any of those strange sounds that used to make me sad, and terrify me with thoughts of coming evil. I most teach you to believe as I do now: or, rather, my *white brother* shall teach you; for he knows the words of Mahneto himself. See, Mailah! There my brother comes—let us go to meet him.'

A flush of joy mounted to the clear olive cheek of Oriana as she said these words, and she sprang to her feet with the lightness of a fawn. Mailah rose more gently, and replacing her infant in the pouch, slung it over her shoulder, and followed her friend, softly whispering in her ear, The white stranger is your Lincoya.'

The Indian beauty smiled, and blushed more deeply: but she did not bound across the glade to meet Henrich as she had purposed doing. She drew her slender figure to its full height, and stood still; and as Henrich galloped across the green meadow, and alighted, full of animation, to tell her of his success in his first essay at hunting the elk, he wondered why she greeted him so coldly.

The fact was that Oriana was beginning to find that the blue-eyed stranger possessed even more interest in her eyes than she had ever felt for her own dark brother, Tekon; and when Mailah had openly alluded to this sentiment—which she thought unknown to all but herself—her natural and instinctive delicacy was wounded. But the feeling quickly wore away; and as Henrich and Jyanough detailed the exciting sports of the day, she forgot all but the pleasure of listening to his voice, and gazing at his fine countenance and bright sweet smile. She was happy; and she though not of the future.

And Henrich was happy, too. He had now found companions whom he could love; and the life of the Indian hunters was all that he had ever pictured to himself of freedom and adventure. The beauty of the scenery—the clearness of the sky—and the glow of health and excitement that animated his whole frame when he joined in the chase with his savage friends, were all so entirely different to the life he had led in damp and foggy Holland, that it was no wonder he enjoyed it, and that his youthful spirits enabled him to subdue the oft-recurring grief that he felt at each remembrance of his family and his home. Hope was strong in his breast; and he trusted once again to meet all whom he loved so dearly: and the present was so bright and inspiring that he could not desire to change it yet.

For many weeks the camp remained pitched in the same lovely situation; and the time of the hunters was fully occupied in the discovery and pursuit of the various wild animals that abounded in the uncultivated, but richly verdant, prairie. Of these, the elk and the buffalo were the most common victims to the spears and arrows of the Indians; and every evening large quantities of meat were brought into the camp, and given to the care of the squaws to dry and cure for winter consumption. These larger animals were too heavy to be transported whole to the huts; end therefore the hunters always skinned them and cut off the flesh where they fell, and left the carcasses to the wolves and the birds of prey that were ever ready at hand. But the smaller animals, and the wild turkeys and other birds, that were killed in great numbers, were brought in and thrown down by the blazing camp fires, that lighted up the glade every night, and were speedily prepared and cooked for the supper of the hungry hunters.

As the leader of the expedition, Tisquantum was always presented with the choicest of the game; and it was Oriana's task to superintend the curing of the elk and buffalo meat, and the cooking that was required for her father's lodge. In all these household cares she was greatly assisted by Mailah, who was both active and skilful in all the duties of an Indian squaw: and eager also to evince her gratitude for the kindness and protection that were afforded to herself and her child by the Nausett Chief, by doing all that she could to lighten Oriana's labors. Time and occupation did not fail to have their usual effect on one so young, and naturally so light-hearted as Mailah; and animated cheerfulness took the place of the mournful expression that had hitherto so frequently sat on her countenance. She did not forget Lincoya; but she forgot the call of the death-bird: and when she sang her child to sleep, it was no longer with the same sad cadence as at first. Sorrow could not strike very deep, or abide very long in the heart of a being so gay, and with a mind and feelings so utterly uncultivated as those of the young Stone Indian. Neither could she live so much in the society of the white stranger, and his two chosen companions, without imbibing something of their intelligence, and becoming sensible of their superiority of mind to all others with whom she had ever associated: and she grew more and more attached to them, and learnt to regret less the friends and companions among whom her youth had been spent.

She was a high-spirited and courageous creature: she would have followed her husband unhesitatingly to death, had she been called on to do so; or she would have died to save him, if her life could have availed to purchase his. But now that he was gone, and she could not even weep over his grave, and deck it with flowers and gifts, her lively spirit rose again, and led her to seek amusement and occupation in everything within her reach.

The accounts which Henrich and Jyanough continually gave to her and Oriana of their exciting adventures in the prairie, had aroused in both of them a strong desire to be spectators of the sport; and they sought and obtained Tisquantum's permission to accompany the hunters one morning to the buffalo ground that lay nearest to the camp, and there to witness the pursuit and capture of some of those magnificent animals.

A short ride through the forest brought the party out upon a vast and glorious prairie, on which the rich autumnal sun was shining in all his strength. On a rising ground that partially overlooked the plain, Oriana and her companion took up their position, beneath the shade of a grove of pines; and they watched the hunters as they examined the foot- prints on the dewy turf, or followed the tracks of the elks and buffaloes through the long prairie-grass, in order to make their arrangements for enclosing the game and driving the animals into an open and central situation.

In the course of this examination, the recent tracks of a number of wild horses were discovered, and fresh excitement was felt by the whole party, for all were desirous to attempt the capture of these most valuable animals; and they resolved, on this occasion, to make them the chief objects of their pursuit. A ring was, therefore, formed by the numerous company of horsemen, enclosing a very large space of the beautiful park-like ground, which was studded with trees, either single or in groups; while underneath them, in the distance, could be seen many buffaloes lying down or grazing. The scene had the appearance of a wide extent of finely-cultivated pasture, ornamented with timber of every kind; end it forcibly recalled to Henrich's memory the fields and the cattle that had surrounded his European home. But the size of the trees, the extent of the natural meadow, and, above all, the wild aspect of the red hunters with their spears, and bows, and tomahawks, soon destroyed the fancied resemblance; while the eagerness and excitement of the novel sport banished all the sad recollections to which it had given rise. A desire also to distinguish himself in the presence of Oriana, and show her that a pale-face could equal her own dark race in courage and dexterity, inspired him with peculiar ardor; and he galloped to the station appointed him by Tisquantum, with a heart that bounded with pride and pleasure.

The hunters were each provided with a long coil of grass rope, with a noose at the end — now called a *lariat* or *lasso* — used by the Indians for casting over the horns of the elks and buffaloes, or the necks of the wild horses, that they desired to capture. These they carried in such a manner as to be ready to throw them off in an instant to their whole length, if necessary; but much practice is required to do this with precision, and Henrich did not yet hope for success in the difficult art. His only chance of capturing a wild courser lay in his skill in casting the spear, which might enable him to pierce the animal through the upper part of the neck, and thus produce a temporary insensibility, during which time he might be secured without any permanent injury. This also requires great precision and address; but Henrich had become an adept in the use of the light lance, and he felt sanguine of success if the opportunity should he afforded him.

The string of horsemen slowly and warily drew in towards the open spot that was intended to be the scene of their operations, and of which Oriana and Mailah had a good view from their safe and elevated position; and soon a troop of wild horses were disturbed by one of the hunters, and burst forth from a thick grove of trees that had previously concealed them. They rushed madly over the plain, mingling with the affrighted buffaloes and American deer, that had not hitherto perceived the stealthy approach of their foes. At every point where they attempted to escape from the enclosure they were met by a mounted huntsman, and were driven back, with shouts and cries, towards the center. All other game was now forgotten; and each hunter singled out, for his own object of pursuit, the steed that pleased him best, and of which he thought he could most easily gain possession. But one there was — the leader of the troop — on which many eyes were fixed with eager desire. He was a noble creature, of perfect form and proportions; and as he pranced before his companions, with neck erect, and throwing his head from side to side, as if to reconnoiter his assailants — while his mane and tail floated in the breeze, and his glossy coal-black skin gave back the rays of the morning sun — he looked like the King of the Prairie, going forth in the pride of perfect freedom.

The ring grew smaller and smaller; and every hand was steady, and every eye was fixed for the moment of trial: and soon the headlong pursuit commenced. At the first scattering of the wild troop, several of the younger and more feeble horses were secured; and some of the hunters, who despaired of nobler game, contented themselves with capturing or slaying either elks or buffaloes. But the finest horses escaped the first assault, and broke through the circling ring into the boundless meadow, where they were followed at mad speed by the hunters, poising their spears, and swinging their nooses round their heads, ready for a cast. Henrich and Jyanough, and several others of the best mounted Indians, had joined in the chase of the black leader, and dashed furiously after him over the plain. The horse that the English boy rode was strong and fleet, and the light weight of his rider enabled him to keep with the foremost of the red hunters' steeds, and, at length, to come almost alongside the noble courser. The spear was poised in Henrich's hand, and was just about to fly, when suddenly his horse fell to the ground, and rolled over on the turf, leaving his rider prostrate, but uninjured, except being stunned for a moment by the shock.

When he opened his eyes, and sprang to his feet, he saw the king of the desert galloping up a rising ground, over which he quickly disappeared, still hotly pursued by Coubitant and several of the hunters. Jyanough and the rest of his companions, had dismounted to assist their fallen friend, and to form conjectures as to the probable cause of the unlucky accident. For some time none could be perceived; but on carefully examining his horse, Henrich at length discovered a small wound in the hind leg, and found that the creature was lame. How, or by whom, the wound had been given, he could not even surmise; for in the eagerness of the chase he had not observed that Coubitant rode close behind him: and that he had passed him at full speed the moment his horse stumbled and fell. But Jyanough had remarked it; and from what he had already seen of the wily Indian, he felt convinced that, prompted by malicious jealousy, he had thus sought to deprive his rival of his hoped-for success, and, perhaps, even to inflict on him some grievous personal injury.

The young Indian had, however, the good sense to conceal his suspicions from Henrich at present, and to allow him to regard the whole affair as accidental; but he determined to keep a strict watch over the conduct of Coubitant for the future, and, if possible, to guard his friend from all his evil machinations.

Soon the Nauset and the rest of the hunters returned from their fruitless chase, and reported the escape of the noble wild coursers and when Jyanough heard the regrets that Coubitant expressed for the accident that had befallen Henrich, and the condolences he offered on his having thus missed the object which otherwise his skill most surely have attained, he could scarcely contain his indignation at such hypocrisy, or refrain from opening the eyes of the unsuspicious young Englishman.

They all returned together, at a slow pace, to the main body of the hunters, for Henrich's horse was too lame to be mounted; and, as soon as the adventure was made known, much sympathy and interest were shown for the disappointment of the pale-face, in which Oriana's countenance and manner showed she partook so warmly, that Coubitant turned aside to conceal his anger and vexation, and heartily wished that his well-aimed blow had not only deprived Henrich of the glory of that day's hunting, but had also put a stop for ever to the success for which he both hated and envied him.

The sport continued, after this interruption, as actively as before, but neither Henrich nor his horse could take any further share in it; and he remained with Oriana and Mailah, enjoying the beauty of the scenery, and gathering flowers and fruit for his companions, and for the little. Lincoya, who, freed from the restraint of his moss-lined bed, now rolled on the turf with Rodolph, and played with the gentle and intelligent animal.

How happy was Oriana that day! She was proud of the gallant bearing of her 'white brother' among the red warriors of her own wild race, and she had exulted at the praises which she had heard bestowed on his address as a hunter, and his shill in horsemanship, by Tisquantum and the elder Indians; and now, though she regretted his accident, and the disappointment which it had caused him, she did not suspect that it had been effected by the malice of a deadly enemy, and she rejoiced that it had given her the pleasure of his society for the rest of the day — a pleasure which she had but seldom enjoyed since their arrival in the prairie.

At the close of the day the game was collected, and, after due preparation, was carried back to the camp, where the squaws had already lighted the evening fires, and made every necessary arrangement for cooking the expected supper. Around these fires the hunters sat in groups, and discussed the events of the day, among which the accident that had befallen the pale-face excited much interest and conjecture. Jyanough listened to the probable and improbable causes that were assigned by all the speakers, especially by Coubitant, to account for so strange a circumstance; but he held his peace, for in his inmost soul he was only more and more convinced that the subtle and dark- brewed savage was the perpetrator of the malicious deed.

In this suspicion, he was the more strongly confirmed by an event that occurred a few days afterwards. It had been discovered that the stream that ran so gently by the side of the encampment fell, at some distance to the west, into a river of considerable size and depth, which then ran on over a descending and rocky bed, forming alternately smooth broad sheets of water and noisy broken falls, until it precipitated itself over a sudden precipice of great depth, and fell dashing and foaming into the basin which its continual fall had worn in the rocks below. The distant roar of this cataract had frequently been heard in the camp, when the wind came from that direction, and when the stillness of the night—broken only by the occasional howl of wild beasts seeking their prey, or the melancholy cry of the goat-sucker[*] succeeded to the sounds of labor or idleness that generally kept the temporary village alive by day. But, hitherto, no one had had leisure or inclination to leave the excitement and novelty of hunting to explore the river, or ascertain its capabilities for fishing.

[Footnote: This mournful sound is believed by the Indians to be the moaning of the departed spirits of women who have committed infanticide; and who are, consequently, excluded by Mahneto from the happy mountains which are the abode of the blessed.]

Now, however, Coubitant brought in a report one evening that the great stream abounded in fish; and proposed in to Henrich that, as he was for the present unable to join in the more active business of the chase, he should assist him in forming a light canoe, in which they could go out and spear the game that lay beneath the clear blue water in the smooth reaches of the river.

To this proposal Henrich readily assented; for the sport was one of which he had beard his Indian friends speak with great pleasure, and he greatly wished to enjoy it. The canoe was immediately commenced; and as it merely consisted of the trunk of a straight tulip-tree, hollowed out by means of fire, and shaped with a hatchet, it was completed in a couple of days.

The light spears that were to pierce the fish were prepared, and long slender lines of twisted grass were fastened to their shafts for the purpose of drawing in their prey; and the following morning, when the hunters were ready to set out on their usual expedition, Coubitant desired Henrich to accompany him to the river side, where their little bark lay ready to receive them. Why, on hearing this proposal, did Jyanough still linger when all the rest of the hunters were mounted, and his own steed was pawing the ground, impatient of his master's delay? And why, after gazing a few moments at Coubitant's dark countenance, did he declare his wish to join the fishing party, and requested the Nausett to allow him to take a place in the canoe? Did he see treachery in that eye of fire? Jyanough could lend his horse to the pale-face, if he should happen to wish to hunt.

His request was, however, negatived decidedly by Coubitant; who assured him, with assumed courtesy, that he regretted the size of the boat was too small to admit of its carrying a third sportsman with safety; but invited him to join him in the same sport the following day, when, he added—with that smile that Oriana hated—Jyanough could lend his horse to the pale-face, if he should happen to wish to hunt.

The young Cree was baffled. He would gladly have pre vented his friend from accompanying Coubitant on the expedition; but be had no means of doing so, or even of putting him on his guard against any possible evil designs on the part of his companion. So he sprang upon his eager horse, and galloped after the hunters, hoping that his fears and suspicions were unfounded.

Oriana and Mailah, attended by their faithful companion Rodolph, walked down to the edge of the river, to see the fishermen embark in their frail vessel; and, for some time, they watched the sport with considerable interest, and admired the skill with which Coubitant pierced and brought up several large fish. These he attracted towards the canoe by means of some preparation that he scattered on the surface of the water; and when the fish appeared within reach of his spear, he darted it with unerring aim, and drew in his struggling victim with the line that was attached to it. Henrich was also provided with weapons; but as the sport was entirely new to him, he found it difficult to take a steady aim, and his success was slight.

Coubitant, however, had soon secured a considerable stock of fish, and he rowed to the shore, and requested Oriana and her companion to convey them to the Sachem's lodge; adding, in a careless tone, that it would not be worth their while to return to the river, as he was going to a reach at some distance down the stream, towards the head of the cataract, where he expected to show Henrich excellent sport.

The two young women returned to the camp; and, having committed the fine fish to the care of the inferior squaws, they agreed to go again towards the river, and take this opportunity of visiting the falls, which they much desired to see, and near which they should probably again meet the fishermen. They rambled through the wood, taking a direct course towards the cataract, the sound of whose waters soon became sufficiently audible to guide them in their unknown way. Sometimes they came in sight of the river; and again they saw the little canoe, either standing motionless on the smooth surface of the water where the stream was wide and unbroken, or else passing, under the skilful guidance of Coubitant, between the rocks that occasionally disturbed its course, and formed foaming rapids, down which the little bark darted with fearful velocity.

The last reach of the broad river was as calm and smooth as a lake. It seemed as if the collected mass of water, which had gathered there from many a broken and troubled stream, and had struggled through many windings and many difficulties, was reposing there, and gaining strength for its last great leap over the dark precipice. As Oriana and Mailah approached the verge of the scattered forest, and stood to gaze on the magnificent scene before them, they perceived the canoe descend a narrow rapid, and then take up a position below an elevated mass of rock, where the water was perfectly still, and where the fishermen could quietly pursue their occupation. They evidently did not perceive their female friends, and the roar of the cataract was now so loud as to prevent all possibility of their hearing their voices. For a short time Oriana and her friend watched their movements, and saw several fish captured; and then proceeded along the steep and rocky bank, in order to obtain a still better view of the waterfall.

It was a beautiful scene on which those two young Indians looked; and they felt its power and grandeur, and stood silent and motionless. The cataract was beneath them; and its roar came up like thunder from the dark deep basin into which its weight of waters fell, and threw up a cloud of foam and spray; and then it rushed away again, as if in gladness at its safe descent and free course, until the shining stream was hidden by the rocks and overhanging trees that marked its winding course. The natural platform on which Oriana and Mailah stood, commanded a view not only of the wild cataract and the lower stretch of the river, but also of the bold steep rocks on the opposite side, and the dark forest that stretched away to the distant mountains that bounded the horizon. It likewise enabled them to perceive the small canoe, lying motionless on the water, in the shadow of the projecting rock.

By and by the boat was rowed into the center of the river, and Coubitant appeared to be seeking for a good fishing spot, as he pointed in different directions, and once or twice darted his spear into the water, and drew it out again without any success. Meanwhile, the canoe floated slowly down the stream, but its motion gradually increased as it approached the fall; and Oriana gazed at it, expecting every moment that Coubitant, who had now taken the oar in his powerful grasp, would turn its course, and either draw towards the shore; or else row back again up the river, and land below the first rapids. To her surprise, and somewhat to her anxiety, he still continued, however, to allow the canoe to proceed; and she saw Henrich take a dart in his hand, and stand erect as if to strike at something beneath the surface, to which Coubitant pointed with the paddle. Another instant, and her white brother was in the water, and struggling to catch the side of the canoe! Breathlessly she gazed; and she distinctly saw the paddle which Coubitant held, extended towards the uplifted hand of Henrich. Still he did not grasp it! O! why was this? And then the boat, which bad already floated perilously near to the fall, was Suddenly turned, and she beheld Coubitant making violent efforts to overcome the force of the current, and row to the opposite and nearest shore. He was alone!

And where was Henrich? Where was the brave young stranger? Battling desperately with the rapid stream which was carrying him onward to destruction. He rose and sank, rose again, and the current bore him on with resistless force. For a moment, Oriana clasped her hands over her eyes, to shut out the dreadful sight; and then, as if inspired by a gleam of supernatural hope, she darted forward, calling Rodolph, and pointing to the stream. The intelligent creature had seen the form of Henrich in the water, and only waited his mistress's command to risk his life in the attempt to save him. But his sagacity taught him that it was useless to enter the river above the fall; and he bounded down the steep bank that led to its foot, and stood eager, and panting, on a point of rock that overhung the basin. Oriana was quickly on the same spot, followed by Mailah; but ere they reached it, the dog had plunged into the foaming waters, and now appeared, upholding the inanimate form of Henrich, and struggling fearfully to drag him from the whirlpool.

O, it was a sickening sight! and Oriana's heart stood still in the agony of suspense She could not aid her brother! She could not cope with that mad whirl of water! But she leaped down the steep rocks, and stood on the narrow ledge of shore below, to wait the moment for action. At length— after what appeared almost a hopeless conflict with the dashing waters— Rodolph appeared through the cloud of foam and slowly and feebly swam towards the shore, still supporting the lifeless burden that seemed almost to drag him beneath the surface.

Now was the time for the Indian girl to prove her skill and courage. Lightly she sprang into the water, and in a moment she was at Rodolphs side; and, with one arm sustaining the drooping head of Henrich, while, with the other, she dexterously swam back to the spot where Mailah stood ready to assist her. With much difficulty they lifted the senseless form of Henrich on the shore, and proceeded to adopt every means in their power to restore suspended animation; while Rodolph—the faithful devoted Rodolph—lay down panting and exhausted, but still keeping a watchful eye on him whom he had so daringly rescued. Long the two young Indians labored in silence, and almost in despair; for no color returned to those pallid lips, and no warmth was perceptible in the chilled and stiffened hands, that fell powerless by his side. Still they persevered: and no tear, no lamentation, betrayed the anguish that wrung the heart of Oriana, while she believed that all was in vain. But her soul was lifted up in prayer to the One True God, in whom she had been taught to put her trust by her beloved white brother: and in His mercy was her only hope.

Nor was that hope in vain. The warm beams of the mid-day sun fell powerfully on that sheltered spot where the little group were gathered, and, combined with the continued friction that Oriana and Mailah employed, at length brought back the life-blood to Henrich's cheeks and lips, and his anxious nurses had the joy of perceiving that he breathed. A few minutes more, and he opened his deep blue eyes, and looked wildly around him, and spoke some English words that Oriana heard amid the din of the falling waters, and knew were of his home and his kindred. And then he uttered her own name, and attempted to rise, but fell back again into her arms, and smiled sweetly and gratefully when her eyes met his, and he saw that she was watching over him. There was joy—deep joy and gratitude—in those young hearts at that moment; but Henrich's weakness, and the noise of, the roaring cataract, prevented them from communicating their feelings in words, and Oriana forbore to ask any questions of Henrich relative to the cause of his perilous adventure.

After some time he seemed greatly to recover, and, rising from the ground, he slowly mounted the bank, supported by Oriana and her friend. But it was evident that he was quite unable to proceed on foot to the camp, and it was agreed that Mailah should return as quickly as possible and bring such assistance as she could procure from thence, while Henrich and Oriana should advance as far as his enfeebled state would admit of.

Mailah's light form soon disappeared in the wood, and it was not long ere she reached the camp, and hastened to the tent of Tisquantum, who, on that day, had not joined the hunting party. She told her story, in which the old Chief showed the deepest interest; and she observed a dark frown on his brow while she related the unsuccessful attempts of Coubitant to draw Henrich from the water with his paddle; but he made no remark.

The hunters were still absent, and few men remained in the camp. These were all engaged in felling wood and other laborious employments, and Tisquantum prepared to lead his own horse out to meet his adopted son. But, just as he and Mailah were leaving the camp for this purpose, Coubitant came rapidly up from the river's brink, and, hurrying towards them, began to relate, with expressions of grief and consternation, the sad fate which he believed to have befallen the young stranger, and the exertions that he had made to save his life, but which had, unhappily, proved unavailing to avert the calamity. The sorrow of the Nausett Indian seemed excessive; and Tisquantum probably considered it so, for he listened with perfect calmness to his recital, and then merely replied, 'Happily, the youth is safe. Mahneto has succored him, and I go to bring him back to the camp.'

Coubitant started: and he looked embarrassed for a moment, when he caught the penetrating eye of Mailah fixed on his countenance. But he quickly recovered his self-possession, and manifested such joy at the escape of the white stranger from a watery grave, that Mailah almost chid herself for her dreadful suspicions.

Coubitant accompanied her and the Sachem on their way through the forest, and when they met Henrich and Oriana, he again assumed such an appearance of pleasure, and so warmly congratulated the former on his miraculous deliverance, that the generous English youth strove to banish from his mind the fearful thoughts that had arisen there while he struggled for life close to the canoe, and wondered at the want of skill and strength displayed by his companion in his abortive attempts to save him. Oriana coldly received his greeting. She had long suspected that he regarded Henrich with hatred and jealousy; and her worst suspicions had that day received a strong confirmation. Still she resolved to conceal them—at least at present—from all but Jyanough, whose friendship for Henrich would, she knew, render him peculiarly alive to all that concerned his safety.

She had not long to wait, for the hunters soon returned; and she observed that, when Jyanough heard the story of the day's adventure, he cast a glance on Coubitant that made the conscious savage quail. But when she related to the young Cree all that she and Mailah had observed, he could restrain his feelings no longer, and plainly told her that he was convinced that Coubitant was the author of the calamity, and that it was not the first attempt he had made at Henrich's life.

They resolved that he should communicate all his suspicions to the Sachem the following morning, and urge him to take measures for the safety of his adopted son: but what was Jyanough's surprise, when he opened the subject to Tisquantum, at being informed that Coubitant had already left the camp with the Pequodees! Jyanough knew that it was their intention that morning, at day-break, to set off on their return to their own woods and plains, and he found that the wily Nausett had expressed a desire to accompany them, and join in the war that was going on between their tribe and some of their neighbors, in order to distinguish himself as a warrior. It was not the Sachem's intention to rejoin his tribe for a considerable time. He was fond of wandering, and proposed to travel towards the north when the hunting season should be over; and he also felt a reluctance to take his now greatly beloved captive back to that part of the country where it was possible he might gain intelligence of his friends, or, perhaps, even make his escape to them. He had, therefore, consented to Coubitant's request, and evidently felt an undefined satisfaction in his absence.

This being the case, and the departure of Coubitant having removed all present danger to Henrich from his malicious schemes, Jyanough forbore to express all he felt to the old Sachem; and he returned to Oriana with the pleasant intelligence that the enemy of her white brother had departed.

To the young Squaw-Sachem this news imparted infinite relief; and even Henrich could not regret it, although he found it difficult to believe that all the suspicions of his friends were well-founded. Still the events of the preceding day were quite sufficient to make him doubt more than ever the sincerity of Coubitant's professed regard; and he felt that he should be happier now that the dark-browed savage was gone. To his pleasant life of freedom we will now leave him, and return to New Plymouth, where many events—deeply interesting to the settlers—had occurred since his involuntary departure, and supposed death.

CHAPTER XI

'There went a dirge through the forest's gloom.

An exile was borne to a lonely tomb,
Brother; — so the chant was sung
In the slumberers native tongue —
Friend and brother! not for thee
Shall the sound of weeping be. HEMANS.

Sadly and slowly the Pilgrim Fathers passed along the scattered village of log huts which was their home in their voluntary exile, and wound up the pathway that led towards the summit of the mount, afterwards called 'the Burying Hill,' on which they had constructed a rude fort or storehouse, and whither they were now bearing to his last earthly home the chief and the most respected of their community. The Governor Carver — he who had presided over their councils, and directed all their movements since the memorable day of their landing, and had been the friend, the physician, the comforter of his little flock, through all their trials and all their sufferings — had fallen a victim to disease and over-exertion, just as spring, with all its brighter hopes for the future, had set in.

It was but a few days after Henrich's capture that this heavy affliction befell the colony, and added greatly to the gloom which the loss of young Maitland had already cast over the whole village. The departure, also, of the vessel in which the Pilgrims had come out to America, occurred at the same time; and, although not one of the exiles desired to return to the land of their birth, and to abandon the enterprise on which they had entered so devotedly, yet it was a melancholy hour when they bade adieu to the captain and his crew, and saw the Mayflower sail away towards their still much-loved, country.

The scurvy and other diseasescombined with the hardships and privations to which they had been exposed during the winter and early spring — had fearfully reduced the number of the ship's company; and of those who remained, the greater part were weakened by illness, and dispirited by the loss of so many of their brave comrades, whose graves they had dug on the bleak shores of New England. The return of spring, and the supply of provisions that the settlers were able to obtain from the friendly Indians, had checked the progress of the fatal complaints that had so fearfully ravaged the colony during the severity of winter; and had restored the survivors of the ship's crew to comparative health and strength. The captain was, therefore, glad to seize the first opportunity of abandoning a shore which had presented to him so cheerless and melancholy an aspect, and of leaving the steadfast and devoted exiles to the fate which they had chosen, and which they were resolved to abide in faith and hope.

On the very day that the Mayflower set sail, and while its white sails could still be distinguished in the eastern horizon, the Governor — who took an active part in every occupation, and even every labor that engaged the settlers — was busily employed in sowing corn in the fields that were considered as the common property of the colony. In directing and superintending this work, he was greatly assisted by the skill and experience of Squanto, the native who, as we have already related, had been so treacherously carried off to England by Hunt, and had, on his return to America, sought out, and attached himself to, the settlers. By them he was greatly regarded, and his knowledge of the English language rendered his services of inestimable value in all their intercourse with the Indian tribes; while his acquaintance with the soil on which they had established themselves, and the native modes of cultivating grain and other vegetable produce, was of the greatest use to men who were only accustomed to European agriculture.

The maize and other grain were sown in the fields that had been richly manured with fish, to ensure an abundant crop;[*] and the laborers returned in a body to the village, led by their venerable and respected President; but no sooner had Carver re-entered his dwelling than he swooned away and never recovered his consciousness. In a few days he breathed his last, to the unutterable grief of his widow, and the deep regret of all the settlers, whose love and confidence he had won during his brief government, by his clear-sighted wisdom and his universal kindness.

[Footnote: It was the custom of the Indians to manure their fields with *shads* or *allezes*, a small fish that comes up the rivers in vast numbers at the spawning season. About a thousand fish were used for every acre of land; and a single alleze was usually put into every corn-hill, when they buried their grain for winter consumption; probably as a charm to keep off the evil demons and hostile wandering spirits.]

As his funeral procession wound up the hill, tears might be seen on the cheek of many a sturdy Pilgrim; and sobs and lamentations broke forth from the women and children. After his remains were laid in their resting-place, a fervent prayer was offered up by Brewster (whose age and character caused him to be regarded as the pastor of the colony, although he had never been called to the ministry after the custom of the Puritans); and then a hymn was sung by the united voices of the whole congregation.

When this simple ceremony was over, and the grave of the departed President was closed, and laid level with the surrounding ground—in order to conceal it from the prowling Indians—the assembly repaired to the fort, or store-house, that stood on the summit of the hill, and which also served the purpose of a meeting-house or chapel. Its rude end unadorned simplicity suited, the peculiar ideas of the Puritans, who, in their zeal to escape from the elaborate ornaments and pompous ceremonial employed by the Papists, had rushed into the opposite extreme, and desired that both their place of worship, and their mode of performing it, should be divested of every external decoration and every prescribed form. The more their place of meeting for prayer resembled an ordinary habitation, the better they considered it suited to the sacred purpose; and they were, therefore, perfectly satisfied to possess no other church than the rude fort, built of logs and posts, and used indifferently as a granary for the public stores, and as a fortress for the defense of the colony from any incursions of the hostile tribes.

In this primitive chapel, Brewster was accustomed to lead the devotions of the Pilgrims and their families, every 'Lord's Day' morning and afternoon;[*] and also on any other occasion of their assembling together. But as they were in continual expectation of the arrival of the venerated John Robinson, to resume his office of regular pastor of the flock, they had not taken any measures to gratify their ardent desire of hearing the 'blessed sermon' three times en every Lord's Day, from some holy man entirely devoted to the service of God. The addresses occasionally delivered to the congregation by Brewster, or by any other of the ruling elders who might preside at a meeting, were called *discourses* not sermons; and the interpretation of certain portions of Scripture, which was sometimes undertaken by any member of the congregation who felt equal to it, was called '*prophesying*.' These were the only modes of spiritual instruction employed by the first settlers, until they procured clergymen from England, or appointed ministers from among their own elders; and these means were highly valued by the settlers, who had abandoned home, and kindred, and the comforts of civilized life, for no other motive than to secure to themselves the privilege of worshipping God according to their own ideas of what was good and profitable to their souls. The talents and the elevated piety of William Brewster rendered him both a very valuable teacher, and also, in the eyes of the Puritans, an efficient substitute for their expected pastor.

[Footnote: The Puritans never used the names *Sunday* or *Sabbath*. They objected is the first as savoring of Paganism and to the second as pertaining to Judaism; and yet they enforced the observance of the Christians day of rest with almost Mosaic strictness.]

On the present mournful occasion he addressed the congregation, in a very impressive manner, on the heavy loss they had sustained in the death of their valued President; and exhorted them to remember and to imitate his piety, his charity, and his exemplary patience and self- denial, under the trying circumstances that had marked the period of his brief government. These circumstances had become less painful, it is true, since their friendly intercourse with the Wampanoges, and the genial change in the weather; but still the trials of the Pilgrims were by no means over, and their need of faith in the good providence of God, and of persevering resolution in the path which they had chosen for themselves, remained as great as ever.

Deeply was the less of their first President felt by the colony, for every individual mourned him as a private friend, as well as a wise end benevolent ruler. But the blow fell with more crushing power on her who had shared his checkered life of joy and sorrow for many years in Europe, and had accompanied him into exile, with the devoted feeling that his presence would make the wilderness a home. His sudden removal, and the cheerless blank that succeeded, were more than the strength of his afflicted widow could endure; and in six weeks she followed him the grave. From that time, it appeared as if the severity of the scourge that had ravaged the infant settlement was exhausted, for scarcely any more deaths occurred during that year; and many who had hitherto suffered from the effects of disease, regained their usual strength, and lived to a remarkably advanced age.

William Bradford was the individual selected by the community to fill the arduous and responsible office that had been held so few months by Carver; and the choice was a most judicious one, for he was a man well suited to be the leader of a colony exposed to the peculiar difficulties that surrounded the Puritan exiles. His uncommon sagacity and penetration of character, and his undaunted resolution in times of danger, caused him to be regarded as the very prop and support of the settlement; and his worth was so generally acknowledged, and so highly appreciated, that he continued to be annually elected Governor for twelve succeeding years: and never did he disappoint the confidence thus reposed in him. His treatment of the Indians was one point on which he showed both the correctness of his judgement, and the right feelings of his heart. He ever acted towards them with true Christian benevolence and equity; and, at the same, he preserved that authority and superiority over them which were necessary to the safety and well- being of the colony; and he also carefully kept from them those

European weapons, the possession of which might render them dangerous to the settlers, and aggravate the frequent hostilities among their own rival tribes. Unhappily, a different course was afterwards pursued by the leaders of the colony of Massachusetts; and the evil con sequences of such short-sighted policy were soon but too apparent, and tended to involve not only the new settlers, but also the original colony of New Plymouth, in quarrels and disturbances with the natives. This however, did not occur for some time after the period of which we are now speaking; and, for the present, Bradford succeeded in maintaining the best possible relations with the already friendly Wampanoges.

William Bradford had been originally brought up as a husbandman; and although he had abandoned this calling to devote himself to the study of the Scriptures, and the writings of the Fathers—for which purpose he had acquired the Latin, Greek, and Hebrew languages—he still retained such a, know ledge of agriculture as proved extremely useful to him as the leader of a young colony, whose support was to be mainly derived from the land of which they had taken possession. He also spoke French and Dutch fluently; and the diary and letters that he has left to posterity show him to have been both a well informed and a truly pious man. When the Puritans left Amsterdam under their pastor, John Robinson, and settled at Leyden, Bradford was scarcely twenty years of age. He there learnt the art of dyeing silk, in order to support himself while he pursued his theological studies, and also performed the part of historian to the community of which he had become a member; and he remained with the congregation during all the years of their residence in Holland, and attached himself with the most affectionate reverence to their generally beloved and respected minister.

One of the first acts of his administration, as Governor of New Plymouth, was to send another embassy to Masasoyt, the Great Sagamore of the whole Wampanoge tribe, in order to strengthen and confirm his present amicable feelings towards the white men, by means of presents, and other marks of friendship. Squanto, as usual, accompanied the party as interpreter; and nothing could be more satisfactory than the interview proved to all parties, especially to the Indian Chief, who was made both proud and happy by the gift of a red military coat, adorned with silver lace. This he immediately put on, over the paint and other savage ornaments in which he was decorated for the state occasion; and he greatly diverted the members of the embassy by the increased air of dignity that he assumed, and the grandiloquous manner in which he began to extol his own power and glory.

'Am I not,' he exclaimed, in a loud voice, 'Masasoyt, the great king? Am I not lord of all the people of the Lowsons; and of such and such places? And he enumerated nearly thirty uncouth Indian names of places over which he claimed sovereignty, his wild subjects uttering a yell of joy and exultation in answer to each word he uttered. The savage monarch then proceeded to ratify and augment the agreement into which he had already catered with Edward Winslow, and promised to guarantee to the English settlers an exclusive trade with his tribe; at the same time entreating them to prevent his powerful enemies, the Narragansetts, from carrying on a commercial intercourse with the French colonists.

Notwithstanding the boasted power of this 'Chief of chiefs,' the scarcity of provisions was so great in his village of Packanokick at the time of this embassy, that he was only able to offer his white friends one meal during their visit to him, which lasted a day and two nights; and this solitary display of regal hospitality consisted of two large fishes just caught in a neighboring lake, and which were divided amongst forty hungry persons. In spite of this temporary distress, he pressed the deputation to remain longer with him; but the object of their mission having been attained, they were glad to leave the residence of the Sagamore, which possessed far less of comfort and civilization than were to be found in the picturesque summer camp of his son and inferior Sachem, Mooanam.

This lovely spot continued to be much frequented by the settlers, between whom and their copper-colored neighbors a strong feeling of mutual regard became established; and this friendship proved a great advantage to both parties, in a social as well as a political point of view. The Wampanoges found the benefit of their alliance with the mighty English during the autumn of that year, when the dread which their name and power had inspired proved a safeguard to the friendly Indian tribe, and preserved them from a combined attack of several other tribes who had, by some mysterious means, been instigated to unite for their destruction.

The intelligence of this conspiracy reached the settlers when a party of them were on the peninsula of Cape Cod, whither they had gone to bring back a young English boy, named Francis Billington, who had lost himself in the forest some time previously, and, after having subsisted for several days on wild fruits and berries, had reached a camp of the Nausett Indians, hitherto so adverse to the Pilgrims. This seemed a good opportunity for endeavoring to establish more friendly relations with the tribe, and Bradford sent off ten men in the shallop to negotiate for the boy's restoration, and to offer gifts to the Nausetts, who, happily, were not so cruel and blood-thirsty a party as those who had kidnapped Henrich Maitland. The overtures of the settlers were well received, and they presented the Chief of the village with a pair of knives, and also returned to the natives a quantity of corn, more than equal to that which they had taken from the graves and huts that they had discovered on their first landing, and which belonged to the Nausetts. This act of justice gained for the settlers the esteem and confidence of the Indians; and as these original possessors of the soil did not dispute the title of the newcomers to the portion of the American soil on which they had established themselves, they considered henceforth that their claim was valid, and that they could stand before the natives on terms of equality.

The lost child was safely restored to Rodolph, who, as usual, shared the conduct of the expedition with Edward Winslow. The joy and gratitude of the boy's father, at being permitted to convey him home uninjured, may be better imagined than described; and while Maitland sympathized in his feelings, he could not help sadly contrasting the fate of his own lost Henrich with that of the more fortunate Francis Billington. But he believed that his son's earthly career had closed for ever; and both he and Helen had submitted to the bereavement with Christian piety and resignation, and had taught their wounded hearts to restrain every impulse to repine, and even to feel thankful that their beloved boy had been spared any protracted sufferings and trials, and had been permitted so speedily to enter into his rest. Had they known his actual late and condition, how much of painful anxiety would have mingled with the sorrow of separation, from which they were now exempt!

The restoration of the little wanderer having been effected, and a good understanding having been established with the Nausetts of Cape Cod, the negotiating party lost no time in returning to New Plymouth, and communicating to Governor Bradford the intelligence of the conspiracy against Masasoyt, to which allusion has already been made, and of which they had been informed by the Nausett Sachem. The news was startling to Bradford and to his council, who all felt the imperative necessity of using immediate efforts for the assistance of the friendly Wampanoges. They were impelled to this resolution, not only in consideration of the alliance that had been formed between themselves and the Sagamore Masasoyt, but also from a conviction that the safety and welfare of the infant colony depended essentially upon their possessing the friendship and the protection of some powerful tribe, like the Wampanoges, whose numbers and warlike character caused them to be both feared and respected by their weaker neighbors. It could only be by a combination of several tribes that any important defeat Of the Wampanoges could possibly be effected: and such a combination the

Nausetts declared they knew to have been already formed; though by what means, and with what motive, remained at present a mystery.

The Indian interpreter, Squanto, was therefore sent off to Masasoyt's residence at Lowams, in order to ascertain the grounds of the quarrel, and to effect, if possible, a reconciliation, without the necessity of the Pilgrims having recourse to arms in defense of their allies. The interpreter was also accompanied by Hobomak, a subject of the Wampanoge chieftain's, who had lately left his own wigwams and settled among the English, and who had already attached himself to the white men with an uncommon degree of devotion. But ere the swarthy ambassadors reached the village of Packanokick, they were suddenly attacked by a small party of Narragansett warriors, who lay in ambush near their path through the forest, and were conveyed away captives to the presence of a fierce looking Indian, who appeared to be a man of power and authority, and who was evidently awaiting their arrival in a small temporary encampment at a little distance.

No sooner had Hobomak glanced at this dark chieftain, than he recognized Coubitant, the bitter foe of the settlers, and the captor of Henrich Maitland. Coubitant had originally been a subject of the Sachem Masasoyt; but some offence, either real or imaginary, had converted him from a friend into a bitter foe; and then it was that he had wandered towards the Spanish settlements, and obtained that prejudiced notion of Christianity to which we have formerly alluded. When tired of his wild roaming life, he had united himself to that portion of the Nausett tribe which was under the guidance of Tisquantum; and his attachment to the Sachem's son, Tekoa, had induced him to remain a member of the tribe during his life, and to devote himself to the object of revenging his death, after that event had occurred at the first encounter with the white settlers.

Hitherto that object had been frustrated by what appeared to him Tisquantum's incomprehensible partiality fur Henrich, which had so entirely prevented his wreaking his vengeance on the innocent son of the slayer. But his was not a revenge that could expire unsatiated, or change to friendship, and expend itself in acts of kindness, as that of Tisquantum had done. No: the thirst for blood remained as strong in the breast of Coubitant as it was on that very hour when he beheld his brother-in-arms fall, bleeding and dying, beneath the mysterious firearms of the white men; and he hoped still to pour forth the white man's blood, as an oblation to the spirit of his friend. Therefore it was that, when he found himself foiled in all his malicious schemes for Henrich's destruction, and also perceived that he was himself becoming an object of suspicion to Jyanough and to the Sachem, he had resolved on quitting the Nausetts, and returning with the Pequodees into the neighborhood of the English settlement. He hoped to stir up several smaller tribes to join with the Narragansetts, and to make war against the Wampanoges—the allies of the Pilgrims—and thus to deprive the hated whites of their aid and protection, and, possibly, also to engage the settlers in the quarrel, and then to find an opportunity of taking one or more of them captive, and slaking the desires of his vindictive spirit in the agonies that he would inflict on his victims. Truly, 'the dark places' of his heart were full of the habitations of cruelty.'

These deep-laid schemes of the wily savage had hitherto met with full success; and by means of deceit and misrepresentation, he had roused up and irritated the feelings of several Sachems and their dependants, and induced them to agree to coalesce for the destruction of the Wampanoges, and then to turn their arms against the settlers, with the view of expelling them altogether from the country. His spies had discovered the intended embassy of Squanto and Hobomak to the village of the great Sagamore of Lowams; and he had, consequently, taken effectual means to intercept it, as he feared its having a favorable aspect.

On the captives being brought before him, he scornfully reproached them as the dastardly tools of the white men, and as traitors to their own nation; and he declared his intention of detaining Squanto as a prisoner, and as a hostage also, in order to ensure the return of Hobomak to New Plymouth, with the message that be designed for the Governor. This message consisted of a threat—which Hobomak well knew he would execute—that if, on being liberated, he proceeded to Packanokick, instead of returning to the settlement, he would flay the unhappy Squanto alive, and send his skin and scalp to the white-hearted English, to show them that the red men scorned their interference, and knew how to punish it.

Hobomak departed, and reluctantly left his companion in the hands of the cruel Coubitant. But he had no power to liberate him, and his only hope of obtaining any effectual succor for him, was in hastening to New Plymouth, and persuading the Governor to send a well-armed force to cut off the retreat of the Narragansetts and their leader, and attempt the rescue of their caked interpreter. Hobomak was fleet of foot, and he rested not until he had arrived in Bradford's presence, and told him of the fate that had befallen Squanto. Weak as the colonists were, and sincerely desirous as they also felt to preserve peace with the natives, they yet deemed it incumbent on them to show the Indians that they would not tamely submit to any insult or injury. Captain Standish was, therefore, immediately dispatched with a body of fourteen men, well armed and disciplined, who were at that time nearly all the men capable of bearing arms of whom the colony could boast. Led by Hobomak, they rapidly traversed the forest, and came upon Coubitant's party soon after they had left their encampment. The Indian leader had anticipated, and desired, this result of his conduct; and his heart swelled with malignant joy when he beheld the hated Rodolph among the foremost of the assailants. Now he deemed the evil spirit whom he worshipped was about to repay him for all his abortive schemes and disappointed efforts, by throwing the very object of his vengeful hatred into his power.

Forward he sprang, whirling his heavy tomahawk round his head, as if it had been a child's toy, and preparing to bring it down on the white man's skull with a force that must have cloven it in two. But Standish saw the impending blow, and, quick as thought, he drew a pistol from his belt, and fired it at the savage. The ball passed through his arm, and the tomahawk fell bloodless to the ground. Had it but drunk the life-blood of Rodolph, Coubitant would have been content to die. But his foe still lived unharmed; and quickly he saw that three of his own followers were also severely wounded, and that his party of naked warriors were altogether incapable of resisting the fierce and well-sustained attack of their civilized assailants. His only chance of safety, and of future vengeance, lay in flight; and to that last resource of a brave spirit he betook himself. He was quickly followed by all his band, who were dismayed at the sound and the fatal effects of the British fire-arms and, leaving Squanto behind them, they were soon concealed from view by the thick underwood of the forest. The object of the expedition having been attained, Standish did not pursue the fugitives, but returned in triumph to the settlement, well satisfied that he had given the Indians a salutary impression of the decisive conduct, and the powerful measures, that would ever be adopted by the white men, when their honor was insulted in the slightest degree.

That such an impression had been made on the red men was soon evident, from the anxiety which was manifested by several of the neighboring tribes to be admitted into the semblance, at least, of an alliance with the mighty strangers. Nine Sachems intimated their desire to acknowledge themselves the subjects of the white men's king, who dwelt on the other side of 'the great water'; and a paper was accordingly drawn up by Captain Standish to that effect, and subscribed with the uncouth autographs of the copper-colored chieftains. Among these— strange to say—the mark of Coubitant, who had been raised to the rank of Sachem by the Narragansetts, was to be seen; but the sincerity of his friendly professions will be shown hereafter. At present, it suited him to unite with the other chiefs in their pledge of allegiance to King James, and of amity towards his British subjects; but he never openly approached their settlement, or made the slightest advance towards becoming better acquainted with them. His evil designs slept, indeed, but they had not expired. They only waited the fitting opportunity to be as actively pursued as ever.

CHAPTER XII

Calm on the bosom of thy God,
  Young spirit! rest thee now!
E'en while with us thy footsteps trod
  His seat was on thy brow.

  Dust to its narrow house beneath!
  Soul to its place on high!
They that have seen thy look in death,
  No more may fear to die.

  Lone are the paths, and sad the bowers,
  Whence thy meek smile is gone
But oh! a brighter borne than ours,
  In Heaven, is now thine own.' HEMANS.

We have observed that very few deaths took place in the colony of
New Plymouth during the second year of their exile, and after the fatal
stroke that deprived them of their President; but among those few, there
was one that carried grief and desolation into the hearts of the family with
whom our story is chiefly connected, and who were already deeply afflicted
by the loss of the first-born. Ludovico Maitland had always been a delicate
child, and on him, consequently, the care and attention of his mother had
been principally bestowed. Helen had watched and tended him through all
the severities of the first winters in the New World, and many had been the
privations that she had voluntarily endured, unknown even to Rodolph,
who would not have suffered her thus to risk her own health, in order to
add to the comforts of her youngest and most helpless child. When the
blessed springtime came, and all nature began again to smile, she hoped
that Ludovico would also be renovated, and bloom again like the flowers he
loved so well. And her hopes appeared to be realized: for the sweet playful
child resumed his sports, and the bright color again glowed on his soft
cheek; and his parents deemed it the hue of health.

At the time when Henrich was stolen away, the little fellow had been
remarkably well, and even Helen's fears for him had almost subsided; but,

whether it was the effect of the shock that he sustained when he saw his brother seized by the fierce savages, and torn away from him, and when he fled so breathlessly to tell the fearful tidings; or whether it was merely the result of his own delicate constitution, which could no longer bear up against the change of climate and food— from that time, he visibly declined. It is true he never complained, and his cheerful spirits were unaltered; but the watchful eye of affection could trace the insidious steps of disease in the changing color, and the too frequently brilliant eye.

Since Edith had lost her constant friend and companion, Henrich, she naturally devoted herself more to her younger brother, and little Ludovico became not only her lively play-fellow, but also her intelligent pupil; and the occupation which she found in the care of the engaging child served to divert her mind from the first real grief she had ever known. Her mother's sorrow, though borne with the most perfect resignation, had greatly affected her health; and as she had entire confidence in Edith's steadiness, she was glad to leave the care of Ludovico principally to her, especially when she observed the good effect which the new responsibility had on her spirits. The two children were, therefore, left much to themselves; and, with their mother's sanction they passed a great portion of their time at the camp of Mooanam, where they were always most kindly received, and where they made rapid progress in acquiring the language, and also many of the useful and ingenious arts, of their swarthy friends.

The departure of Coubitant and his savage band, after their cruel design against the peace of Rodolph's family had been accomplished, removed all fears of injury or molestation from the minds of the settlers; for no hostile Indians now remained in their immediate neighborhood, and the path from New Plymouth to the village of the friendly Wampanoges became a beaten and frequented track; so that Edith and her little charge could go to and fro in safety, under the protection of Fingal, a magnificent dog belonging to their father, and their constant companion and playfellow; and frequently they were accompanied, on their return to the British village, by the Chieftain's wife, Apannow, and her little boy, Nepea, who was the darling of both Edith and Ludovico.

A strong attachment also sprang up between Apannow and Helen; for the Squaw-Sachem was possessed of much natural gentleness of disposition, and was most ready to adopt all those habits of civilized life that she saw practiced among her English friends, and that it was possible for her to transplant to her Indian home. She was, likewise, willing to listen to the doctrines and precepts of the Gospel, and to admit their beauty and their holiness, although it was long—very long—ere she, or any of the adults of her tribe, were so far converted to the Christian truth as to be either desirous or fit to be baptized. But there was no bigotry or opposition in the mind of Apannow; and she became a kind and sympathizing friend to Helen and to her children.

Rodolph was necessarily much engaged in agricultural occupations, and also in the business of the government, as he was one of the council who were appointed to assist the President, and to share the labors and responsibilities of his frequently very difficult office. The gradual change in little Ludovico's health was, therefore, not so soon observed by his father as by Helen and Edith; and when he returned to his much- loved home after the toils and cares of the day, his wife forbore to arouse fresh anxiety in his breast, by telling him of her own fears. On the contrary, she rejoiced to see the pleasure and animation that lighted up the sweet child's expressive countenance, as he ran to meet his father, and the happiness of both as they played under the wide- spreading trees that shaded their now luxuriant garden. At such times, while listening to Ludovico's ringing laugh, and watching his light footsteps as he chased his father and Edith from tree to tree, she flattered herself that all must be well with the joyous child, and that her apprehensions were unfounded. But, again, when the following day found him pale and exhausted, and all the more so for the excitement and exercise of the previous evening, these foreboding fears would return, and her heart would sink heavily at the prospect of the coming woe.

The short summer of North America attained its height; and, as the heat increased, so did Ludovico's young life wane away, and his strength become daily less. Rudolph now saw, as plainly as his afflicted wife, that their only remaining son was soon to be taken from them; and he strove to arm both himself and her with the only power that could support them under such an aggravated calamity. He constantly led her to look only to Him who 'gave,' and who also 'takes away,' and without whom 'not a sparrow falleth to the ground'; and to trust Him even in the depth of sorrow: and he had the satisfaction of seeing her become more and more resigned, and more and more strong in faith to meet the coming trial.

Slowly and gently it came; but it came at last: and though his parents and his sister had long given up all hope of retaining their loved Ludovico on earth, and had endeavored to resign him into the hands of his Heavenly Father, yet, when the blow came, they felt it sudden, and found how little they were prepared for it. One warm summer evening the sweet child was carried by Rodolph to Edith's bower, that he might look once more at the flowers he had helped to plant and to tend; and his soft eyes seemed to take a last farewell of every cherished object, and to follow the setting sun with a fixed gaze, that said those eyes would never see it set again. But there was no sadness—no regret—in the gentle countenance; and the infantine lips still smiled, as they whispered the evening prayer that he had so often repeated with Edith. Young as he was, Ludovico had learnt to love his Redeemer, and to feel that to 'depart, and be with Christ, was far better than to abide on earth; and the 'valley of the shadow or death,' which the Lord so mercifully made easy to his flesh, had no terrors for his young spirit.

Could his parents, then—could even his broken-hearted sister—bear to disturb his angelic calmness by any display of their own grief? No: they restrained it; and even tried to smile again as they replied to his touching remarks, and spoke of the happy day when they should all meet again in heaven, and dwell for ever in the presence of that gracious Savior, who was new taking him, as they believed, to join his dear brother Henrich.

As twilight came on, his father bore him back to the house, and laid him again on his little couch; and ere the glorious sun arose to lighten the earth once more, his spirit had passed away into that realm of perfect light where they 'have no need of the sun, neither of the moon, to shine in it; for the glory of God does lighten it, and the Lamb is the light thereof.' And many tears were shed for him, when the sight of the grief of those he loved so dearly could no longer disturb his peace, or check the willing spirit in its heavenward flight.

The sorrows of the Maitlands—thus renewed and aggravated—excited the warmest sympathy throughout the colony; for they were universally respected and beloved, and their calm and pious resignation drew forth the admiration of the whole community of Puritans, who deemed any strong expressions of grief to be altogether unsuitable to Christians. But Rodolph and Helen did not the less feel their chastisement, because they forbore to express their feelings to any other than to God, and to their revered friend and minister, Brewster. On Edith, this second blow fell even more heavily than the first; for, since Henrich's loss, she had devoted herself to her younger brother, and felt for him almost a mother's love: and now her pupil, her playfellow—the sunshine of her life—was taken away from her! Truly, the Lord was preparing her in the furnace of affliction for the future lot to which He had appointed her; and sorrow did net visit her in vain. Her character was strengthened and matured, and her mind was taught to find resources in itself that proved hereafter of inestimable value to her, and to those most nearly connected with her.

The thoughts and attention of her parents—and indeed of the whole colony—were at this time diverted greatly from their own private cares and interests, by an event of much importance to the settlement. This was the arrival of a vessel, called the Fortune, from the mother- country, bringing out to the colony a new and more comprehensive charter, obtained for them by the Society of Plymouth, and also twenty- five fresh settlers, who were chiefly friends and relatives of those already established in New England. How welcome these familiar countenances, that recalled days of happiness long passed but not forgotten, were to the hearts and memories of their brethren, none but exiles can tell! The new comers were indeed joyfully received, and hospitably entertained by the Pilgrim Fathers; who invited them to take up their quarters in their rude but comfortable dwellings, and to share their scanty stores. Unfortunately, the new settlers were unable to contribute any thing to these stores; for all their own provisions were already consumed on the voyage. This accession to their numbers, therefore, added greatly to the inconvenience of the colony, and occasioned such a scarcity of food, that the Governor was obliged to put the whole community upon a daily allowance; an arrangement to which they all submitted without a murmur. And not only did the original settlers thus consent to endure privation for the sake of their newly- arrived friends and relatives, but they also contributed more liberally than their narrow means could well afford, to provision the Fortune for her voyage home. This was the occasion of the first mercantile adventure of the Pilgrims, who took the opportunity of the return of the ship to England, to send to the Society with which they were connected a quantity of furs and timber to the value of five hundred pounds. But success did not attend their speculation; for the vessel fell into the hands of the French, and all their hopes of profit were, for the present, blasted.

It is needless to dwell on all the continued and various hardships that these brave men, and their families, had to endure for several ensuing winters. A few circumstances that more especially exemplify their manners and mode of life, will be sufficient for the purposes of our narrative, the course of which must necessarily be somewhat interrupted by these details. Some knowledge of the habits of the adventurers, and of the events that befell them at this early period of their history, is however needful for the illustration of the story; and they shall be briefly given, before we take up the thread of the narrative a few years subsequent to the period of which we are now speaking.

For some time the friendly relations with the Wampanoges, which had been established by Carver and further cemented by Bradford, remained undisturbed, and no signs of hostility were shown by any other of the neighboring Indian tribes. This was probably owing, in a great degree, to the wholesome example of decided measures that had been given to the natives on the occasion of the capture of Hobomak and Squanto, and also to the efficient means of defense that were now adopted by the settlers. On their first arrival in New England, they had planted their guns on the hill which commanded the rising city of New Plymouth, and which afterwards received the name of 'the Burying Hill.' There, as we have seen, the remains of the venerable Carver were deposited; and there the infant form of Ludovico Maitland was laid in its last narrow resting-place, and shaded by shrubs and plants that Edith, and the faithful servant Janet, delighted to place there, and to tend and water with untiring care and watchfulness.

This hill was converted, during the first year of the Pilgrim's residence in New England, into a kind of irregular fortification. The storehouse—which was also the chapel and the council hall—stood on the summit, and this was surrounded by a strong wall of timber, well furnished with batteries, on which a watch was kept night and day, to look out for the approach of any hostile parties of Indians. At a considerable distance from this building ran a strong wooden palisade, that enclosed the height entirely, and was divided into four portions, the entrance to which was securely fastened every night; and the able- bodied men of the colony, under the command of Miles Standish, were arranged in four squadrons, to the care of each of which one quarter was entrusted. The occupation which this charge entailed on the limited number of men who were capable of undertaking it, in addition to their necessary labors and employments in building their dwellings, cultivating their fields, and procuring provisions by hunting and fishing was both heavy and incessant; but disease had nearly left the colony, and want, though occasionally felt to a painful degree, was not always their portion; and the Pilgrim Fathers were cheerfully contented with their lot.

Still, it was a lot that involved much of hardship and personal privation, as a drawback to the liberty, both religious and political, that had been obtained by emigration. The harvests were scanty, and not nearly sufficient to provide bread for the increasing community, and also seed for the following year, and the supplies that were occasionally procured from the Wampanoges, and their allies, were very uncertain. At one time, every species of grain became so scarce that the settlers had recourse to pig-nuts as a substitute for bread; and the last pint of corn that remained to the colony, after the fields were sown, was counted out among the whole community, when *five grains* fell to the share of each person, and these were looked upon as a rare treat, and eaten as a particular dainty. Cattle were, as yet, unknown in the colony; and their chief subsistence consisted of game, wild fowl, and fish, of which the supply was frequently both scanty and precarious. 'Often,' we are told in the diary of the Governor Bradford, 'we do not know in the evening where we shall get a meal next morning; but yet we bear our want with joy, and trust in Providence.' And strong, indeed, must have been the faith and patience of these Pilgrim Fathers, which sustained their spirits amidst such long-continued trials, and enabled them to meet and overcome such complicated difficulties without hesitation and without a murmur!

At one period their only food was fish, and occasionally merely shellfish; but never was this miserable fare partaken of by the emigrants, who assembled to receive their respective portions, without a blessing being asked, and thanks being offered by the pious Brewster, who, with a spirit of gratitude too often unknown to those who revel in abundance, praised God for having permitted them 'to suck out of the fullness of the sea, and for the treasures sunk in the sand.' While such an example of holy trust, and patient submission to the will of God, was set by the leading men of this suffering colony—men who were both loved and respected—not a complaining word was uttered by the rest. All felt that they were bound to emulate the faith and piety of their high-souled Governor, and their venerated elder.

And, truly, they had need of every motive, and of every aid—both human and divine—that could keep their souls in peace, when actual famine at length stared them in the face. The second winter had been endured; and, in spite of cold and privation, the health of the colony had improved; and spring again brought brighter hopes, and better prospects of the summer's harvest. But before the grain was well grown up, a drought came on, that threatened the utter destruction of the crops. For six long weeks not one drop of rain fell on the thirsty land. 'The sky was as brass' to the fainting emigrants, and 'the earth was as iron' to them. Yet these men of God did not despair. They were accustomed to regard every dispensation of Providence, whether prosperous or afflictive, either as a special blessing from the hand of God, to support and encourage His believing people, or as a Fatherly chastisement, to punish their iniquities, and excite them to greater piety and watchfulness. 'It pleased God,' said Edward Winslow, in speaking of this inflict ion, 'to send a great dearth for our further punishment.' Under this conviction, the congregation were called on by the Governor and the elders to set apart a day for special humiliation and prayer, in order to entreat the Lord to remove from them his chastening hand, and to 'send a gracious rain upon His inheritance.'

The call was universally obeyed; and men, women, and children assembled themselves together, fasting, on 'the Burying Hill,' to listen to the solemn address delivered by Brewster, and to unite in fervent prayers and humble confessions to their God and Father. The sky that morning was clear and bright as ever; and the sun walked in unclouded brilliance and majesty through the deep blue vault of heaven. For eight hours, the devotions of the assembly continued almost without interruption; and it seemed as if 'none regarded, neither was there any that answered.' But as the sun was sinking towards the western horizon, a cloud, 'as it were a mans hand,' was seen to rise as if to meet the glowing orb; and, ere he sank, his rays were obscured by a heavy bank of clouds. Joy and gratitude now filled the breasts of the suppliants, and the dim and anxious eye of many a mother, who had watched the declining forms of her little ones in silent anguish, was lighted up with hope, and glistened with a tear of thankfulness. Such, indeed, had been the sufferings of the younger children, although the greatest sacrifices had been made by their parents in order to provide them with the food so necessary to their existence, that Helen had frequently poured forth her heartfelt thanksgivings to her Heavenly Father, that He had seen fit to remove her gentle and idolized Ludovico from a scene of so much distress; and had called him away to a land where want, as well as sorrow, is unknown, in a manner, and at a time, which allowed her to ensure his ease and comfort to the last. To have seen her darling pine for food, which she could not procure for him — to have watched that fondly-cherished child sinking into his grave from the actual want of proper nourishment, and to know that in the land they had abandoned all that was needed to prolong his precious life was teeming in profusion — would, she weakly thought, have been more than her faith could have endured. But Helen erred in that doubting thought. She was a *Christian:* and had her Lord and Savior seen fit thus to try her, He would also have given her grace to meet the trial as a *Christian;* for His promise to each one of His people is sure: 'As thy day is, so shall thy strength be.'

Edith, her only remaining child, was strong and energetic in mind and body; and she was no burden to her mother. Cheerfully she had borne her share of privation; and, uncomplainingly, she had assisted Helen and Janet in seeking for roots and berries hour after hour in the forest, when no other food was to be obtained. Now, on this day of fasting and prayer, she stood beside her mother and Rodolph, and lifted up her young voice in prayer for heavenly succor, and in praise, when the first signal of coming aid was seen in the crimson west.

The whole congregation had risen from their posture of supplication, and were gazing with deep interest and emotion at the gathering clouds, when they were startled at observing a large party of Indians emerging from the thicket below, and advancing towards the palisade that formed their outer fortification. At first they imagined them to be a hostile body of Narragansetts, or Pequodees, who had discovered the manner in which that day was being spent among the pale-faces, and had resolved upon breaking the recently-formed treaty, and attempting their destruction while they were thus assembled together and unarmed. But these apprehensions were soon removed by the appearance of their friend Mooanam, who advanced from the rest of his party, and hurried forward, holding in his hands a fine fish, and calling on his allies to open their gates and admit him and his followers into the fortress, for that he had brought them food.

Joyfully his summons was answered, and the generous red men entered the enclosure, and laid before the Governor a quantity of, fish, sufficient to supply the whole community with several wholesome and acceptable meals. The kindness of this offering was highly estimated by the settlers; for they well knew that their Indian friends had long been suffering privations little less than what they had themselves endured, and that their prospects for the future were hardly more cheering than their own. The native and untaught courtesy, also, with which the seasonable gift was offered, added not a little to its value.

'Behold!' said Mooanam to the President, when he and his attendants had placed the fresh spoils of their lake in order before him—'Behold what the good Mahneto has given to his children in their day of distress! And the red men could not eat and be in plenty, while they knew that the faces of their white brethren were pale with want, and their little children were crying for food. Take this, my brother, and let the hearts of your people be glad, and bless Mahneto while they eat. I and my young men will return to the supper that our squaws are preparing.'

'We do bless Mahneto, who is the God and father both of the red and white men!' replied Bradford with solemnity; for he was deeply impressed by the pious feelings of the Sachem, and touched by his considerate kindness. 'We do bless Mahneto; and we bless you also, our faithful and generous friends, who have thus so promptly shared with us the produce of your labors, instead of reserving it for your own future wants. But here is enough for you and us; and you and your young men must abide tonight in our village, and partake with us of the abundance that you have provided. We leave the future in the bountiful hands of Him who has thus made you His instruments to provide for us a table in the wilderness.'

'We will remain,' said Mooanam, 'and to-morrow some of your people shall go with us to our lakes, and fish in our canoes. The clouds are rising, and we shall, perhaps, have even better success than we have met with today. But tell me, my white brother,' he continued—while he looked inquiringly at Bradford—'tell me why your village is deserted this evening, and why no sounds of labor met our ears as we passed through the silent street? This is not the white men's day of rest; and the white men do not leave their work to sleep or dance, as the red men too often do. Why, then, are you and your people—even your squaws and your little ones—assembled here today, and what caused that joyful song that died away as we came to the foot hill?'

We have spent the day in fasting and prayer,' replied the President. 'We know that our Great Father has sent this long drought upon us, to chasten us for our sins: and we have met to humble ourselves before Him, and implore Him to send us the fruitful showers from heaven, before our crops are altogether withered in the ground. He alone can command the clouds to drop fatness; and when He sees that His punishment has done its appointed work, He surely will take it away. Even now, while we were making our prayers and supplications unto Him, and confessing our sins, He has sent a token that He has heard our cry, and will grant our request. Look at those clouds that are rising over the western hills, and gradually spreading like a curtain across the sky. For six weary weeks those clouds have been withheld, and we have been humbled; and, at times, our faith has well nigh failed. But the faithfulness of our God never fails; and now we are confident that, ere long, His blessing will descend upon us.'

Mooanam made no reply; but he gazed intently on the gathering clouds, and then looked searchingly into Bradford's fine expressive countenance, as if to be assured that he had heard and understood aright. Squanto stood beside him; and his aid had been several times required by both parties, in order to the carrying out the above discourse: and now the Sachem drew him aside, and conversed earnestly with him in a low voice. He was making him repeat, in his own tongue, the words of the white man; and Bradford heard him say to the interpreter, as he turned away to rejoin him, 'Now we shall see whether the Great Spirit really hears the prayers of the white men.'

The President understood this remark, and fervently he lifted up his own heart to the Lord, and prayed that the hopes of His suffering and trusting people might now be fulfilled; not only for their own relief, but also that the minds of the dark heathen might be impressed, and that they might see and feel the power and the goodness of the Christians' covenant God.

While Mooanam and the Governor were engaged in conversation, the assembly had dispersed to their own homes; each family carrying with them their respective portion of the food so liberally offered by their Indian friends, and eager to partake of the first plentiful meal that they had enjoyed for several weeks; The hope of coming rain also cheered the hearts of the Pilgrims; and there was joy and gratitude throughout the village that evening.

The Sachem and his people were gladly received and entertained in the dwellings of the Governor and principal inhabitants; and when Mooanam lay down to rest, he long gazed through the opening in the wooden wall of the chamber that formed its only window, and watched the heavy clouds as they sped across the sky, and observed the face of the glimmering moon, that looked out so calmly and brightly between their dark moving masses. The soul of the Sachem was deeply impressed; and he thought of all that Bradford had said to him, and wondered whether the God of the white men was indeed the God of the Indians also.

CHAPTER XIII

'It shall come to pass, that before they call, I will answer; and while they are yet speaking, I will hear.' ISA. lxv, 24.

Mooanam awoke from his sleep soon after the dawn of day appeared. He looked up at the open window, and a strange feeling of awe came over his soul, as he beheld the rain falling gently and steadily from the dull grey sky. He sprang to his feet, and hurried into the next apartment, where he found the President and his family already assembled, and gazing at the descending shower in silent admiration.

The Sachem caught the hands of Bradford in both his own; and while a tear of deep emotion glistened in his dark eye he exclaimed —

'Now I see that your God loves you. When the red men ask for rain, and use their conjuring arts to induce the Great Spirit to hear their wild cries, he gives it, it is true; but he gives it with hail and thunder, which makes the evil still greater. Your rain is of the right kind; it will restore the drooping corn. Now we see that your God hears you, and cares for you.'

The same impression, to a certain degree, was made on all the Indians, who were taught to regard this seasonable rain as the settlers themselves regarded it — as a special interposition of Providence for their relief. And were they wrong in thus looking upon it as an answer to their prayers, from a prayer-hearing God? And was it vain superstition that led them to rejoice as much in this proof of the goodness and benevolence of the God whom they served, and of His guiding and protecting hand being outstretched for their succor, as in the prospect of coming plenty that was thus afforded to them? Surely not. Their faith, and love, and confidence in God were all animated and strengthened by their conviction that the relief thus seasonably received came directly from Him who has promised in his faithful Word, that *all things,* whether joyous or grievous, 'shall work together for good to them that love Him; to them that are called according to His purpose.

So deeply was Hobomak, the Wampanoge interpreter, impressed by this instance of the pious trust of his white friends in the providence of their God, and of the protection they enjoyed under His guidance and government, that he gave himself up to a serious consideration of their religion and so sincere was his desire for spiritual knowledge, and so humble and teachable did he show himself, that, after a time, he was judged fit to be admitted into the pale of the Christian church. He was baptized as the first fruits of the settlers' efforts to evangelize the heathen among whom they had cast their lot: and he lived a firm friend of the white men, and died, after residing many years among them, 'leaving a good-hope that his soul went to rest.

The welcome rain continued to fall for several hours without intermission, on the morning that succeeded the Pilgrim's day of prayer and humiliation; and Mooanam sent his young men home to fish in the lake, while he remained with his white friends, intending to follow them in the afternoon, with a party of the settlers, to share their sport. As the day advanced, the clouds broke, and warm sunshine, interrupted by frequent refreshing showers, succeeded to the settled rain of the morning. So favorable, altogether, was the change, that Winslow gratefully remarks: 'It is difficult to say whether our withered corn, or our depressed spirits, were most refreshed and quickened. So great was the benevolence and goodness of our God!'

The Pilgrims had prayed for rain; and when their prayers were granted, they did not neglect the equally incumbent Christian duty of thanksgiving. Again the congregation ascended 'the Burying Hill'; and again their united voices rose to heaven in prayers and songs of praise. Mooanam formed one of the assembly; and he listened with deep and reverent attention to the devotions of his friends, frequently applying to Hobomak, who stood at his side, to explain to him the words and sentences that he did not comprehend.

The service concluded, and the women and children were descending the hill by the path that led to the village, leaving the Governor and his council to discuss some public business, and the other men to arrange themselves as usual into companies, for the manning of their fortification and other necessary employments. Just at that moment a native, attired in the costume and equipments of a Narragansett, was seen to approach the foot of the hill, bearing a bundle of strange appearance in his hands. With a quick and decided step he mounted the height, and glanced fiercely at the females and their children, whom he passed in the winding path, and who all involuntarily shrank from the gaze of his piercing and singularly expressive eye. In the breast of Janet that glance struck a chill of horror; for she had once before encountered it, and never could she forget or mistake it again. It seemed that Fingal recognized it also, and knew the evil that it foreboded. He was bounding down the hill by Edith's side, and, with expressive looks and actions, inviting the pensive child to join in his gambols, when the savage approached. Instantly he paused, and took his stand close to his young mistress, as if to guard her from some apprehended danger; and, as the red warrior passed, and bent his eye on Edith, the sagacious creature uttered a low deep growl, and seemed ready to spring at his throat, if the hand and voice of his young companion had not restrained him. Fingal was a noble specimen of the St. Bernard breed of dogs, whose sagacity is such as frequently to appear like human reason, and his intelligence was not inferior to that of the best of his race. In this instance it did not mislead him.

The dark warrior strode on without one sign of courtesy, and paused not until he had entered the group of elders and councilors who stood around the President, prepared to attend him to the public hall. The white men made way for him to approach the Governor; and, as he did so, his keen eye met that of Rodolph Maitland, and instantly kindled with a deeper fire, and gleamed with an expression of almost diabolical vengeance, which was seen by Rodolph, and understood by him for he, too, could not fail to recognize in the Narragansett warrior that same Coubitant who had fought so well at 'the first encounter,' and who had afterwards attended the Nausett Chief, Tisquantum, when he and his people were repulsed in their attack on New Plymouth. It was evident to Maitland that this savage entertained towards him and his race a peculiar sentiment of hatred; but the cause of this feeling was unknown to him.

The idea, however, that Henrich's loss was in some way connected with this man—or that he could give him some information respecting the nature of his son's death, and the place where his remains had been deposited—came forcibly to his mind; and, regardless of the cold malignant gaze that Coubitant fixed on him, he hastily approached him, and exclaimed in the Indian tongue—'Surely you are the Nausett warrior whom I saw with the Sachem of that tribe. If so, you can tell me the fate of my son—the boy who was carried off, and, I fear, cruelly slain when Tisquantum and his people retired from these woods. O, tell me how my boy was murdered, and where his dear remains were laid!

Rodolph's fine countenance was lighted up with eager animation. A tear of fond regret and affection glistened in his eye, and he could have grasped the hand of the swarthy savage, and almost have blessed him, if he would have told him that his darling Henrich had died by a single blow, and that his body had been laid unmolested to rest. But Coubitant drew back, and with a smile of fierce mockery and infernal triumph, replied briefly—

'Ha! you found his bloody coat then. May your heart's blood soon flow forth as his did; and may my eyes see your body equally mangled and defaced!'

At the same moment, he placed the bundle that he carried on the ground before the President, saying, 'This comes from the Chief of the Narragansetts!' and, turning away, hastily descended the hill, and was lost to view among the trees of the skirting wood, before the council had time to resolve on the course they should pursue respecting his detention, or Rodolph had recovered the shock that his cruel words had inflicted.

The curiosity of the Governor and his friends was now directed to the strange-looking package that lay on the ground. On examination, they found the envelope to be composed of a dried snakeskin, which was quickly opened, and disclosed several Indian arrows. Squanto gazed on these with a significant look; and on being questioned by Bradford as to the meaning of so singular an offering, he informed him that it was the native mode of declaring war.

The well-known enmity of the Narragansetts towards the Wampanoges — the friends and allies of the settlers — rendered this hostile declaration no surprise to the Governor and his council. But the fact of its being conveyed by Coubitant, who had so lately, in the character of a subordinate Narragansett chieftain, subscribed the written acknowledgement of King James's supremacy, excited no small astonishment. It was a source, also, of regret, as it proved how little dependence could be placed in the professions of the natives. To enter on a war with the numerous and powerful tribe of the Narragansetts, was likewise far from being desirable in any point of view; for the Pilgrims were little prepared either to meet such formidable antagonist's in the field, or to resist the continual attacks and aggression's that constitute the greatest share of Indian warfare.

A consultation was therefore held as to the best method of replying to the challenge of the Narragansett Sachem; and it was finally determined that the most prudent and effectual course would be to show a resolute appearance, and give no cause to the native's to suppose that they dreaded their enmity. A bold acceptance of the challenge might, it was urged both by Squanto and Hobomak, strike terror into the savages, and deter them from prosecuting their present hostile intentions.

Bradford, therefore, adopted the Indian method of communicating this reply by expressive signs; and, taking the arrows — which appeared to be poisoned — from the snakeskin, he placed some gunpowder and balls in the significant wrapper. He then inquired who among his trusty warrior's would volunteer to take the packet to the dwelling of Cundincus,[*] the Chief of the Narragansetts. Several offered their services; and, among those, none was so eager to be employed as Rodolph Maitland. He felt an earnest desire to see and speak with Coubitant once more: and no fear of the personal risk that he might incur in the expedition could deter him from thus making another attempt to obtain some certain information respecting his lost son.

[Footnote: Afterwards called by the settlers, Canonicus.]

Had the President known how much reason there was to fear that treachery might be exercised towards Maitland, he would surely not have suffered him thus to risk his valuable life. Rut he was ignorant of all the peculiar circumstances that had occurred to show that he was a special mark for the vengeance of Coubitant: and the confidence he felt in his courage and ability led him—on this occasion, as on many others—to select him as his ambassador. Two companions were assigned to him, and Squanto was desired to attend the party as interpreter.

When Helen heard that her husband was appointed to convey a reply to the war-like message of the dark savage whom she had met on the hill, and whose aspect had filled her with terror, she felt an involuntary dread; and gladly would she have dissuaded him from accepting the office of ambassador—which she knew not he had so earnestly solicited—had she not been well aware that all such attempts would be useless. Rodolph was not a man to shrink from any service that was required of him for the public good; and least of all from any service that involved danger and difficulty. He, however, concealed from his anxious wife the fact that he had recognized in the Narragansett messenger a deadly and determined foe, knowing how greatly—and perhaps how justly—her fears would be increased, if she suspected that the Indian champion was one of those who had planned and executed the capture of her eldest son.

But Janet had, as we have seen, remembered the swarthy savage, and the scene with which his countenance was associated in her mind; and when she had an opportunity of speaking to her master in private, she implored him to resign the embassy into other hands, and not thus rashly to encounter a foe, whose public conduct had proved him to be unworthy of confidence, and whose expression of countenance betokened both cruelty and treachery. But all her arguments were unavailing. Maitland had undertaken the charge of the expedition at his own request; and he would have felt himself dishonored in now declining it from any personal motives, even had he been, in the least degree, inclined to do so. On the contrary, his spirit was roused and excited by the very perils he was conscious he might have to encounter; and his desire to obtain, and convey to Helen, some intelligence of Henrich— even if that intelligence should still for ever the doubts end hopes, that, in spite of every past circumstance, would sometimes arise in his own heart, and that of his own wife—was so great that nothing could have turned him from his purpose. He, therefore, desired the faithful Janet to preserve the same silence on the subject of Coubitant that she had already so judiciously adopted towards her mistress; and assured her that he would neglect no precaution that might preserve him from the treacherous intentions of the Indian, should any such be actually entertained by him.

The next morning Rodolph started at break of day, to convey the reply of the Governor to the Narragansett Sachem, whose tribe inhabited the district now called Rhode Island, lying to the south-west of New Plymouth. He was accompanied by two friends, and likewise by the interpreter, Squanto. His faithful dog, Fingal, also showed such a strong desire to follow his master, that, although it was Maitland's usual custom to leave him at home as a guard, during any of his occasional absences, when his services in hunting were not required, he could not, in this instance, resist his eager pleadings. Helen, also, assured him that she should feel no apprehension at being deprived of her usual protector, as no danger was likely to menace her dwelling; and the increase in the population of the village, from the arrival of the new settlers, had added an inmate to the family, in the person of Claude Felton, a stout young laboring man, who had become the useful assistant of Maitland in his agricultural occupations, and proved a good and faithful servant.

To his protection and watchful care Rodolph Maitland committed his little family; and, taking a cheerful farewell of his wife and Edith, he commenced his journey through the wild and almost trackless woods. Guided by Squanto, the party reached the village of Cundineus, and were received into the presence of the Sachem and his nephew Miantonomo, who shared with him the cares and the dignity of his chieftainship.

With the assistance of the interpreter, Rodolph informed the Chiefs that he was the bearer of the reply of the mighty strangers to the bold challenge that had been sent to them on the part of Cundineus and Miantonomo; and he invited them to open the packet which he laid before them, in order that they might fully understand the nature of that reply, and judge whether the subjects of the powerful king of Great Britain were terrified at the audacity of the red men. Probably Squanto made some additions of his own to the harangue of the ambassador; for a very ludicrous change of expression appeared on the countenances of the savage Chieftains. The looks of fierce defiance with which they had received the embassy gave way to anxious and timid glances, which they hastily cast at the ominous snake-skin, while they involuntarily drew back, as if they feared it would explode, and punish their rash temerity.

Rodolph saw the effect of Squanto's version of his speech, and resolved to increase it. He understood enough of the native tongue to perceive that the interpreter had alluded to the potent and deadly properties of the contents of the snake-skin, and he desired him to inform the Chiefs that the musket which he carried in his hand contained a very small portion of the same substance, and he would give them proof of its power. He then glanced for a moment into the lofty trees that surrounded the place of audience, and perceiving a monkey that was clinging to one of the wide-spreading branches, nod chattering angrily at the intrusive foreigners, he took a deliberate aim, and in another instant the creature lay lifeless and motionless on the ground. The Indians were startled at the report, and amazed at the effect of the invisible messenger of death. They hastened to examine the dead animal but one drop of blood issuing from its skull was the only indication that some missile had pierced its brain; and the veneration of the Narragansetts and their Chiefs for the prowess of the white men evidently rose in a great degree.

But there was one among them who did not share the wonder or the awe of the assembly. He stood silent and motionless, at a little distance from the group, with his eyes intently fixed on Rodolph's countenance, and a smile of malignant scorn and triumph on his own dark features. His arms were folded across his scarred and painted breast, and his right hand grasped the handle of a long knife that was stuck into his deerskin belt. The action seemed to be involuntary, and without any present purpose; for he remained in the same position, unobserved by Rodolph, until he and his attendants had retired to the hut appointed them by Cundineus, to rest and refresh themselves, end await the reply of the Chief.

Rodolph then desired Squanto to make inquiries for Coubitant, and, if possible, to bring him to the hut. But the sagacious interpreter had seen and recognized the white mans face; and he earnestly entreated Maitland not to give him any opportunity of executing the vengeance which was evidently burning at his heart, and ready to break forth in some deed of fatal violence. Rodolph's English friends also joined so warmly in these entreaties that he at length consented that Squanto should seek the savage, and endeavor to draw from him all the information that he could give respecting Henrich's death. He did so, and a long conversation took place that evening, the result of which was that he assured Rodolph that his son had indeed been murdered in the wood, as he had always supposed, and that his scalp had been torn off even before life was extinct, whilst his body had been conveyed to the next encampment, and burned with many heathen rites, to appease the troubled spirit of Tisquantum's son Tekoa.

The father shuddered, and turned away to hide the rising tear, as he listened to this harrowing but false account. He, however, fully believed it; and felt that, henceforth, it would be vain to cherish any hope concerning his son, except that blessed hope which is the privilege of the Christian — the sure and certain hope of meeting hereafter, in the presence of the God and

Savior in whom he had taught his child to place his trust. He said no more; he did not even question Squanto as to the cause of his having spent so long a time in conferring with Coubitant, when all the information he had obtained amounted merely to the sad assurance that his son had suffered a dreadful death. Had he done so, the interpreter might have found it difficult to account for his conduct, as he had professed a strong dislike to Coubitant, and a distrust of all his motives and actions. The fact was, that the wily savage had discovered Squanto's love of importance, and his desire to be supposed to possess the confidence of the white men, and by flattering his vanity, he had drawn from him all the information he could give with respect to the strength of the settlers, and their capability of resisting an attack of the natives. Squanto took care to exaggerate the numbers and the power of his employers; but still it appeared to Coubitant, that if he could once more induce the neighboring tribes to combine and invade their territory, there was every probability of their being utterly exterminated and nothing short of this could satisfy the feeling of hatred that he entertained towards the whole race of the strangers. By way of exalting the might of the settlers in the minds of the native, Squanto assured Coubitant that the white men kept the plague, of which the Indians well knew the desolating effects, imprisoned in a cellar, where they also stowed, their gunpowder, and that they could let it loose upon their foes at their pleasure. This strange evidence was heard also by Miantonomo, whom Coubitant called to join the conference, as he, knew that he already hated the English; and he desired to strengthen that feeling to the utmost, for the furtherance of his own plans.

From Coubitant, Squanto also received some intelligence, which, in the minds both of the superstitious interpreter and his heathen informant, was of vital importance to the settlers, and calculated to inspire them with dread. This was the awful fact that, a short time previous, several of the neighboring tribes had met in the adjacent forest, and that the Powows of the whole district had passed three days and nights in cursing the strangers, and uttering against them the most horrible imprecations. The effect of this diabolical proceeding, in causing the defeat of their foes, Coubitant did not do not; and, in spite of his veneration for the English, and his conviction that their deities were more powerful than the Indian demons, Squanto was filled with apprehensions on their account. He communicated the circumstance to Rodolph, and was surprised and almost offended at the smile of indifference and contempt with which the Christian listened to him. But he found it impossible to make him attach any importance to what seemed to him so serious a calamity; and, by degrees, his own fears subsided and his mind was reassured by the arguments and the cool composure of Maitland.

Rodolph and his companions lay down to rest for the night in the Indian hut, across the entrance of which Squanto placed several strong boughs, and spread a cloak of deer-skin over them. This was done ostensibly for the purpose of keeping out the cold night wind, but really to serve as a screen from the prying eyes of Coubitant, whose intentions he much mistrusted, and also as an obstacle to any attempt he might possibly make to violate the laws of honor and hospitality, by a secret attack on the person of the ambassador. Whether the savage actually meditated any such act of treachery, was not known; but if he approached the hut with a murderous purpose, he was probably deterred more by the fierce growlings of Fingal—who lay at the entrance, but scarcely slept that night—than by the barrier of boughs and deerskin.

Several times were the party awakened by the trusty watch-dog's angry bark; and once, when Rodolph hastened to the entrance, and drew aside the curtain, he thought he could descry more than one retreating figure in the uncertain darkness. The continued uneasiness of Fingal prevented his master from again giving way to sleep until after day had dawned, when his faithful guard became tranquil, and he likewise sought the repose which he greatly needed before recommencing his fatiguing journey.

Ere he set out on his homeward way, Rodolph again repaired, with Squanto, to the presence of the Chief; to demand his message to the British Governor; and he was informed by Cundincus, that he had already dispatched a messenger to restore the dreaded packet, and to deprecate the wrath of the pale-faced Chieftain. This was all the ambassador could desire; and, taking a courteous leave of the Sachem, he and his attendants resumed their journey without further delay.

For a considerable distance their path lay through the forest; and the underwood was so close and thick that the road consisted of a narrow track, scarcely wider than would admit of two persons passing one another along it, and only calculated for travelling in 'Indian file,' which is so much practiced by the natives. In this manner our party proceeded, Rodolph leading the way, and his attendants following singly; while Fingal, who seemed rejoiced to have left the village, bounded along at his master's side, ever and anon leaping up to express his joy by licking his face and hands.

'Down, Fingal!' said his master, kindly patting his favorite's head, and stroking his thick shaggy mane. 'Down, my good fellow; your joy is too boisterous for this narrow, thorny path. You shall expend your superfluous strength and spirits on the plain yonder; for I think I detect some game scudding across the green meadow before us.'

Rodolph paused to adjust his gun; and the sagacious dog ceased his wild demonstrations, end paused also until the task was completed. Then as his master rose to proceed, he once more sprang up to his shoulder, end his intelligent eyes asked leave to dash through the covert, and drive out the expected game.

But why did that bound of pleasure change instantaneously into a convulsion of agony? and why did the noble creature fall by his master's side and look so earnestly up into his face? Surely, in the midst of his own death struggle, he sought to tell him, with that mute eloquence of love, that danger was near. Rodolph knew that it was so; but no danger could then have compelled him to leave his dying friend— the friend whose life was now ebbing away as a sacrifice for his own. Yes! the shaft that had pierced through the neck of Fingal was designed for Rodolph's breast; and he who cast it deemed that it had found its intended mark, when, through the bushes, he saw the white man's form bend quickly and suddenly to the ground. Then Coubitant fled exultingly, and his savage heart beat high with joy and triumph.

But Rodolph thought not of him, or of his malice. He only saw his faithful dog expiring at his side, and knew that he had no power to aid him. It was evident that the arrow was poisoned, for the wound, otherwise, appeared too slight to be mortal; and the foam that gathered on Fingal's jaws, and the convulsive struggle that shook his form, showed too plainly that his sufferings would soon be over. The companions of Rodolph urged him to join them in instant flight; for they felt the peril of their present situation, where the surrounding thicket gave such ample opportunity to their lurking foes to take a deadly aim, while, at the same time, it prevented them from either discovering or pursuing their assailants. But all their arguments, and all their entreaties, were unavailing so long as Fingal continued to lick his master's caressing hand, and to reply to his well-known voice, by looks of intelligent affection.

Soon, however, his head sank powerless on Rodolph's knee, and the bright glance of his eye faded away, and life and motion ceased. Was it unmanly in his master to brush a tear from his eye, as he rose from the ground, and turned away one moment from the lifeless form of his favorite?

I will not leave him here,' he said. 'The savages shall not mangle his body, as they would gladly have mangled mine. His death has saved my life; and all that remains of him shall be carried to a place of safety, and buried beyond the reach of those who slew him.'

'Yes,' replied Squanto readily—for he desired the removal of the dog from that spot, for other reasons beside the gratification of Maitland's feelings—' Yes; we will carry him away, and hide him from Coubitants eyes. Doubtless he will return here, as soon as all is quiet, to see the success of his murderous attempt; and when he finds the path thus stained with blood, he will be satisfied, and pursue us no further than to see whether we bury our dead companion in the forest, or bear him to his home. We must, therefore, carry Fingal all the way to New Plymouth, lest he should follow on our trail, and discover that he has only slain a dog.'

Rodolph's English companions concurred in this view, and willingly lent their aid to convey the body of Fingal from the place of his death. A couple of poles were cut hastily, and a rude light litter was formed; for Squanto wished that Coubitant should find traces of such preparations, as they would help to convince him that they had thus borne away the wounded or dead form of the ambassador.

'Now,' said he, when all was ready, 'not another moment must be lost. Even now the keen eye of the foe may be upon us, and our stratagem may be in vain. Two of you must bear the litter, and must carefully place your feet in the same spot, so as to form but one track; and lead our pursuers to believe that only three men have passed along. And there, throw that bloody handkerchief on the path, and Coubitant will take it as a trophy of success. Stay, he exclaimed, as Rodolph and one of his friends were about to raise the lifeless form of Fingal from the ground 'stay one moment, and I will completely deceive that deceiver.'

He smiled as he spoke, for he felt it a pleasure and a triumph to outwit the wily Coubitant. Then, while the body of the dog was supported, he carefully pressed his feet on the soft path, so as to leave a distinct impression, and convince any who should examine the trail that it was not the dog who had been wounded. This cunning device he practiced again and again until they had passed through the wood, and entered the grassy meadow, where such precautions were no longer needed. Then the party quickened their steps, and paused not again until they had struck deeply into the forest that succeeded to the undulating reach of meadowland.

The way seemed long to Rodolph. He desired to reach his cherished home; and yet he dreaded to return and sadden the heart of his little Edith with the story of Fingal's death, and the sight of the inanimate form of her last and much-loved playfellow. Had it not been for this catastrophe, he would have kept from his wife and child the knowledge of the cruel attempt that had been made on his life as such knowledge could only distress them, and cause them needless anxiety and alarm in future. But the death of Fingal must be accounted for; and, let the consequence be what it might, it must be accounted for truly, and without prevarication. Therefore it was that Rodolph dreaded meeting those whose presence was the joy and the sunlight of his life.

He reached his home, and silently entered his blooming garden; and, with Squanto's assistance, laid the body of Fingal, now cold and stiff, beneath the venerable tree that shaded Edith's bower. Then he entered his dwelling, and found its inmates busily employed at their usual domestic occupations, and overjoyed at his sudden and unexpected arrival. But, in spite of his own pleasure, a shade of sadness and anxiety was on his brow, which he could not hide from the quick eye of Helen; and she eagerly inquired the cause.

Sadly Rodolph told his story; and joy and deep gratitude for the preservation of her beloved husband so filled and engrossed the heart of Helen, as, for a time, to overpower every feeling of regret for the loss of the faithful animal, who seemed to have been providentially directed to accompany his master, and save his life at the sacrifice of his own.

But Edith keenly felt the loss she had sustained. She was thankful—very thankful—that her father had been restored to their home in safety; but she did not the less deplore the death of her dear companion: and, unable to restrain her tears, she hurried from the house, and ran to hide her grief in her lonely bower. For some time her parents did not perceive her absence, for they were occupied with their own feelings of pious gratitude; but presently Rodolph remarked that she had left the room, and remembered where he had deposited the body of her favorite. He rose, and went towards the spot, accompanied by Helen; and tears of sorrowful sympathy arose in the eyes of both, as they beheld the desolate child lying on the ground by Fingals side, with her arms around his neck, and her long waving hair hanging over his inanimate face, that had never before met her gaze without an answering look of intelligence and affection.

Gently they raised her, and spoke to her words of love and comfort; but she long refused to be comforted. And though, at length, she became calm and resigned, and never was heard to utter one murmur at this fresh stroke of sorrow, yet her pensive sadness became more confirmed, and plainly showed that she mourned for Fingal, not only as her lost companion, but also as a connecting link between her own heart and the memory of her lamented brother. Poor Edith! her early life was one of trial and disappointment; but it was good for her to be afflicted.'

CHAPTER XIV

'O Christian warriors! wherefore did you thus
Forget the precepts of your Lord and Chief,
And lend yourselves to deeds of guilt and blood!
Did ye not know — or, knowing, did not heed —
Those solemn words of His, when death was nigh,
And He bequeathed a *legacy of "peace"*
To His disciples? They that take the sword
Shall perish with the sword. O, well it were
If ye who left your native land, and sought
A desert for the liberty of faith,
Had acted more according to that faith,
And sought to win the souls you rashly sent
To meet their God and yours!' ANON.

Yes, well, indeed, lied it been if the settlers had been able and willing to preserve, unbroken, the friendly relations with the Indians, which, after the first natural distrust felt by the natives towards the white strangers had subsided, they were, in several instances, able to establish. But such was not the case. They received many provocations from the natives, even from those who professed to be most friendly towards them, and also from the settlers who followed them from the mother-country; and they did not always meet these provocations in the truly Christian spirit which, it must be allowed, generally pervaded their councils, and actuated their public and private proceedings with the wild tribes by whom they were surrounded.

Even Masasoyt — their friend and ally — was about this time nearly estranged from them, and on the point of joining the Narragansetts in a project for their destruction. This change in his sentiments was the result of the machinations of Coubitant, assisted by the foolish pretensions and love of interference which rendered Squanto almost as dangerous as he was useful to his employers. His boasting tales about the power of the English settlers to imprison and to let loose the desolating plague at their will and pleasure, had been told to the Sagamore of the Wampanoges, as well as to Coubitant and Miantonomo; and suspicions had arisen in the breast of Masasoyt, which he vainly strove to infuse into his more enlightened and trustworthy son, Mooanam. Nothing that his father could say had any effect in weakening the friendship entertained by the young Sachem, and his brother Quadequina, towards the emigrants; and it was owing to this steady friendship that they were made acquainted with the altered feelings of the Sagamore in time to prevent their ripening into open hostility.

Mooanam communicated to the President the doubts and suspicions that had taken possession of his father's mind, and advised him immediately to send the faithful and devoted Hobomak to Packanokick, to endeavor to remove the evil impression, and restore his confidence in the Pilgrim Fathers. He also convinced both Bradford and his council that the conspiracy which Squanto had represented as already formed, and only waiting the concurrence of Masasoyt to be carried into deadly effect, was as yet in its infancy, and might, by judicious management, be altogether broken up. The Pokanokit interpreter had greatly exaggerated, in his report to the Governor, all that he had heard from Coubitant while at the Narragansett village; and had persuaded him, in spite of the opinion expressed by Rodolph, to believe not only that he and his people had been cursed by the Powows, but also that the tribes to which these satanic conjurors belonged were uniting for the common purpose of attacking and destroying the British settlement.

All this was done by Squanto, with no serious intention of injuring his new friends, but from a vain desire to make himself important, and show the extent of his knowledge and sagacity. His vanity was, however, very near proving fatal to him: for when the trusty Hobomak had explained to the Sagamore the real motives and intentions of the settlers towards the natives, and had convinced him that all the strange and mysterious stories that Squanto delighted to tell were either pure inventions or gross exaggerations, a second change was effected in the old Chief's feelings, and he sent to demand that the faithless interpreter should be immediately delivered up to him.

The Governor was extremely reluctant to comply with this demand, as he well knew how cruel and how summary were the judgements of the native Chiefs; and he, as well as the whole of the colony, felt a regard for Squanto, notwithstanding his folly and his errors. Nevertheless, the Pokanokit was a subject of the Sagamore, who had made an express stipulation in his treaty with the settlers that any of his people, who might take up their abode in the colony, should be given up to him whenever he required it; and therefore Bradford felt himself compelled to abandon Squanto to his fate.

The messengers who accompanied Hobomak on his return to New Plymouth were loaded with a quantity of valuable beaver-skins, which they laid in a pile at the Governor's feet, as a bribe to induce him to comply with

Masasoyt's demand. These the Governor rejected with indignant scorn, observing that no man's life could be purchased from the English; and that if he resigned the interpreter into the power of his native sovereign, it was only because truth and justice required it, and not from any base motives either of fear or advantage.

Then the messengers approached the wretched man, who stood calmly awaiting the decision of the Governor; and he saw one of them draw from his belt the knife that Masasoyt had commanded him to plunge into the culprit's heart. But Squanto did not tremble. All the native fortitude, so characteristic of his race, was manifested in this awful moment; and the bystanders felt a respect for the Pokanokit that he had never before inspired.

Gladly would each individual have interposed to save him; and breathlessly they watched the movements of the President, whose signal was to fix the moment of Squanto's death. Bradford hesitated: the word trembled on his lips, when suddenly looking towards the sea from the summit of the Burying Hill,' on which the assembly stood, he espied a shallop bounding over the waves, and advancing directly towards the shore beneath.

He made this a pretext—certainly, not a very well grounded onefor delaying the execution of Squanto's sentence; and declared that he would not give the fatal signal until he had ascertained the object and the contents of the approaching vessel. This faltering on the part of the Governor excited great wrath in the messengers of Masasoyt; and, without any farther parley, they took up their beaver skins, and departed to their home. Squanto's forfeited life was thus providentially spared; and the conduct of Bradford was, through Mooanam's good offices, overlooked b the Sagamore. But that life was not greatly prolonged. Very soon after this event he was seized with I virulent fever, while on a short journey with the Governor, and, in spite of all the care and attention that were bestowed on him, he died, much regretted by the whole colony.

The boat, whose seasonable approach had been the means of arresting the fatal stroke, was found to have been sent from some English fishing vessels, many of which now constantly frequented the shores of New England. It conveyed to the colony an addition of several able-bodied men, who were joyfully welcomed by the settlers, as laborers were just then much wanted, both in the fields and in the increasing town. These men were sent out by an English merchant named Weston, who had long endeavored to encourage the colonization of New England; but from very different motives to those which had actuated the Pilgrim Fathers, and led them to forsake the comforts of a European home for the toils and uncertainties of an American wilderness. A desire for profit appears to have been the ruling principle in

Weston's mind. He was, therefore, very indifferent as to the moral character of the men whom he sent out to join the emigrants, and was only solicitous to secure a quick return of the money that he had expended: and, finding that the prospect of gain from a connection with the New Plymouthers was doubtful and tardy, he had resolved to found a colony himself.

For this purpose he had, some time previously, obtained a grant of a portion of land in Massachusetts, and sent over sixty men to cultivate it, in two ships, which he placed under the command of his brother-in- law. The arrival of this fresh band of emigrants had proved a fruitful source of trouble and annoyance to the first settlers, for they were chiefly idle and profligate vagabonds, who had no settled occupation at home, and no characters to sustain. Weston himself described them in a letter to Bradford, as 'tolerably rude and profane.' And a friend of the Pilgrims wrote from England to warn them against having any connection with the new colony: and recommended them to have it distinctly explained to the Indians, that they were a new and independent society, for whose conduct and good faith they could in no way be responsible.

Notwithstanding all these warnings, and the very unprepossessing appearance of the new emigrants, the Plymouthers had shown more kindness and hospitality than they had prudence and caution: and had received their countrymen into their own settlement on their arrival in America. They had even permitted on half of their number to reside at New Plymouth during the whole summer, while the strongest and healthiest had proceeded to Massachusetts to fix on a spot for their settlement, and prepare habitations. They had decided on a place called Wessagussett,[*] a little to the south of Boston; and thither they were afterwards followed by their companions from New Plymouth. The long residence of these men among the pious and high-minded Pilgrims had not, however, made any salutary impression on their minds: and all the kindness and hospitality they had received were most ungratefully forgotten.

[Footnote: New Weymouth]

In various ways the new colony vexed and annoyed the men of Plymouth; but in no way more seriously than by their conduct towards the natives, which was so different to the just and upright dealings of the Pilgrims, that the Indians began to lose their confidence in the white men, and to suspect deceit and imposition where hitherto they had only found truth and justice. Weston's colony was, indeed, scarcely settled at Wessagussett, before complaints were sent by the Indians to their friends at Plymouth, of the repeated depredations that were committed by the new settlers, who were continually carrying off their stores of corn, and other property: and these accusations were by no means surprising to Bradford and his council, as they had already detected them in many acts of theft during their stay at New Plymouth.

The harvest of this year was poor and scanty; and the great accession to their numbers, caused by the visit of Weston's settlers, had entirely consumed the stores of the Plymouthers, and reduced them again to actual want. Joyfully, therefore, they hailed the arrival of two ships from the mother country, laden with knives, beads, and various other articles, that would be acceptable to the Indians in the way of barter, and enable the settlers to purchase from them the necessary supply of provisions, for which they had hitherto been compelled to pay very dear in skins and furs. Meanwhile, the colony of Wessagussett was in a still worse condition. They had quickly consumed all the food with which the generous Plymouthers had supplied them, and had then stolen everything on which they could lay their hands. They had also sold almost all their clothes and bedding, and even their weapons; and were brought to such extreme necessity that they did not refuse to do the meanest services for the Indians who dwelt near their settlement, in return for such means of subsistence as the red men were able to furnish them with. For this condescension—so unlike the dignified yet kind deportment of the Plymouthers—the natives despised them, and treated them with contempt, and even violence. Thus early was the British name brought into disrepute with the Indians, when men bearing that name came among them for mere purposes of speculation and profit, and ware not governed by the Christian principles of humanity and justice that distinguished the earliest settlers in New England from all those who followed them. Nor did the evil consequences of their ill conduct rest with themselves. They fell also on the peaceably-disposed colony of Plymouth, and were the means of involving them in hostilities with the natives, which had hitherto been warded off by the kind and judicious management of the Governor and his assistants.

The general state of peace which had, up to this period, been maintained with the Indians, was greatly to be attributed to the bold and decisive measures that were always adopted by Miles Standish, the military chief of the little community, and the leader of every warlike expedition. He well knew how to impress the natives with a due respect, for he never tolerated the slightest injury or insult, and yet he never permitted his men to be guilty of any act of injustice or oppression towards the red men.

Since the arrival of Weston's disorderly colony, Captain Standish had shown himself even more decided in maintaining the rights and the dignity of the Plymouthers, and had endeavored to show the natives that they were not to identify the new comers with those whom they had already learnt to know and to respect. But at length, in spite of all these judicious measures, the Pilgrims were drawn into the quarrel that subsisted between their countrymen of Wessagussett and the natives; and, having drawn the sword, they certainly forgot the principles of mercy and humanity that had hitherto guided them. Active measures were, undoubtedly, called for; but cruelty and stratagem were unworthy of these Christian warriors.

The continued marauding expeditions of the men of Wessagussett had exasperated the neighboring tribes to the last degree; and the state of weakness to which they were reduced by their own thoughtless and improvident conduct, led the natives to suppose that they would fall an easy prey to their combined force. They, therefore, again formed a combination to attack and utterly destroy these oppressive intruders into their country. Probably the council of Chiefs, who met in the depths of the forest to arrange their plan of operations, would have contented themselves with contriving the destruction of the new and offending colony, which they might easily have effected had they confined their projected operations to that object alone. But there was one in the council who could not rest satisfied with such a partial vengeance on the white strangers; and his fiery eloquence, and false assertions and insinuations, prevailed over the rest of the Chiefs to disregard every treaty, and every obligation that ought to have bound them to the settlers of New Plymouth, and to include them also in their savage scheme of massacre and plunder.

The argument by which he finally overcame the scruples of those Chiefs who had allied themselves with the first emigrants, and had acquired a regard and respect for them, was one of self-preservation. He boldly asserted that the men of New Plymouth would never either pardon or forget the destruction of their countrymen of Wessagussett, but would immediately lay aside the mask of kindness and forbearance with which they had hitherto concealed their undoubted project of acquiring the dominion of the whole country, and gradually destroying the red men; and would call forth all their supernatural powers, and blast them with fire and plague, unless they were taken by surprise, and annihilated at one fell swoop. All the superstitious fears of the ignorant natives were thus aroused, and if there were any in the assembly who were too well acquainted with the white men to credit all that Coubitant asserted, they thought it either unsafe or unwise to express their opinions any further.

Happily for the settlers, one such faithful and friendly spirit was there to watch for their interests, and provide for their preservation. Masasoyt had resumed all his kindly feelings towards his English allies, since the misunderstanding occasioned by Squanto's meddling propensities had been explained away by the trusty Hobomak. He had also recently been visited by Edward Winslow, when he was afflicted with a severe illness, and the Christian soldier had ministered to his relief in a way that had excited both the wonder and the lively gratitude of the Sagamore. When, therefore, he obeyed the summons of Coubitant to join the general council of Chiefs, he had no intention of consenting to any hostile measures being undertaken against his powerful and beneficent friends. Weston's wild and disorderly crew had excited his anger in common with that of all the other neighboring Sachems; and he was quite willing to combine with his red brethren for their chastisement—perhaps, even for their utter destruction: but he did not confound the Pilgrim Fathers, who had never failed in truth and honesty, with the deceitful and marauding vagabonds who wore white faces, and called themselves Christian subjects of King James, while they acted like heathen savages.

At first, Masasoyt met the malignant arguments and false assertions of Coubitant with an open and generous statement of the upright conduct of the strangers towards himself and his tribe, during the three years of their residence in New England; and urged the assembled Chiefs to beware how they attempted to molest men whose power to resist and punish any such attempt was only equaled by their willingness and ability to benefit those who treated them with confidence and integrity. But he soon perceived that his arguments in favor of mercy and justice were powerless, when opposed to the fierce and crafty harangues of Coubitant; and he, therefore, forbore to make any further reply, and even appeared to acquiesce in the decision of the council, that the only means of securing the safety and independence of the Indian tribes was utterly to exterminate the invaders.

The proposed plan for accomplishing this barbarous project, was first to surround and fall on the miserable and sickly colony of Wessagussett; and then, before the news of the massacre could reach New Plymouth, to hasten thither, and wreak on its unsuspecting and unprepared inhabitants the same fierce vengeance.

The day and hour were fixed, and every necessary preliminary was minutely arranged; and then the council broke up, and the Chiefs returned to their respective dwellings, to collect and fully arm their followers, and prepare to meet again at the appointed time and place, with both hands and hearts read to execute the bloody deed.

Masasoyt retired like the rest; and, attended by the little band of warriors who formed his bodyguard, be took the forest path that led to his dwelling at Packanokick. But he did not long pursue that path. When he had proceeded such a distance through the forest as to feel sure that he should not, by turning to the right, cross the route of any of the other Chiefs, he dismissed all his followers, except two of the most trusty and confidential. The rest he desired to proceed immediately to Packanokick, and inform his people that they must prepare for a warlike expedition, and that he was going to visit his son, Mooanam, in order to give him directions to join in the enterprise with that portion of the tribe that was under his authority.

This was very far from being the truth; but the Indian Sagamore considered that every falsehood and stratagem was allowable, and even meritorious, that could further a desired object, especially if that object was so undoubtedly good in itself as that which now engrossed his thoughts and wishes. He did not know that it is sin to do evil that good may come; and therefore we must judge him by his generous motives, and not by his heathen practice.

Having thus freed himself from those on whose discretion and fidelity he could not fully rely, he changed his course, and traveled straight towards New Plymouth. There was no beaten track through the tangled woods in that direction; but the position of the sun, and the appearance of the trees, were sufficient guides for the sagacious Indian Chief, and, in spite of his advanced age, he pursued his way with vigor and activity. Frequently his path was obstructed by the luxuriant growth of underwood, or by the cable-like creepers that hung in every direction, crossing each other like the rigging of a ship, and presenting obstacles that nothing but the tomahawks that hung from the girdles of the natives enabled them to overcome. With these weapons — ever ready, in the hand of an Indian, either to cut his way through the forest, to fell the timbers for his wigwam or his canoe, to slay the game that his arrows have brought to the ground, or to cleave the skull of his enemy — did old Masasoyt and his devoted followers divide the large tough climbing plants that obstructed their passage. Sometimes, also, when the sun was totally obscured and the necessary windings in their course would hive rendered them uncertain whether they were following the right direction, these useful tomahawks enabled them to consult the Indian compass.

The manner in which these children of the wilderness supply to themselves the want of that invaluable instrument is both curious and ingenious, and it proved of essential use to the Wampanoge Chief on this occasion. Whenever he found himself at fault from the absence of the sun, or any other direct indication of the proper course, he raised his battle-axe, and struck a heavy blow at some neighboring pine or birch tree, on each side of which he cut a deep notch, and then, by examining the grain of the wood, he could tell which was the north, and which the south side—the former being easily ascertained by the greater closeness of the concentric rings, and consequent hardness of the fiber. The sap being more drawn to the south side by the action of the sun, causes the rings on that side to swell more; and this operation of nature has been observed by nature's children, and employed by them as a sure guide in their long wanderings through the pathless forests where they find a home.

The journey to New Plymouth was rather a long one; but the Sagamore and his companions were each provided with a small quantity of their usual travelling food, *nokake* — or meal made of parched maize — which they carried, in true Indian fashion, in their hollow leathern girdles. When they came to a pond, or brook, they paused to eat a few handsful of this simple provision, which is so dry that it can only be swallowed when either water or snow is at hand, ready to wash down each mouthful; and, consequently, in summer the natives have sometimes to travel long distances before they can avail themselves of the food that is already in their hands.

Immediately on his arrival at New Plymouth, the Sagamore repaired to the dwelling of Bradford; and, requesting a private interview — at which no one was allowed to be present except the Wampanoge interpreter Hobomak — he informed him of the conspiracy of the natives, and warned him to be well prepared for the intended attack. Could he have given this warning, and ensured the safety of his allies, without betraying the whole of the conspirators' projects, he would gladly have done so; for he both despised and hated the men of Wessagussett, and he was willing that they should he treated as they seemed disposed to treat such of his race as they could get into their power. He even made an attempt to persuade Bradford to leave them to the fate they so well deserved, and to connive at their destruction, which would remove an increasing evil from the first colony.

But the President soon convinced him that such a course would be altogether at variance with the precepts and principles of that religion in which he gloried, and which it was his chief aim, and that of all his Christian brethren, to exalt and make honorable in the eyes of the natives: and that, therefore, no selfish considerations could induce them to abandon their countrymen to destruction, notwithstanding their ingratitude towards themselves, and their ill conduct towards the Indians.

With this decision Masasoyt was extremely dissatisfied: but he could not now withdraw the information he had imparted, even if he desired it; and he also felt it to be most politic to secure the friendship of the white men, even if it should involve the sacrifice of the lives of some of his own countrymen, and interfere with their projects of vengeance on their foes. This was most likely to be the case in the present instance; for the Governor was excited to great indignation by the intelligence f this second conspiracy, in which several of the Chiefs who had signed the treaty with Captain Standish were concerned; and he immediately summoned the gallant soldier, and the rest of his council, to deliberate on the best means of defeating it.

It now only wanted three days of the time appointed for the gathering of the red warriors, and the attack on Wessagussett. No time was, therefore, to be lost; and it was soon determined that Standish, with a band of eight men, should march the following morning at day-break, and come stealthily upon the savages before they could he fully prepared for the assault. It was a bold—perhaps a rash—measure, for so small a party to go forth, and encounter the native forces thus combined. But Standish, though a man of prudence and discretion, was a stranger to fear; and he and his followers had already learnt the power of order and discipline, in compensating for any disadvantage of numbers. It was, therefore, with cheerful confidence that the military force of the settlement prepared for their march and they plainly showed on what that confidence was founded, by requesting the prayers of the congregation for their success.

A great part of the night was, accordingly, spent in prayer; and the blessing of the God of truth and mercy was solemnly asked upon an enterprise that the leaders well knew was about to be carried out by fraud and cruelty.

At sunrise, the soldiers met on 'the Burying Hill,' and the staff of office was given, with much solemnity, to Captain Standish, by the pious and venerable Brewster. They had already taken leave of their wives and families, who did not altogether share the cheerful exultation displayed by the Puritan warriors; and who were not permitted to be present at this final ceremony, lest their anxious fears should disturb the composure of their husbands and fathers. Notwithstanding this characteristic prohibition, Helen, and her younger daughter Edith, had ventured to station themselves in the path that led down 'the Burying Hill,' in the direction in which Standish and his men were to march, that they might take one more farewell of Rodolph before he left them on an expedition which, to their minds, seemed fraught with danger and uncertainty; and where they feared he might again be exposed to the vengeance of his untiring foe.

The gallant little band marched down the hill, and came where Edith and her child stood waiting, beneath a tree, for what might be their last look on one most dearly loved; and when Rodolph saw them he forgot the strictness of discipline and order required by his commander, and left the ranks to indulge the feelings of his heart, by again embracing his weeping wife and child.

The stern captain instantly recalled him; and when he saw a tear glistening in the eye of the husband and father, a slight expression of wonder and contempt passed over his countenance. He marveled that so brave a soldier and so strict a Puritan as Rodolph Maitland should still remain subject to so much worldly weakness. But Standish was not, at that time, a married man; and he was very deeply imbued with all the severe and unbending principles of his sect, which even went so far as to demand the suppression of all natural feelings—making it a fault for a mother to kiss her children on the Lord's day—and inflicting actual punishment on the captain of a ship for having embraced his wife on 5 Sunday, when, after a long separation, she hurried to meet him, as he landed from the vessel! To such puerile littlenesses will even great minds descend.

Rodolph was unmoved by the commander's contemptuous glance. He knew his own unflinching Puritan principles, and his own undaunted courage; and he knew his value in the eyes of Standish. The captain knew it also, for he never liked to go on any enterprise that required bravery and cool judgement without securing the aid of Maitland; and although the tenderness of his friend's feelings, and the warmth of his domestic attachments—so different to the coolness and apathy which was so prevalent in the community—were a continual subject of surprise and pity to the iron-hearted leader, yet he highly respected him, and even loved him, as much as such a gentle feeling as love of any kind could find admittance to his breast.

They journeyed on thenthat stern captain, who had no tie to life, and deemed it a privilege to die with 'the sword of the Lord and of Gideon' in his hand, fighting for the cause of his own peculiar sect, in which alone he thought salvation could be found; and that warm-hearted husband and father, who felt that he had left behind him what was far dearer than life itself—those who alone made life precious to him-and who yet was willing to sacrifice all, if honor and duty demanded it. Which was the braver man of the two?

Both were brave; but Standish was the most unscrupulous. He considered that any stratagem was lawful which could place his heathen enemies in his power; and no arguments of the high-minded and truthful Maitland could convince him that deceit and treachery, even towards their infidel foes, were unworthy of Christian warriors. Miles Standish was resolved to use some device to get the chiefs of the conspiracy off their guard, and, by destroying them, to break up the hostile confederacy altogether: and as Maitland was bound to obey his orders, and also knew the utter impossibility either of changing the resolves of his captain or of deserting the enterprise, he was compelled to join in proceedings that he could not approve.

When the little band had arrived at the spot indicated by Masasoyt, and within a short distance of the Indian place of rendezvous, Standish commanded his men to halt for rest and refreshment for the last time before the expected encounter with the army of savages who were assembling for their destruction. This halting-place was situated on the summit of a considerable elevation, well covered with trees and bushes, and overlooking a plain, on the further side of which the Indian camp was formed. The advantageous position in which the emigrants were posted enabled them to obtain a full view of their enemies without being perceived by them; and Captain Standish resolved to remain there quietly that night, in order to recruit the strength of his men after their rapid and toilsome journey, and to mature his plans for subduing the horde of natives before him with so small a band as now surrounded him, and who waited but his orders to rush on to the most desperate enterprise.

The Wampanoge interpreter, Hobomak, accompanied the party at his own desire, and that, also, of his sovereign, Masasoyt. Standish was glad of his assistance in his capacity of interpreter: he had already shown such devoted attachment to the English, that they entertained no fears of his either betraying or deserting their cause; and, on this occasion, he fully justified their confidence.

Early in the morning, the leader announced his intention of going himself to the Indian camp, to make overtures of peace, and to invite the Chiefs to a conference; and he desired his men to construct a strong and spacious wigwam for their reception, and to make a door to it, which could be closed and fastened securely. He did not then explain his project more clearly; but Rudolph understood it, and his soul revolted from the treachery he suspected. 'Now,' said the captain, having finished his directions to his well-disciplined followers, 'who will volunteer to go down with me and Hobomak to the heathen camp, and to carry the flag of truce before me? It may be a service of danger to enter that hornet's nest; and no one who has left his soldier's heart at home with his wife or his children, had better attempt it.'

Rudolph felt the sarcasm, though it was uttered good humoredly, and he instantly replied —

'I am ready, my chief, to attend you wherever you may go; and if I have left my heart's affections at New Plymouth, you shall see that I have brought with me none the less of courage and fidelity to my leaders and my countrymen. The dearer my home, the more energetic shall be my efforts to preserve it from desolation. Besides,' he added, In an undertone, so that only Standish should hear: 'I much prefer going boldly into the midst of the enemy, even at the risk of my life, to remaining here to assist in constructing a trap for their destruction.'

'You are a brave fellow, Maitland,' said the captain, grasping his hand with warmth and energy, 'but you have brought some peculiar prejudices over from Europe with you, and do not yet perceive the difference of warring on equal terms with civilized troops—as you were accustomed to do in your youth—and contending with a horde of savages, who know nothing of the laws of honor, and who are even now combined to destroy us all, without either challenge or preparation. Come along with me, and leave the rest to do as I have directed. Necessity has no law; and if we do not meet those cunning natives with equal cunning, we shall have no chance against them.'

'Truth and sincerity appear to me the strongest necessity; and the God of truth will order the results as he pleases,' answered Rodolph. 'But I have sworn to obey your orders, and you need not fear the constancy of either my heart or hand. I know my duty as a soldier, and I will do it.'

'I know you will, Maitland,' replied his commander; and his respect for his conscientious friend rose higher than ever, while a slight misgiving as to the righteousness of his own projected plan passed through his breast. It did not abide there, however, for he was really satisfied that he was acting in conformity to the will of God, and that he was fully justified in asking for His blessing to crown his murderous schemes with success.

Maitland took the flag of truce, which consisted of a long spear, with a white handkerchief attached to the summit, and preceded the captain, who followed in full uniform, attended by his swarthy interpreter. As soon as they emerged from the wood that covered the halting-place, and entered the open plain, they were espied by the keen and watchful eyes of the natives; and a messenger was dispatched to meet them, and bring them to the presence of the Indian leader, Wattawamat, who was regarded as the chief of the conspirators.

Captain Standish assumed a pacific air, and desired Hobomak to advance before him, and inform the Chiefs that he came to propose terms of reconciliation and peace. He then himself approached them; and, with the aid of the interpreter, made to them a rather lengthy harangue on the benefits that would accrue to them from preserving peace with the white men; and his sorrow, and that of his employers, on having accidentally discovered that the tribes of Massachusetts entertained feelings of enmity towards the British settlers at Wessagussett.

Ever and anon, during the translations of the various paragraphs of this speech, Rodolph observed the keen eyes of the captain, as they carefully surveyed the surrounding force, and examined the individuals who appeared to be their leaders. And once, when his own eye followed the direction of his commander's, his glance encountered one that instantly riveted it, and excited in his breast some sensations—not of *fear*, for Rodolph knew not the feeling—but of inquietude and distrust. Yes; Coubitant was there, gazing at his supposed victim with amazement and hatred; and half inclined to believe that some supernatural power must belong to the man who could have been wounded with his deadly arrow, and yet survive to confront him once more. There he stood—with disappointed vengeance in his heart, and fury flashing from that eye of fire.

But while he kept a continual watch on every movement of Rodolph's, his quick ear lost not one word of the speech that Hobomak was rendering into his native tongue. He heard when, in Standish's name, he invited the Chiefs to meet him in the wigwam that his men were constructing on the border of the thicket, and where, he said, he would smoke with them the pipe of peace, and give to them the presents that the Governor had sent, as pledges of his friendly intentions.

The moment this invitation had been delivered, Coubitant approached Wattawamat, and whispered a few words in his ear, to which the Chieftain gave a sign of acquiescence; and then the Nansett left the assembly, and disappeared among the trees and bushes that bounded the plain on every side.

Wattawamat gave no immediate reply to the proposal of the English Chief; but, as is not unusual with the Indians, kept up a long discourse, and contrived to lengthen the audience for a considerable time. Another Indian then approached the Sachem, and again whispered to him some words that gave him evident satisfaction, for he smiled grimly, and displayed his fine row of ivory teeth for a moment, as he nodded approbation to the messenger. Then, resuming his wonted gravity of demeanor, he replied to Captain Standish that he was satisfied, by his assurances, of the good faith of the white men, and that he and his brother Chiefs would avail themselves of his invitation, and meet in the wigwam a little before sunset; where he hoped so to arrange all the little disagreements that had occurred between the red men and the mighty strangers, as to be able to establish between them and all his countrymen the same friendship and alliance that appeared to exist with the Wampanoge tribe, whose Chief, he observed, with a slight curl of his lip, had failed in his promise to attend their meeting that day.

The cause of this favorable decision on the part of Wattawamat was the report that Coubitant had just sent him of the insignificant force of the English, which that crafty and swift-footed warrior had contrived to ascertain, by running round the border of the weed to the place where Standish's men were at work, and taking an accurate and unobserved survey of their numbers.

He felt convinced that it would be easy for the Chiefs, and such of their attendants as might be allowed to follow them to the place of conference, to overpower and destroy every one of the little band of whites, and then to prosecute their original intention of carrying fire and slaughter into both the British settlements. In all this scheme there was nothing so grateful to the ruthless heart of Coubitant as the idea of Rodolph's death; and that too, as he trusted, by his own hand. O, how he panted for the devilish joy of tearing off his scalp, and carrying it back to throw it triumphantly at Henrich's feet! We shall see whether such joy was accorded to him.

Standish and his companions took their leave, and returned to the hill, where they found great progress had been made in building the wigwam; and two hours before sunset it was completely wattled round, leaving only a small aperture near the top to admit light, and a narrow place of entrance, to which a strong door was affixed.

The captain then explained his plan, which was approved by all but Maitland; and he forbore to urge any further opposition, which, he felt, would now be useless. A temperate meal was partaken of, and a hymn sung by the undaunted little company; and pipes and tobacco having been plentifully placed in the hut, the sides of which were decorated with pieces of gay colored calico, and a few knives and trinkets, as pretended gifts to the Chiefs, nothing remained but to await the arrival of the victims.

Soon the Indian Chiefs, decked in all their bravery of feathers and embroidered skins, came marching a cross the plain, followed by a few attendants less richly adorned. Standish and his party went to meet them, and conducted them with much courtesy to the wigwam, which was soon obscured by the clouds of smoke that issued from the pipes of the grave and silent assembly. But this silent gravity did not long continue. Captain Standish addressed the Chiefs, and strove to speak kindly to men whose deaths he was compassing all the while: but, whether his resolution somewhat failed as the moment for the execution of his bloody purpose drew on, or whether he was disconcerted by the absence of Rodolph, who refused to enter the wigwam, and assist at the slaughter, so it was that he manifested evident signs of weakness and indecision.

The Chiefs were emboldened by this, and they were troubled by no qualms of conscience on the subject of shedding the white men's blood. They rose from their seats on the ground, and began to taunt the captain with his want of eloquence, and also with the smallness of his stature, which was despicable in their eyes. Then, growing still bolder as they became excited, they drew their knives, and whetted them before the eyes of their hosts: flourishing them round their heads, and boasting how they had already shed the blood of many white men in the distant European settlements.

It was a fearful scene: but the real peril of his situation instantly restored the commander to his wonted resolution and firmness. He called on his men to be ready, and not to allow one of the Chiefs to escape from the wigwam, and with his hand on his pistols, he waited the proper moment for action. The Indians continued to pour forth the most abusive epithets: but they did not begin the expected attack, and it was evident that they were a little intimidated by the undaunted bearing of the white men. One of them, however, seemed actuated by some desperate purpose, and to be regardless of aught else. From the moment of his entrance into the wigwam, his eyes had sought some object that they did not find: and now, in all the excitement of the approaching conflict, his only aim seemed to be to make his way through the entrance in search of some person on whom he desired to wreak his fury. It was Rodolph whom Coubitant sought, and who was now, providentially, out of his reach, and waiting the result of the deed against which he had vainly protested.

At length the wrath of Standish broke loose. He gave the appointed signal, and the door was closed—shutting in friends and foes in one small field of battle, or, rather, of carnage. The scene in the dimly-lighted wigwam was terrific; and the yells of the infuriated natives broke, with a sickening effect, on the ears of Rodolph Maitland, who could not consent to share in what he considered a murderous conflict, and not an honorable war; and who yet felt as if he was deserting his countrymen, by thus remaining inactive.

But if he felt undecided as to his proper course of action, that indecision did not last long. In a few moments the door of the wigwam was violently burst open, and the combatants rushed out, struggling and bleeding, from the den of slaughter. All the white men came forth, for, though many of them were wounded, not one had fallen. But three of the Indians lay dead and dying on the floor of the hut; one of them being the mangled body of Wattawamat, who was slain by Standish with his own knife—that very knife which the savage had sharpened for the purpose of plunging it into the heart of the white chief!

Where was Rodolph now? In the midst of the fray, fighting desperately and successfully. The moment he saw the battle raging in open field, and beheld the blood flowing from the wounds of his countrymen, he forgot all else except that his strong right arm wielded a trusty blade; and its skilful stroke soon brought another of the red warriors to the ground, and chased away those who sought to secure their wounded comrade. The Indians saw that they were overmatched, and that nothing but flight could save the remainder of their party; they therefore uttered their wild war-cry once more, and commenced a rapid retreat down the hill, pausing several times to send back a volley of arrows on their victorious foes; which, however, fell harmless to the earth, though more than one was aimed at Rodolph, by the strong and skilful hand of Coubitant.

But rest was not to be afforded to the little conquering band. While they were securing the wounded Indian, and binding up their own wounds, they discovered a movement in the body of savages on the other side of the plain, and truly surmised that they were preparing to attack them in greater numbers. Standish instantly gave orders that the Indian whom Rodolph had brought to the ground should be hung to a neighboring tree, which was as instantly executed; and he re-entered the tent, to make sure that no life remained in those three who lay on its bloody floor. All were dead: and Standish, approaching the body of the Chieftain Wattawamat, raised his good broad sword, and at one blow severed the head from the trunk. Then seizing the gory head by the long scalp-lock, he carried it forth as a trophy, and desired one of his men to secure it, and carry it back to New Plymouth.

No time remained for further parley. A band of Indians were approaching across the plain; and Standish disdained to fly, even before such superior numbers. Every musket and pistol was hastily loaded, and the undaunted party marched down the hill to meet the coming foe. They met: and in spite of the furious onset of the savages, they were again made to feel that their undisciplined hordes were no match for the well- aimed fire-arms of the white men, and had no power to break the order of their steady ranks. Once more they fled, leaving another of their number dead on the field, and they returned no more to the charge. During all this affair, Hobomak had remained a quiet spectator of the combat, and of the defeat of his countrymen; and now he approached the English captain, and complacently praised his bravery and military prowess; and he remained as devoted as ever to his Christian friends.

The triumphant soldiers returned to New Plymouth, and were received with joyful exultation by the Governor and the inhabitants, who felt deeply grateful for the deliverance that had been accorded to them, and the safety of the brave men who had fought in their defense. All the little band had been preserved from serious personal injury; but Rodolph Maitland had also been preserved from blood-guiltiness, and that was more to him than life and safety, and to his Christian and devoted wife also.

The head of Wattawamat was brought to New Plymouth, and the dreadful trophy was conspicuously placed over the entrance to the fortress, as a warning to the natives against any future conspiracies for the destruction of the white men. So great, indeed, was the terror inspired by the power and the severity of the settlers, that many of the natives—who were conscious of having been engaged in the conspiracy, though undiscovered—left their wigwams, and fled into the woods, or concealed themselves in reedy morasses, where a great number of them perished from hunger and disease. The settlers were much distressed at this result of their proceedings, which, at the same time, they considered to have been perfectly justified by the necessity of self- preservation. But when their venerated pastor Robinson— to whom they had, ever since their emigration, looked for guidance and sympathy— heard of these sad events, he expressed the deepest sorrow, and begged them never again to be led away by the fiery temper of their leader; adding these touching and impressive words—' How happy a thing had it been, if you had *converted some* before you had killed any!'

CHAPTER XV

A change came o'er the spirit of my dream:
The boy was sprung to manhood; to the wilds
Of distant climes he made himself a home.
And his soul drank their beauties; he was girt
With strange and dusky aspects; he was not
Himself like what he had been: — on the sea,
And on the shore, he was a wanderer.' BYRON.

On the border of a green meadow, watered by a narrow stream, the wigwams of a large Indian settlement were lighted up by the slanting beams of the setting sun, as they shone, soft and bright, through the tall dark pines and gently-waving birch trees beneath which the village was erected. The deep red trunks of the ancient fir trees contrasted beautifully with the silvery bark of the birch; and between the shadows which were cast by the gigantic boles of these, and many other varieties of timber, the sunbeams played on the smooth soft turf, and illuminated a scene of peaceful joy and contentment.

Towards the center of the broken and irregular semi-circle in which the huts were arranged, rose two wigwams, of a size and construction superior to the rest; and around them were planted many flowering shrubs and fruit-bearing plants, that clearly showed the habitations to have been permanently fixed for some seasons, and to have been occupied by persons who possessed more of good taste and forethought than are commonly displayed by the improvident natives. Many climbing plants also threw their luxuriant branches over the sides and roof of these rude, but picturesque dwellings, and the brilliant blossoms hung gracefully around the eaves and the doorway, and moved gently in the evening breeze.

On a neatly-carved bench, in front of one of these wigwams, sat an aged Indian Chief, and by his side a young woman, who seemed to possess all the ease of manner and refinement of a European, but whose clear brown skin, and glossy jet-black hair and eyes, at once showed her to be of the same race as her venerable companion. Her dress was also Indian, but arranged with a taste and delicacy that rendered it eminently becoming to her graceful figure; while her hair, instead of being either drawn up to knot on the crown of the head, or left loose and disheveled in native fashion, was braided into a truly classical form, and simply adorned with a beautiful white water-lily—a flower that Oriana always loved.

Two other figures completed the group that was formed near the wigwam door. One of them was a young man of tall end muscular form, whose dress and richly-carved weapons would have proclaimed him to be an Indian warrior and chieftain, had not his curling brown hair, and deep blue eyes, spoken of a Saxon lineage. Courage and intelligence gleamed in those fearless eyes, but no Indian fierceness or cunning were there; and as the tall warrior stooped towards the ground, and lifted up in his arms a laughing little child that was reclining on the mossy turf, and tearing to pieces a handful of bright-colored flowers that his father had gathered for him, the smile of affection and happiness that lighted up those clear blue eyes, showed that a warm and manly heart was there.

'Ah! Ludovico!' said the happy young father, as he fondly kissed the child, whose azure eyes, and long black eyelashes and curling raven hair, showed his descent both from the fair race of Britain, and America's wild wandering children. 'Ah, Ludovico! how well I remember your uncle, when he was a merry infant like you, and used to roll on the grass in my sweet sister Edith's garden, and tear its gaudy blossoms, as you do these flowers of the forest. Those were happy days,' he added—and the bright smile of careless mirth changed to one of pensive sadness—'yes; those were happy days that never can return. If my sisters, and my playful little brother, yet live, they must be changed indeed from what they were when last I saw their sweet faces on that eventful evening, that fixed the course of my destiny. Edith must now be a woman—a lovely woman, too; and little Ludovico a fine open- hearted boy. And my beloved parents, too: O, that I knew they were alive and well and that ere long they would see and bless my Oriana and my child!'

And Henrich seated himself by the side of his young Indian wife, and gazed in the face of his laughing boy, with an expression at once so sad and sweet, that the child became silent and thoughtful too; and, dropping the flowers that filled his little hands, he gently clasped them as if in prayer, and looked long and searchingly into his father's eyes.

'There, now you look exactly as my brother used to do when he knelt at my mother's knee, and she taught him to lisp his evening prayer,' exclaimed Henrich and his eyes glistened with emotion, as home, and all its loved associations, rushed into his mind.

Oriana saw his sadness; and felt—as she often had done before on similar occasions—a pang of painful regret, and even of jealousy, towards those much-loved relatives whom her husband still so deeply regretted. She laid her hand on his, and raising her large expressive eyes to his now melancholy countenance, she gently said—

'Does Henrich still grieve that the red men stole him away from the home of his childhood, and brought him to dwell among the forests? Is not Oriana better to him than a sister, and are not the smiles of his own Ludovico sweeter to his heart than even those of his little brother used to be? And is not my father his father also? O Henrich—my own Henrich'—she added, while she leaned her head on his shoulder, and tears burst from her eyes, and chased each other down her clear olive checks, to which deep emotion now gave a richer glow—'tell me, do you wish to be set free from all the ties that bind you to our race, and return to your own people, to dwell again with them; and, perhaps, to lift the tomahawk, and east the spear against those who have loved you, and cherished you so fondly? Often have you told me that your Indian wife and child are dearer to you than all that you have left behind you at New Plymouth. But tell it to me again! Let me hear you say again that you are happy here, and will never desert us; for when I see that sorrowful look in your dear eyes, and remember all you have lost, and still are losing, to live in a wilderness with wild and savage men, my heart misgives me; and I feel that you were never made for such a life, and that your love is far too precious to be given for ever to an Indian girl.'

The smile returned to Henrich's eyes, as he listened to this fond appeal; and he almost reproached himself for ever suffering regret for the blessings he had lost to arise in his mind, when those he still possessed were so many and so great.

'Dear Oriana, you need not fear,' he replied, affectionately; 'I speak the truth of my heart when I tell you that I would not exchange my Indian home, and sacrifice my Indian squaw, and my little half-bred son, for all the comforts and pleasures of civilized life—no, not even to be restored to the parents I still love so dearly, and the brother and sister who played with me in childhood. But still I yearn to look upon their faces again, and to hear once more their words of love. I well know how they have all mourned for me: and I know how, even after so many years have passed, they would rejoice at finding me again!

'Yes; they must indeed have mourned for you, Henrich. That must have been a sad night to them when Coubitant bore you away. But I owe all the happiness of my life to that cruel deed—and can I regret it? If my "white brother" had not come to our camp, I should have lived and died an ignorant Indian squaw—I should have known no thing of true religion, or of the Christian's God—and,' continued Oriana, smiling at her husband with a sweetness and archness of expression that made her countenance really beautiful, 'I should never have known my Henrich.'

'Child!' said old Tisquantum, rousing himself from the half-dreamy reverie in which he had been sitting, and enjoying the warm sunbeams as they fell on his now feeble limbs, and long white hair. 'Child, are you talking again of Henrich leaving us? It is wrong of you to doubt him. My son has given me his word that he will never take you from me until Mahneto recalls my spirit to himself, and I dwell again with my fathers. Has he not also said that he will never leave or forsake you and his boy? Why, then, do you make your heart sad? Henrich has never deceived us—he has never, in all the years that he has lived in our wigwam, and shared our wanderings, said the thing that was not: and shall we suspect him now? No, Oriana; I trust him as I would have trusted my own Tekoa: and had my brave boy lived he could not have been dearer to me than Henrich is. He could not have surpassed him in hunting or in war: he could not have guided and governed my people with more wisdom, now that I am too old and feeble to be their leader: and he could not have watched over my declining years with more of gentleness and love. Henrich will never desert us: no, not if we return to the head-quarters of our tribe near Paomet,[*] as I hope to do ere I close my eyes in death. So long as I feared my white son would leave us, and return to his own people, I never turned my feet towards Paomet; for he had wound himself into my heart, and had taken Tekoa's place there: and I saw that he had wound himself into your heart too, my child; and I knew that he was more to us than the land of our birth. Therefore I have kept my hunters wandering from north to south, and from east to west, and have visited the mountains, and the prairies, and the mighty rivers, and the great lakes; and have found a home in all. But now our Henrich is one of us, and never will forsake us for any others. Is he not Sachem of my warriors, and do they not look to him as their leader and their father? No; Henrich will never leave us now!'

[Footnote: The native name for Cape Cod, near which the main body of the Nausetts resided.]

And the old man, who had become excited during this long harangue, smiled at his children with love and confidence, and again leaned back and closed his eyes, relapsing into that quiet dreamy state in which the Indians, especially the more aged among them, are so fond of indulging.

Tisquantum was now a very old man; and the great changes and vicissitudes of climate and mode of life, and the severe bodily exertions in warfare and hunting, to which he had been all his life exposed, made him appear more advanced in years than he actually was. Since the marriage of his daughter to the white stranger—which occurred about three years previous to the time at which our narrative has now arrived—he had indulged himself in an almost total cessation from business, and from every active employment, and had resigned the government of his followers into the able and energetic hands of his son-in-law. Henrich was now regarded as Chieftain of that branch of the Nausett tribe over which Tisquantum held authority; and so much had he. made himself both loved and respected during his residence among the red men, that all jealousy of his English origin and foreign complexion had gradually died away, and his guidance in war or in council was always promptly and implicitly followed.

And Henrich was happy—very happy—in his wild and wandering life. He had passed from boyhood to manhood amid the scenery and the inhabitants of the wilderness; and though his heart and his memory would still frequently revert to the home of his parents, and all that he had loved and prized of the connections and the habits of civilized life, yet he now hardly wished to resume those habits. Indeed, had such a resumption implied the abandoning his wife and child, and his venerable father-in-law, no consideration would ever have induced him to think of it. He had likewise, as Tisquantum said, on obtaining his consent to his marriage with Oriana, solemnly promised never to take her away from him while he lived; therefore, at present he entertained no intention of again rejoining his countrymen, and renouncing his Indian mode of life.

Still 'the voices of his home' were often ringing in his ear by day and by night; and the desire to know the fate of his beloved family, and once more to behold each fondly-cherished member of it, would sometimes come over him with an intensity that seemed to absorb every other feeling. Then he would devise plan after plan, by which he might hope to obtain some intelligence of the settlement, or convey to his relatives the knowledge of his safety. But never had he yet succeeded. Tisquantum had taken watchful care, for several years, to prevent any such communication being effected; and it was, as we have seen mainly with this object that he had absented himself from the rest of his tribe, and his own former place of abode.

He had led his warriors and their families far to the north, and there he had resided for several years; only returning occasionally to the south-western prairies for the hunting season, and again travelling northward when the buffalo and the elk were no longer abundant in the plains. In all these wanderings Henrich had rejoiced; and his whole soul had been elevated by such constant communion with the grandest works of nature — or rather, of nature's God. He had gazed on the stupendous cataract of Niagara, and listened to its thunders,[*] till he felt himself in the immediate presence of Deity in all its omnipotence.

[Footnote: O-ni-ga-rah, the Thunder of Waters, is the Indian name for these magnificent falls.]

He had crossed the mighty rivers of America, that seemed to European eyes to be arms of the sea; and had passed in light and frail canoes over those vast lakes that are themselves like inland oceans. And, in the high latitudes to which the restless and apprehensive spirit of Tisquantum had led him, he had traveled over boundless fields of snow in the sledges of the diminutive Esquimaux, and lodged in their strange winter-dwellings of frozen snow, that look as if they were built of the purest alabaster, with windows of ice as clear as crystal. And marvelously beautiful those dwellings were in Henrich's eyes, as be passed along the many rooms, with their cold walls glittering with the lamp-light, or glowing from the reflection of the fire of pine branches, that burnt so brightly in the center on a hearth of stone. Well and warmly, too, had he slept on the bedsteads of snow, that these small northern men find so comfortable, when they have strewn them with a thick layer of pine boughs, and covered them with an abundant supply of deerskins. And then the lights of the north — the lovely Aurora, with its glowing hues of crimson and yellow and violet! When this beauteous phenomena was gleaming in the horizon, and shooting up its spires of colored light far into the deep blue sky, bow ardently did Henrich desire the presence of his sister — of his Edith who used to share his every feeling, and sympathize in all him love and reverence for the works of God! But in all those days and months and years that elapsed between the time when we left Henrich in the hunting-grounds of the west, and the time to which we have now carried him, Oriana had been a sister — yes, more than a sister-to him; and she had learnt to think as he thought, and to feel as he felt, till he used to tell her that he almost fancied the spirit of Edith had passed into her form, and had come to share his exile.

Certainly, the mind and feelings of the Indian girl did ripen and expand with wonderful rapidity; and, as she grew to womanhood, her gentle gracefulness of manner, and her devoted affection towards Henrich, confirmed the attachment that had been gradually forming in his heart ever since he had been her adopted brother, and made him resolve to ask her of the Sachem as his wife.

Since the conduct of Coubitant had excited—as we saw in a former chapter—the suspicions of Tisquantum, and had so evidently increased the dislike of Oriana, the Chieftain had abandoned all idea of bestowing his daughter's hand on him or of making him his successor in his official situation; and the departure of the cruel and wily savage had been to him, as well as to Oriana and Henrich, a great satisfaction and relief. None of them wished to see his dark countenance again, or to be exposed to his evil machinations; and all were fully aware that the marriage of the white stranger to the Sachem's lovely daughter was a circumstance that would arouse all his jealousy and all his vengeance. Nevertheless, this apprehension did not deter the old Chief from giving a joyful consent to the proposal of Henrich to become his son in fact, as he had long been in name and affection; and the summer of the year 1627 had seen the nuptials celebrated in Indian fashion. On the same day, also, the young widow, Mailah, became the wife of Henrich's chosen friend and companion, Jyanough, who had never left the Nausetts since first he joined them, but had followed his brother-in-arms in all his various wanderings.

It was a joyful day to the tribe when this double marriage took place; and great was the feasting beneath the trees on the shores of the mighty lake Ontario, where their camp was pitched. Game was roasted in abundance, and much tobacco was consumed in honor of the happy couples, who were all beloved by their simple followers; and for whom fresh wigwams were built, and strewed with sweet sprays of pine and fir, and furnished with all that Indian wants demanded, and Indian art could furnish. With some difficulty, Henrich prevailed on the Sachem to permit his daughter to forego the native custom of cutting off her hair on the day of her marriage, and wearing an uncouth head-dress until it grew again; but at length he was successful, on the plea that Oriana, being a Christian, and about to unite herself to a Christian also, could not be bound to observe the superstitious and barbarous ceremonies of her race. Her fine black locks were, therefore, spared; but Mailah was a second time robbed of hers, and appeared for many months afterwards with her head closely shrouded in the prescribed covering.

Much did Henrich wish that he and his bride could have received the blessing of a minister of the Gospel, as a sacred sanction of their union. But this could not be: and he endeavored to supply the deficiency, and to give a holy and Christian character to what he felt to be the most solemn act of his life, by uniting in earnest prayer with Oriana, Mailah, and Jyanough, that the blessing of God might rest upon them all, and enable them to fulfil their new and relative duties faithfully and affectionately and 'as unto the Lord.'

Three years had elapsed since that day, and no event had occurred to interrupt the domestic happiness of those young couples, or to disturb the perfect friendship and unanimity that reigned between them. They were a little Christian community — small indeed, but faithful and sincere, and likely to increase in time; for little Lincoya was carefully instructed in the blessed doctrines which his mother and his step-father had received, and when Henrich's own son was born, he baptized him in the name of the Holy Trinity, and gave him the Christian name of his own loved brother Ludovico; and earnestly he asked a blessing on his child, and prayed that he might be enabled to bring him up a Christian, not in name only, but in deed and in truth.

CHAPTER XVI

Wrath is cruel, and anger is outrageous; but who is able to stand before envy?
'Open rebuke is better than secret love.
'Faithful are the wounds of a friend; but the kisses of an enemy are deceitful.'
PROV. xxii, 4—6

Tisquantum still sat dozing on his favorite seat before his dwelling, and Henrich and Oriana remained beside him, silently watching the peaceful slumbers of their venerable parent, and the playful sports of their child, who was again roiling on the soft green turf at their feet, and busily engaged in decking the shaggy head and neck of a magnificent dog with the gay flowers that were scattered around him.

It was Rodolph—the faithful Rodolph—who had once saved Henrich's life from the treacherous designs of Coubitant, and who had often since proved his guard and his, watchful protector in many seasons of peril and difficulty. His devotion to his master was as strong as ever; and his strength and swiftness were still unabated, whether in the flood or the field. But years had somewhat subdued the former restless activity of his spirits, and, now that he had dwelt so long in a settled home, his manners had become so domestic, that he seemed to think his chief duty consisted in amusing the little Ludovico, and carrying him about on his bread shaggy shoulders, where he looked like the infant Hercules mounted on his lion. They were, indeed, a picturesque pair, and no wonder that the young parents of the beautiful child smiled as they watched him wreathing his little hands in the long curling mane of the good-tempered animal, and laying his soft rosy cheek on his back.

Such was the group that occupied the small cultivated spot in front of the chief, lodges of the village: and thus happy and tranquil might they have remained, until the fading light had warned Oriana that it was time to lay her child to rest in his mossy bed, and to prepare the usual meal for her husband and her father. But they were interrupted by the approach of Jyanough and Mailah, accompanied by the young Lincoya; and also by a stranger, whose form seemed familiar to them, but whose features the shadow of the over-hanging trees prevented them at first from recognizing.

But, as the party approached, a chill struck into the heart of Oriana, and she instinctively clung closer to her husband's arm, as if she felt that some danger threatened him; while the open, manly brow of Henrich contracted for an instant, and was crossed by a look of doubt and suspicion that was seldom seen to darken it, and could not rest there long. In a moment that cloud had passed away, and he rose to greet the stranger with a frank and dignified courtesy, that showed he felt suspicion and distrust to be unworthy of him. Rodolph, also, seemed to be affected by the same kind of unpleasant sensations that were felt by his more intellectual, but not more sagacious fellow-creatures. No sooner did the stranger advance beyond the shadow of trees, and thus afford the dog a full view of his very peculiar and striking countenance, than he uttered a low deep growl of anger; and, slowly rising from the ground, placed himself between his little charge and the supposed enemy, on whom he kept his keen eye immovably fixed, while his strong white teeth were displayed in a very formidable row.

Coubitant—for it could be no other than he—saw clearly the impression that his appearance had excited on the assembled party of his old acquaintances; but he was an adept in dissimulation, and he entirely concealed his feelings under the garb of pleasure at this reunion after so long a separation. The candid disposition of Henrich rendered him liable to be deceived by these false professions of his former rival; and he readily believed that Coubitant had, during his absence of so many years, forgotten and laid aside all those feelings of envy and jealousy that once appeared to fill his breast, and to actuate him to deeds of enmity towards the white stranger, whose father had slain his chosen friend and companion.

But was it so? Had the cruel and wily savage indeed become the friend of him who had, he deemed, supplanted him—not only in the favor of his Chief, but also in the good graces of his intended bride—and who was now, as he had learnt from Jyanough, the husband of Oriana, and the virtual Sachem of Tisquantum's subject warriors? No: 'jealousy is cruel as the grave; the coals thereof are coals of fire, which hath a most vehement flame'; and in the soul of Coubitant there dwelt no gentle principles of mercy and forgiveness to quench this fiery flame. He was a heathen: and, in his eyes, revenge was a virtue, and the gratification of it a deep joy: and in the hope of attaining this joy, he was willing to endure years of difficulty and disappointment, and to forego all that he knew of home and of comfort. Therefore had he left the tribe of his adoption, and the friends of his choice, and dwelt for so many winters and summers among the Narragansetts, until he had acquired influence in their councils, and won for himself rank in their tribe. And all this rank and influence he had, as we have seen, exerted to procure the destruction of the white men, because one of their number had caused the death of his friend, and he had vowed to be revenged on the race. He hated the pale-faces, and he hated their religion and their peaceable disposition, which he considered to be merely superstition and cowardice; and now that he had failed in all his deep-laid schemes for their annihilation, all his hatred was concentrated against Henrich, and he resolved once more to seek him out, and, by again uniting himself to the band of Nausetts under Tisquantum, to find an opportunity of ridding himself of one who seemed born to cross his path, and blight his prospects in life.

Until Coubitant had traced his old associates through many forests, and over many plains, and had, at length, found the place of their present abode, he knew not that all his former hopes of becoming the Sachem's son-in law, and succeeding to his dignity, were already blasted by the marriage of Oriana to Henrich, and the association of the latter in the cares and the honors of the chieftainship. For some years after his abrupt departure from the Nausetts—and while he was striving for distinction, as well as for revenge, among the Narragansetts—he had contrived, from time to time, to obtain information of the proceedings of those whom he had thought it politic to leave for a time; and, as he found that no steps were taken towards connecting the pale-faced stranger with the family of the Sachem by marriage, after he had attained the age at which Indian youths generally take wives; and it was even reported that Tisquantum designed to unite him to the widow of Lincoya—his jealous fears were hushed to sleep, and he still hoped to succeed, ultimately, in his long-cherished plans.

It was not that he loved Oriana. His heart was incapable of that sentiment which alone is worthy of the name. But he had set his mind on obtaining her, because she was, in every way, superior to the rest of her young companions; and because such a union would aggrandize him in the estimation of the tribe, and tend to further his views of becoming their chief.

After the failure of his schemes for the utter destruction of the British settlements, and all his malicious designs against Rodolph in particular, his personal views with regard to Oriana and Henrich, and his desire to rule in Tisquantum's stead, returned to his mind with unabated force, and he resolved again to join the Sachem, and endeavor to regain his former influence over him, and the consideration in which he had once been held by his subject-warriors. But the removal of the tribe to the north, and their frequent journeyings from place to place, had, for a great length of time, baffled his search; and when, at last, he was successful, and a Nausett hunter—who had been dispatched from Paomet on an errand to Tisquantum—met him, and guided him to the encampment, it was only to have all his hopes dashed for ever to the ground, and his soul more inflamed with wrath and malice than ever.

On reaching the Nausett village Coubitant had met Jyanough, and been conducted by him to his hut, where he learnt from him and Mailah all that had happened to themselves and their friends since he had lost sight of them; and it had required all the red-man's habitual self- command and habit of dissimulation to enable him to conceal his fury and disappointment. He did conceal them, however; and so effectually, that both the Cree and his wife were deceived, and though that the narrative excited in him no deeper interest than former intimacy would naturally create. But this was far from being the case. Oriana and the chieftainship were lost to him at present, it is true; but revenge might still be his—that prize that Satan holds out to his slaves to tempt them on to further guilt and ruin. To win that prize—and, possibly, even more than that—was worth some further effort: and deceit was no great effort to Coubitant.

So he smiled in return to Henrich's greeting, and tried to draw Oriana into friendly conversation, by noticing her lovely boy; who, however, received his advances with a very bad grace. He also addressed Tisquantum with all that respectful deference that is expected by an aged Indian—more especially a Sachem—from the younger members of his race; and, at length, he succeeded in banishing from the minds of almost all his former acquaintances those doubts and suspicions that his conduct had once aroused; and he was again admitted to the same terms of intimacy with the Chief and his family that he had enjoyed in years long gone by.

Still, there was one who could not put confidence in Coubitant's friendly manner, or believe that the feelings of enmity he once so evidently entertained towards Henrich were altogether banished from his mind. This was Jyanough, whose devoted attachment to the white stranger had first led him to mistrust his rival; and who still resolved to watch his movements with jealous care, and, if possible, to guard his friend from any evil that might be designed against him.

For some time, he could detect nothing in Coubitant's manner or actions that could, in any way, confirm his suspicions, which he did not communicate to any one but Mailah; for he felt it would be ungenerous to fill the minds of others with the doubts that he could not banish from his own.

The summer advanced, and became one of extreme heat. The winding stream that flowed through the meadow—on the skirts of which the Nausett encampment was formed—gradually decreased, from the failure of the springs that supplied it, until, at length, its shallow waters were reduced to a rippling brook—so narrow, that young Lincoya could leap over it, and Rodolph could carry his little charge across without any risk of wetting his feet. The long grass and beautiful lilies, and other wild flowers, that had grown so luxuriantly along the river's brink, now faded for want of moisture; and the fresh verdure of the meadow was changed to a dry and dusky yellow. Day by day the brook dried up, and it became necessary for the camp to be removed to some more favored spot, where the inhabitants and their cattle could still find a sufficient supply of water.

For this purpose, it was resolved to migrate southwards, to the banks of the broad Missouri, which no drought could sensibly affect; and there to remain until the summer heat had passed away, and the season for travelling had arrived. Then Tisquantum purposed to bend his steps once more towards the land of his birth, that he might end his days in his native Paomet, and behold the home of his fathers before his death. To this plan Henrich gave a glad assent; for he surely hoped that, when he reached a district that bordered so nearly on the British territories, he should be able to obtain some information respecting his relatives, and, perhaps, even to see them. And Oriana no longer dreaded returning to the dwellings of her childhood, for she felt assured—notwithstanding the occasional misgivings that troubled her anxious heart—that Henrich loved her far too well ever to desert her; and that he loved truth too well ever to take her from her aged father, let the temptation be never so great.

All, therefore, looked forward with satisfaction to the autumn, when the long journey towards the east was to commence: but they well knew that its accomplishment would occupy several seasons; for the movement of so large a party, of every age and sex, and the transport of all their baggage across a district of many hundreds of miles in extent, must, necessarily, be extremely slow, and interrupted by many pauses for rest, as well as by the heat or the inclemency of the weather.

Coubitant also expressed his pleasure at the proposed change, which would afford occupation and excitement to his restless spirit, and which, likewise, promised him better opportunities for carrying out his ultimate schemes than he could hope for in his present tranquil mode of life. His constant attention to Tisquantum, and his assiduous care to consult his every wish and desire, had won upon the old man's feelings, and he again regarded him rather as the proved friend of his lost Tekoa, than as the suspected foe of his adopted son Henrich. He frequently employed him in executing any affairs in which he still took an active interest, and he soon came to be looked upon by the tribe as a sort of coadjutor to their white Sachem, and the confidential friend of the old Chieftain. This was just what Coubitant desired; and he lost no opportunity of strengthening his influence over the Nausett warriors, and making his presence agreeable and necessary to Tisquantum.

The time appointed for the breaking up of the encampment drew near, and both Henrich and Oriana felt much regret at the prospect of leaving the peaceful home where they had spent so many happy days, and where their little Ludovico had been born. Their comfortable and substantial lodge, shaded with the plants that decorated it so profusely and so gaily, had been the most permanent dwelling that they had ever known since their childhood: and though they hoped eventually to enjoy a still more settled home, they could not look on this work of their own labor and taste without affection, or leave it for ever without sorrow.

In order to lessen the fatigue of Tisquantum it was arranged, at the suggestion of Coubitant, that he should precede the old Sachem, and his immediate family and attendants, to the place of their intended encampment; and should select a suitable situation on the banks of the Missouri, where he and the Nansett warriors could fell timber, and prepare temporary huts for their reception. This part of the country was familiar to him, as he had traveled through it, and dwelt among its plains and its woods in the days of his wandering youth: and he gave Henrich minute directions as to the route he must take, in order to follow him to the river, which, he said, lay about three days' journey to the southward.

To the south of the present encampment arose a considerable eminence, that was thickly wooded to the summit on the side that overlooked the Nausett village, and partially sheltered it from the heat of the summer sun. On the other side it was broken into steep precipices, and its banks were scantily clothed with shrubs and grass, which the unusual drought had now rendered dry and withered. A winding and narrow path round the foot of this hill was the only road that led immediately into the plain below; and by this path Coubitant proposed to conduct the tribe, in order to avoid a long detour to the west, where a more easy road would have been found. He described it to Henrich, who had often been to the summit of the range of hills that overlooked it in pursuit of game, but who was ignorant of the proposed route into the Missouri district; and, after some conversation on the subject, he proposed that the young Sachem should accompany him the following morning to the brow of the mountain, from whence he could point out to him the road he must take through the broken and undulating ground that lay at the bottom of the hill; and the exact direction he must follow, after he reached the wide and trackless prairie that intervened between that range and the hills that bordered the Missouri.

At break of day the march of the tribe was to commence; but as several of the Nausetts were acquainted with the intricate path round the base of the hills, it was not necessary for Coubitant to lead them that part of their journey in person. He therefore proposed, after pointing out to Henrich all the necessary land-marks which could be so well observed from the summit, to find his own way down the steep side of the rugged precipice, and rejoin the party in the plain.

This plan was agreed to; and Coubitant invited Oriana to accompany her husband, that she also might see and admire the extensive view that was visible from the heights, and observe the track that her countrymen would follow through the valley beneath.

Oriana readily acceded to this proposal, not only because she loved to go by Henrich's side wherever she could be his companion, but also because—in spite of the present friendly terms to which Coubitant was admitted by her father and Henrich—she never felt quite easy when the latter was alone with the dark-browed warrior.

The morning was clear and bright; and before the sun had risen far above the horizon, and ere the sultry heat of the day had commenced, Coubitant came to Henrich's lodge, and summoned him and his wife to their early walk up the mountain. With light and active steps they took their way through the wood, and Rodolph followed close behind them—not now bounding and harking with joy, but at a measured pace, and with his keen bright eye ever fixed on Coubitant.

In passing through the scattered village of huts, the dwelling of Jyanough lay near the path. Coubitant ceased to speak as he and his companions approached it; and Oriana thought he quickened his pace, and glanced anxiously at the dwelling, as if desirous to pass it unobserved by its inmates. If such was his wish, he was, however, disappointed; for, just as the party were leaving it behind them, they heard the short sharp bark of Rodolph at the wigwam door, and immediately afterwards the answering voice of Jyanough.

'Rodolph, my old fellow, is it you?' exclaimed the Cree, as he came forth from his hut, and looked anxiously at his friends, who now, to Coubitant's inward vexation, stood to greet him.

'Where are you off to so early? he inquired of Henrich; and why is Coubitant not leading our warriors on their way?'

'We are but going to the brow of the hill,' replied Henrich, 'that Coubitant may point out to me the path by which we are to follow him. He will then join his party in the plain, and I will quickly return to accompany you on our projected hunting scheme. We must add to our stock of provisions before we commence our journey.'

'I will ascend the hill with you,' said Jyanough; and Coubitant saw that he took a spear in his hand from the door of the wigwam. Forcing a smile, he observed, as if carelessly —

'It is needless, my friend. Henrich's eye is so good that he will readily understand all the directions that I shall give him. Do you doubt the skill of our young Sachem to lead his people through the woods and the savannas, being as great as his prowess in war and his dexterity in hunting? Let him show that he is an Indian indeed, and wants no aid in performing an Indian's duties.'

'Be it so,' answered Jyanough; and he laid aside the spear, and reentered the hut, rather to Henrich's surprise, and Oriana's disappointment, but much to the satisfaction of Coubitant.

Rodolph seemed displeased at this change in the apparent intentions of his friend; and he lingered a few moments at the door of the lodge, looking wistfully at its master. But Jyanough bade him go; and a call from Henrich soon brought him again to his former position, and his watchful observation of every movement of Coubitant.

The brow of the hill was gained: and so grand and extensive was the view to the south and west, that Oriana stood for some time contemplating it with a refined pleasure, and forgot every feeling that could interrupt the pure and lofty enjoyment. Beneath the precipitous hill on which she stood, a plain, or wide savanna, stretched away for many miles, covered with the tall prairie-grass, now dry and yellow, and waving gracefully in the morning breeze. Its flat monotony was only broken by a few clumps of trees and shrubs, that almost looked like distant vessels crossing the wide trackless sea. But to the west this plain was bounded by a range of hills, on which the rising sun shed a brilliant glow, marking their clear outline against the deep blue sky behind. And nearer to the hill from which she looked, the character of the view was different, but not less interesting. It seemed as if some mighty convulsion of nature had torn away the side of the hill, and strewed the fragments in huge end broken masses in the valley beneath. Over these crags the hand of nature had spread a partial covering of moss and creeping plants; and many trees had grown up amongst them, striking their roots deeply into the crevices, and adorning their rough surfaces by their waving and pendant boughs. Through the rock-strewn valley, a narrow and intricate path had been worn by the feet of the wandering natives, and by the constant migrations of the herds of wild animals that inhabited the prairie, in search of water or of fresher herbage during the parching heat of an Indian summer.

Along this difficult path the Nausett warriors and their families were now slowly winding their way, many of them on horseback, followed by their squaws and their children on foot; and others, less barbarous, leading the steeds on which the women and infants were placed on the summit of a pile of baggage, and carrying their own bows and quivers, and long and slender spears.

It was a picturesque scene: and the low chanting song of the distant Indians—to which their march kept time—sounded sweetly, though mournfully, as it rose on the breeze to the elevated position occupied by Oriana and her two companions. The latter seemed fully occupied—the one in pointing out, and the other in observing the route of the travelers. But the eye of Henrich was not unobservant of the beauties of the prospect; and that of Coubitant was restlessly roving to and fro with quick and furtive glances, that seemed to indicate some secret purpose, and to be watching for the moment to effect it.

Some of the Nausetts in the path below looked upwards; and, observing their young Sachem and his companions, they raised a shout of recognition, that caused the rocks to echo, and also made the brows of Coubitant to contract. He saw that he must delay his purpose until the travelers were out of sight: and this chafed his spirit: but he controlled it, and proposed to Henrich and Oriana to seat themselves on the verge of the precipice, and watch the course of the travelers, while he went to reconnoiter the steep path by which he designed to join them. They did so, and the hushes that grew to the edge of the steep declivity shaded the spot, and hid them from the retreating form of Coubitant.

For some time they sat together, admiring the beauty of the scene before them, and watching the long procession in the defile below, as it wound, 'in Indian file, between the rocks and tangled bushes that cumbered the vale, until it was almost out of sight. Rudolph lay beside them, apparently asleep; but the slumber of a faithful watch-dog is always light, and Rodolph was one of the most vigilant of his race. Why did he now utter a low uneasy moan, as if he dreamt of danger? It was so low that, if Henrich heard it, he did not pay any heed to it, and continued talking to Oriana of their approaching journey, and of their plans for the future, in perfect security.

But their conversation was suddenly and painfully interrupted. A fierce bark from Rodolph, as he sprang on some one in the bush close beside Henrich, and the grasp of a powerful hand upon his shoulder at the same instant, caused the young Sachem to glance round. He found himself held to the ground by Coubitant, who was endeavoring to force him over the precipice; and would, from the suddenness and strength of the attack, have undoubtedly succeeded, but for the timely aid of Rodolph, who had seized on his left arm, and held it back in his powerful jaws. He was, however, unable to displace the savage, or release his master from the perilous situation in which he was placed; and, owing to the manner in which Henrich had seated himself on the extreme verge of the rock that overhung the precipice, it was out of his power to spring to his feet, or offer any effectual resistance. The slender but not feeble arm of Oriana, as she clung frantically to her husband, and strove to draw him back to safety, was, apparently, the only human power that now preserved him from instant destruction. Not a sound was uttered by one of the struggling group; scarcely a breath was drawn—so intense was the mental emotion, and the muscular effort that nerved every fiber during these awfully protracted moments.

But help was nigh! He, in whose hands are the lives of His creatures, sent aid when aid was so needful. A loud cry was heard in the thicket; and, as Coubitant made one more desperate effort to hurl his detested rival from the rock, and almost succeeded in flinging the whole group together into the depths below—he felt himself encircled by arms as muscular as his own, and suddenly dragged backwards.

Henrich sprang on the firm ground, and beheld his faithful friend Jyanough in fierce conflict with the treacherous Coubitant, and powerfully assisted by Rodolph, who had loosed the murderer's arm, but continued to assail and wound him as he struggled to draw his new antagonist to the brink, and seemed resolved to have one victim, even if he shared the same dreadful fate himself. Henrich flew to the aid of his friend, leaving Oriana motionless, and almost breathless, on the spot where she had endured such agony of mind, and such violent bodily exertion. For once, her strength and spirit failed her; for the trial had been too great, and faintness overcame her as she saw her husband again approach his deadly and now undisguised foe.

Coubitant saw her sink to the ground, and, with a mighty effort, he shook off the grasp of Jyanough, and darted towards Oriana. He had thought to carry her off, a living prize, after the murder of her husband; but now his only hope was vengeance and her destruction would be vengeance, indeed, on Henrich.

But love is stronger even than hate. The arms of Henrich snatched his unconscious wife from the threatened peril; and, as he bore her away from the scene of conflict, Jyanough again closed on the villain, and the deadly struggle was resumed. It was brief, but awful. The strength of Coubitant was becoming exhausted—his grasp began to loosen, and his foot to falter.

'Spare him!' cried Henrich, as he saw the combatants on the verge of the craggy platform, and feared they would fall together on the rocks beneath.

'Spare him; and secure him for the judgement of Tisquantum.' And again he laid Oriana on the ground, and rushed to save alike his friend and foe.

'He dies!' exclaimed Jyanough. 'Let him meet the fate he merits!' And springing backwards himself, he dashed his antagonist over the rock. One moment Henrich saw his falling form, and met the still fiery glance of that matchless eye—the next, he heard the crash of breaking branches, and listened for the last fatal sound of the expiring body on the rocks below. But the depth was too great: an awful stillness followed; and, though Henrich strove to look downwards, and ascertain the fate of his departed foe, the boughs and creepers that clothed the perpendicular face of the rock, entirely prevented his doing so.

'He is gone!' he exclaimed; and not in a voice of either joy or triumph, for his soul was moved within him at the appalling fate of such a man as Coubitant and at such a moment! 'He is gone to his last account: and O! what fearful passions were in his heart! Thank God, he did not drag you with him to death, my faithful Jyanough! But tell me,' he added—as they returned together to where Oriana lay, still unconscious of the dreadful tragedy that had just been enacted so near her—' tell me, my friend, how it was that you were so near at hand, when danger, which I could not repel, hung over me, and your hand was interposed to save me?'

'My mind misgave me that some treachery was intended,' replied Jyanough, 'when I saw that wily serpent leading you to the mountain's brow; and my suspicions were confirmed by his evident reluctance to my joining the party. Rodolph's expressive countenance told me, too, that there was danger to be feared; and no red man can excel Rodolph in sagacity. So I resolved to be at hand if succor should be needed; and, having waited till you were all fairly out of sight and hearing, I followed slowly and stealthily, and reached the verge of the thicket just in time to hear the warning cry of your noble dog, and see that dastardly villain spring upon you from the bush. The rest you know: and now you will believe me, when I own my conviction that your destruction has been his object since the time I joined your camp: and that, to accomplish it, and obtain possession of Oriana, he returned to Tisquantum's tribe, and has worn the mask of friendship for so many months. My soul is relieved of a burden by his death; and forgive me, Henrich, if I own that I glory in having executed on him the vengeance he deserved, and having devoted him to the fate he designed for you.'

Henrich could not regret the death, however dreadful, of one who seemed to have been so bent on the destruction of his happiness and his life; but the thought of all the guilt that lay on Coubitant's soul, unrepented of and unatoned, saddened and solemnized his spirit; and he only replied to

Jyanough's exulting words by a kindly pressure of his friend's hand, as they approached Oriana.

Her senses bad returned, and, with them, a painful sense of danger and of dread, and she looked anxiously, and almost wildly, around her, as Henrich knelt beside her, and gently raised her from the ground.

Where is he?' she exclaimed. 'Where is that fearful form, and those eyes of unearthly fire that glared on me just now? You are safe, my Henrich,' she added; and, as she looked up in his face, tears of joy and gratitude burst from her large expressive eyes, and relieved her bursting heart. You are safe, my Henrich: and oh that that dark form of dread and evil might never, never, cross my path again!'

'Fear not, Oriana,' replied Jyanough, 'he never more will darken your way through life. He has met the death he designed for Henrich, and let us think of him no more. It is time to return to the camp; and your husband and I will support you down the hill.'

'I am well, quite well, now !' cried Oriana, and she rose from the ground, and clung to Henrich's arm, as if to assure herself of his presence and safety. 'I could walk through the world thus supported, and thus guarded, too,' she added, as she stroked the head of the joyous Rodolph, who now bounded round her and Henrich with all his wonted spirit. 'I owe much to my two trusty friends; for, but for their care and watchfulness, what would now have been my dreadful fate! Let us leave this spot—so beautiful, but now so full of fearful images!'

CHAPTER XVII

Hither and thither; hither and thither!
Madly they fly!
Whither, O, whither! Whither, O, whither? -
'Tis but to die!
Fire is behind them: fire is, around them:
Black is the sky?
Horror pursues them; anguish has found them:
Destruction is nigh!
And where is refuge? where is safety now?
Father of mercy! None can Save but Thou?' ANON.

'What is that distant cloud, Henrich?' inquired Oriana, as they rode by Tisquantum's side on the evening of the day of their journey towards the Missouri. 'It seems like the smoke of an encampment, as I see it over the tall waving grass: but it must be too near to be the camp of our people; unless, indeed, they have tarried there, waiting the arrival of Coubitant, who never will rejoin them more.'

'I see the cloud you speak of, Oriana; and I have been watching it with some anxiety for several minutes. It cannot be what you suggest, for you know your father received a message from the trusty Salon—next in command to Coubitant—to tell him that their leader not having joined the party as he promised, a search had been made, and his mangled body found at the foot of the rock, where, it was supposed, he must have fallen in attempting the sleep descent. Salon's messenger further stated that, having buried the corpse where it lay, he had led the people on, and should pursue the path pointed out by Coubitant, and hasten to prepare the necessary huts for our reception. I dispatched the messenger again with further directions to Salon; and ere this, no doubt, the encampment is formed on the shores of the great river to which we are journeying. 'Father,' he added, as he turned towards Tisquantum, your eye is dim, but your sagacity is as keen as ever. Can you discern that rising smoke, and tell us its cause?'

The aged Sachem had been riding silently and abstractedly along. The tall dry grass—now ripe, and shedding its seeds on every side—rose frequently above his head; for he was mounted on a low strong horse, and he had not observed the cloud that had attracted the attention of the younger travelers. He now paused, and looked earnestly to the south, in which direction the smoke appeared right before the advancing party, and from whence a strong and sultry wind was blowing. As the prairie grass rose and fell in undulating waves, the old man obtained a distinct view of the smoke, which now seemed to have spread considerably to the right and left, and also to be approaching towards the travelers.

The narrow, zigzag track of the deer and the buffaloes was the only beaten path through the prairie; and this could only be traveled by two or three horsemen abreast. The old Sachem, and Henrich, and Oriana, led the party; and Jyanough, and Mailah, and young Lincoya, all well mounted, rode immediately in the rear. The attendants of the two families, and a few experienced warriors, some on foot and some on horseback, followed in the winding path.

On the halt of the foremost rank, the rest rode up, and were immediately made aware of the ominous signs which hitherto they had not noticed. Instantly terror was depicted in every countenance; and the deep low voice of Tisquantum sank into every heart, as he exclaimed, 'The prairie is on fire!'

'Turn!' cried Henrich, 'and fly! Let each horseman take one of those on foot behind, and fly for your lives. Cast the baggage on the ground— stay for nothing, but our people's lives.'

He was obeyed: men and women were all mounted; and Henrich snatched his boy from the arms of the woman who carried him, and, giving the child to Oriana, took up the terrified attendant on his own powerful steed.

The wind rose higher: and now the roar of the pursuing flames came fearfully on the fugitives, growing louder and louder, while volumes of dense smoke were driven over their heads, and darkened the sky that had so lately shone in all its summer brightness.

Headlong the party dashed along the winding path, and sometimes the terrified horses leaped into the tall grass, seeking a straighter course, or eager to pass by those who had fled before them. But this was a vain attempt. The wild pea-vines, and other creeping plants that stretched among the grass, offered such impediments to rapid flight, as forced them again into the path.

And now the wild inhabitants of the broad savanna came rushing on, and joined the furious flight, adding difficulty and confusion to the horror of the scene. Buffaloes, elks, and antelopes, tore madly through the grass, jostling the horses and their riders, and leaving them far in the rear. The screaming eagle rode high above among the clouds of smoke, and many smaller birds fell suffocated to the ground; while all the insect tribe took wing, and everything that had life strove to escape the dread pursuer.

It was a desperate race! The strength of the fugitives began to fail, and no refuge, no hope, seemed near. Alas! to some the race was lost. The blinding effect of the dense smoke that filled the atmosphere, the suffocating smell of the burning mass of vegetable matter, and the lurid glare of the red flames that came on so rapidly, overpowered alike the horses and their riders: while the roaring of the fire — which sounded like a mighty rushing cataract — and the oppressive heat, seemed to confuse the senses, and destroy the vital powers of the more feeble and ill-mounted of the fugitives. Several of the horses fell, and their devoted riders sank to the ground, unable any longer to sustain the effort for life; and Henrich had the agony of passing by the wretched victims, and leaving them to their fate, for he knew that he had no power to save them.

Many miles were traversed — and still the unbroken level of the prairie spread out before them — and still the roaring and destructive flames came borne on the mighty winds behind them. A few scattered trees were the only objects that broke the monotony of the plains; and the hills, at the foot of which they had traveled that morning, and where alone they could lock for safety, were still at a great distance. At length, the aged Tisquantum's powers of endurance began to give way. The reins almost fell from his hands; and, in trembling accents, he declared his total inability to proceed any further.

Leave me, my children!' he exclaimed, 'to perish here; for my strength is gone; and what matters it where the old Tisquantum breathes his last. Mahneto is here, even in this awful hour, to receive my spirit; and I shall but lose a few short months or years of age and infirmity.'

'Never, my father!' cried H enrich, as he caught the reins of the Sachem's horse; and while he still urged his own overloaded steed to fresh exertions, endeavored also to support the failing form of his father-in-law. 'Never will we leave you to die alone in this fiery desert. Hold on, my father! hold on yet a little longer till we gain the defile, where the flames cannot follow as, and all will yet be well!'

'I cannot, my son!' replied the old man. 'Farewell, my dear, my noble boy! — farewell, my Oriana! And his head sank down upon the neck of his horse.

He would have fallen to the ground but for Henrich, who now checked the panting steeds, and sprang down to his feet in time to receive him in his arms.

Fly, Oriana!' he exclaimed, as his wife also drew the bridle of her foaming horse by his side. 'Fly, Oriana, my beloved! save your own life, and that of our child! If possible, I will preserve your father— but if not, farewell! and God be with you!'

One moment Oriana urged her horse again to its swiftest pace, as if in obedience to her husband's command—the next, she was at Mailah's side, holding her infant in one arm, white with the other she guided and controlled the terrified animal on which she rode.

'Here, Mailah!' she cried—and she clasped the child to her breast, and imprinted one passionate kiss on its cheek—' Take my Ludovico, and save his life, and I will return to my husband and father. If we follow you, well. If not, be a mother to my child, and may the blessing of God be on you!'

She almost flung the infant into the extended arms of Mailah; and then, having with difficulty turned her horse, and forced him to retrace his steps, she again rejoined those with whom she was resolved to live or die.

One glance of affectionate reproach she met from her Henrich's eyes: but he did not speak. With the assistance of Ludovico's nurse, who rode behind him, he had just lifted Tisquantum to his own saddle, and was preparing to mount himself, and endeavor to support the unconscious old man, and again commence the race far life or death. But it seemed a hopeless attempt—so utterly helpless was the Sachem, and so unable to retain his seat. Quick as thought Oriana unbound her long twisted girdle of many colors; and, flinging it to Henrich, desired him to bind the failing form of her father to his own. He did so: and the nurse having mounted behind Oriana, again the now furious steeds started forward. All these actions had taken less time to perform than they have to relate; but yet the pursuing flames had gained much way, and the flight became more desperate, and more hazardous. Again the prostrate forms of horses and their riders met the eyes of Henrich and Oriana; but in the thickness of the air, and the wild speed at which they were compelled to pass, it was impossible to distinguish who were the unhappy victims.

'Heaven be praised!' at length Henrich exclaimed—and they were the first words he had uttered since the flight had been resumed—' Heaven be praised! I see the rocks dimly through the clouds of smoke. Yet a few moments, and we shall be safe. Already the grass around us is shorter and thinner: we are leaving the savanna, and shall soon reach the barren defile, where the flames will find no fuel'

The horses seemed to know that safety was near at hand, for they bounded forward with fresh vigor, and quickly joined the group of breathless fugitives, who, having reached the extremity of the prairie, had paused to rest from their desperate exertions, and to look out for those of their companions who were missing, but who they hoped would soon overtake them.

Oriana snatched her now smiling boy from Mailah's arms, and embraced him with a fervency and emotion that showed how little she had hoped to see his face again. But her own happy and grateful feelings were painfully interrupted by her friend's exclamation of agony —

'Where is my Lincoya?' she cried. 'Did he not follow with you? I saw him close to me when I paused to take your child: and he is not here! O, my Lincoya! my brave, my beautiful boy! Have you perished in the flames, with none to help you?' And she broke forth into cries and lamentations that wrung the heart of Oriana.

She could give her no tidings of the lost youth, for she knew not whose fainting forms she had passed in the narrow shrouded path; and it was utterly impossible now to go and seek him, for the flames had followed hard upon their flight, and were still raging over the mass of dry herbage, and consuming even the scattered tufts that grew among the stones at the entrance to the ravine. So intense was the heat of the glowing surface, even after the blaze had died away, that it would not be practicable to pass over it for many hours; and the party, who had reached a place of safety, were compelled to make arrangements for passing the night where they were, not only that they might be ready to seek the remains of their lost friends the next morning, but also because their own weary limbs, and those of their trembling horses, refused to carry them any further. All the provisions and other baggage, which they had carried for their journey, had been abandoned in the flight, end had become a rapid prey to the devouring flames. But several of the scorched and affrighted prairie fowls, and a few hares — exhausted with their long race — were easily secured by the young hunters, end afforded a supper to the weary company.

The horses were then turned loose to find fodder for themselves, and to drink at the little brook that still trickled among the rocks; and large fires having been lighted to scare the wild beasts that, like our travelers, had been driven for refuge to the ravine, all lay down to sleep, thankful to the deities in whom they respectively trusted, for their preservation in such imminent peril.

Fervent were the prayers and praises that were offered up that night by the little band of Christians, among whom Henrich always officiated as minister: and even the distressed spirit of Mailah was comforted and calmed as she joined in his words of thanksgiving, and in his heartfelt petitions that the lost Lincoya might yet be restored to his parents; or that, if his spirit had already passed away from earth, it might have been purified by faith, and received into the presence of its God and Savior.

Mailah was tranquilized; but her grief and anxiety were not removed: and she passed that sad night in sleepless reflection on the dreadful fate of her only child, and in sincere endeavors so to realize and apply all the blessed truths she had learnt from Henrich, as to derive from them that comfort to her own soul, and that perfect resignation to the will of God, that she well knew they were designed to afford to the Christian believer. And that night of watchfulness did not pass unprofitably to Mailah's spirit.

But where was Lincoya? Where was the youth whose mother mourned him as dead? He was safe amid the top most boughs of a lonely tree, that now stood scorched and leafless in the midst of the smoldering plain, several miles from the safe retreat that had been gained by his friends.

The horse on which he rode that day, though fleet and active, was young, and uninured to long continued and violent exertion; and, at length, its foot getting entangled in some creeping plant that had grown across the pathway, it had fallen violently to the ground, and thrown its young rider among the prairie-grass, where he lay, stunned, and unable to rise, until all his companions had passed by. Then he regained the path, and attempted to raise the exhausted creature from the earth: but all in vain. Its trembling limbs were unable to support it; and Lincoya saw that he could no longer look to his favorite steed for the safety of his own life, and must abandon it to perish in the flames.

But the boy was an Indian, and accustomed to Indian difficulties and Indian expedients. He glanced rapidly around for some means of preservation; and, seeing a tree of some magnitude, and at no great distance, he resolved to try to reach it ere the coming fire had seized on the surrounding herbage, and seek for a refuge in its summit. With much difficulty, he forced his way through the tall rank grass that waved above his head, and the wild vines that were entangled with it in every direction; and he reached the foot of the tree just as the flames were beginning to scorch its outmost branches. He sprang upward; and, climbing with the agility of a squirrel, he was soon in the highest fork of the tree, and enabled to look down in security on the devastating fire beneath him. All around was one wide sea of ruddy flames, that shot up in forked and waving tongues high amid the heavy clouds of smoke. Happily for Lincoya, the herbage beneath his tree of refuge grew thin and scanty, and did not afford much food for the devouring elements; otherwise it must have consumed his retreat, and suffocated him even in its topmost boughs. As it was, the lower branches only were destroyed, and the boy was able to endure the heat and smoke until the roaring flames had passed beneath him, and he watched them driving onward in the wake of his flying friends.

To follow his companions that night was hopeless, for how could he traverse that red-hot plain? He, therefore, settled himself firmly among the sheltering branches, to one of which he bound himself with his belt of deer skin, and prepared to pass the night in that position, as he had passed many similar ones when he had been out on hunting expeditions with his father-in-law Jyanough.

Long he gazed on the strange aspect of the wide savanna, as it glowed in the darkness of night, with a lurid and fearful glare, that only made the gloom more visible. But weariness and exhaustion at length overcame him, and he fell asleep, and did not awake until the sun was high in the heavens. The prospect around him was changed, but the plain looked even more dreary and desolate than it appeared while the fire was at work on its clothing of grass. Now all was laid low, and smoking ashes alone covered the nakedness of the savanna. Lincoya gazed earnestly in every direction, that he might make sure of the route he must follow in order to rejoin his friends; and his attention was attracted by the figures of two men approaching towards the tree in which he sat, and apparently engage d in earnest conversation. For a moment his hopes led him to believe that they were Jyanough and Henrich, who had returned, probably, in search of him; and he was about to hail them with a loud and joyful cry. But the caution so early instilled into the mind of an Indian restrained him: and well it was for him that he had not thus given vent to his feelings. The men drew nearer, and he saw, to his amazement, that they were Coubitant—he whose death and burial had been so confidently reported, and Salon—the trusty Salon—to whom the conduct of the tribe had been deputed after the supposed death of the appointed leader.

They came beneath the tree; and, seating themselves at its foot, proceeded to refresh themselves with food and water, that looked tempting to the eyes of the fasting and parched Lincoya, as he gazed noiselessly and attentively at their proceedings, and listened to their discourse.

'At last I have been successful, Salon,' said Coubitant to his companion. 'At last I may rejoice in the destruction of those I hate with so bitter a hatred. Those burnt and broken weapons were Henrich's, end this ornament belonged to Oriana.' As he said this he displayed in his hand a girdle clasp, that Lincoya recognized as having been worn by the Squaw-Sachem on the previous day. It had fallen to the ground when she gave the girdle to Henrich: and many of his personal accoutrements had also been cast there, unheeded, in his anxiety to save Tisquantum.

'I would I could have been more sure of all the bodies that lay just beyond,' continued the savage; 'but I think I could not be mistaken in those I most wished to find, burnt and disfigured as they were. And the horses, too, were surely those they rode; for I knew the fragments of Tisquantum's trappings, and recognized the form of Lincoya's pony. Yes! they are all destroyed; I know it, and I exult in it! Now, who shall prevent my being Sachem of the tribe, and leading my warriors to the destruction of the detested white invaders of our land?

'Truly,' replied Salon, 'your last scheme has succeeded better than any of the others you have tried; and I now gladly hail you as Sachem of our tribe. I have made sure of the fidelity of many of our bravest warriors; and when those who would have taken the white man's part, and followed him in obedience to Tisquantum's wishes, find that he is dead, they will readily take you for their leader, as the bravest of our tribe, and the most determined foe of the pale-faces. But it is possible that Henrich has even yet escaped us. The bodies that lie scorched on the ashes are fewer than the number that were to follow us. We must, therefore, take measures to seize and destroy those who yet live, if they are likely to disturb our scheme. Of course, they will again set out on the same track, as being that which will most quickly bring them where food and water are to be found. We have only to lie in wait at the other side of the savanna, where the narrow mountain pass leads to the river, and our arrows and spears will be sufficient to silence every tongue that could speak against your claims.

'You are right, nay faithful Salon,' answered Coubitant, with a sign of warns approbation of the forethought of his accomplice. 'Let us lose no time in crossing the plain; for, doubtless, the survivors of this glorious fire will be early on their march, and it would not do for them to overtake us in the midst of the ruin we have wrought. We will set all inquiries to rest, and then we will report to our tribe that the dreadful conflagration has deprived them of both their Chiefs, and that it rests with themselves to choose another. O, Salon! my soul burns to lead them to Paomet, that stronghold of our country's foes!'

The murderers arose, and took their way directly across the prairie: for all the rank herbage being now reduced to ashes, they were no longer obliged to follow the winding course of the buffalo track. They proceeded at a rapid pace; but it was some time ere Lincoya ventured to descend from his hiding-place, as he feared being observed on the level plain, if either of those ruthless villains should east a glance behind them. At length their retreating forms appeared to him like specks in the distance; and he came down from his watch-tower, and fled as fast as his active young limbs could carry him, towards the spot where he hoped to rejoin his friends. He had not very long continued his flight, when he perceived several persons on horseback approaching towards him; and soon he found himself in the arms of his joyful mother, and was affectionately greeted by Jyanough and Henrich, who, with several others, had come out to look if any of their missing companions were still within reach of human aid.

All but Lincoya had perished! The fire and the smoke had not only destroyed their lives, but had so blackened and disfigured them that it was impossible to identify a single individual. A grave was dug in the yet warm earth; and all the victims were buried sufficiently deep to preserve their remains from the ravages of wild beasts; and then the party returned in all haste to those who anxiously awaited them at their place of refuge.

On the way, Lincoya related to his father-in-law and Henrich the whole of the conversation which he had heard between Coubitant and Salon, while he was in his safe retreat; and their surprise at finding that the former had survived his desperate fall from the brow of the precipice, and still lived to plan and work out schemes of cruelty and malice, was only equaled by their indignation at thus discovering the treachery and deceit of Salon. They had hitherto put the most entire confidence in the fidelity of this man: and if they had still entertained any doubts or suspicions as to the honesty of Coubitant's intentions, they had relied on Salon to discover his plans, and prevent any mischief being accomplished.

The whole story was told to Tisquantum; and his counsel was asked as to the best mode of now counteracting the further schemes of the traitors, and escaping the snare which they found was yet to be laid for their destruction. It would be impossible for them to reach the camp on the banks of the Missouri, by the path which Coubitant had pointed out, without passing through the defile where the villain and his confederate now proposed to lie in wait for them, and where, in spite of their superior numbers, many of their party would probably be wounded by the arrows and darts of their hidden foes, without having any opportunity of defending themselves. That route was therefore abandoned. But the old Sachem remembered having traversed this part of the continent many years ago, and he knew of a track to the west, by which the mountains that skirted the course of the Missouri might be avoided, and the rivers reached at a considerable distance above the place at which the encampment was appointed to be formed. This road was, indeed, much longer than that across the prairie, and would occupy several days to traverse; so that it was doubtful whether Coubitant would wait so long in his lurking-place, or whether he would conclude that the Chiefs were dead, and return to take the command of the tribe.

Nevertheless, no other course was open; and, with as little delay as possible, the journey was commenced. A scanty supply of food was obtained by the bows and arrows of the hunters, and water was occasionally met with in the small rivulets that flowed from the hills, and wandered on until they eventually lost themselves in the broad Missouri.

Inured to privations and to toilsome journeys, the Indian party heeded them not, but cheerfully proceeded on their way until, at length, they beheld the wigwams of their tribe standing on a green meadow near the river's side. They hastened on, and were received with joyful acclamations by the inhabitants, who had almost despaired of ever seeing them again. The conflagration of the prairie was known to them; but almost all of them were ignorant of the true cause of the awful calamity, and attributed it entirely to accident. Nor were any suspicions aroused in their minds by the conduct of Coubitant and Salon, who had pretended the greatest alarm and anxiety for the fate of the Chiefs and their party, and had set out as soon as it was possible to traverse the savanna, in the hope, as they declared, of rendering assistance to any of the Sachem's company who might have survived the catastrophe.

Much to the relief of all the party, they found that neither Coubitant nor his accomplice had yet returned to the camp; and their prolonged absence was becoming a source of uneasiness to the rest of the tribe, who were preparing to send out a party of men to search for them, the very day that Henrich led his detachment into the village.

It was agreed by the Sachems and Jyanough, that they would not communicate to the rest of their people all they had discovered of the treachery of Coubitant and Salon; as they knew not yet how many of the warriors might have been induced to join in the conspiracy, and connive at their crimes. They, therefore, accounted for having traveled by so circuitous a route, on the plea of their inability to cross the prairie without any supply of either provisions or water; and they commanded the party who were about to search for Coubitant and. Salon, to set out immediately, and to use every possible exertion to find them, and bring them in safety to the camp. They could have told their messengers exactly where the villains were to be found; but that would have betrayed a greater knowledge of their movements than it would have been prudent to disclose; and they only directed the men to shout aloud every now and then, as they traversed the mountain passes, that the lost travelers might know of their approach; and also to carry with them a supply of food sufficient to last several days.

The messengers departed: and then Jyanough set himself to work, with all an Indian's sagacity, to find out the extent to which the conspiracy had been carried among the warriors of the tribe. He succeeded in convicting four men of the design to elevate Coubitant to the chieftainship, and of a knowledge and participation in his last desperate scheme for the destruction of the Sachem and all his family. Summary justice was, therefore, executed on the culprits, who scorned to deny their crimes when once they were charged with them; and submitted to the sentence of their Chief with a fortitude that almost seemed to expiate their offence. The most daring of the four openly exulted in his rebellious projects, and boasted of his long-concealed hatred towards the pale-faced stranger, who presumed to exercise authority over the free red men; and Tisquantum deemed it politic to inflict on him a capital punishment. He was, therefore, directed to kneel down before him, which he did with the greatest composure; and the aged Chief then drew his long sharp knife, and, with a steady hand and unflinching eye, plunged it into the heart of the criminal. He expired without a groan or a struggle; and then the other three wretches were led up together, and placed in the same humble posture before the offended Sachem. At Henrich's request, the capital sentence was remitted; but one of agony and shame was inflicted in its stead— one that is commonly reserved for the punishment of repeated cases of theft. The Sachem's knife again was lifted, and, with a dexterous movement of his hand, he slit the noses of each of the culprits from top to bottom, and dismissed them, to carry for life the marks of their disgrace. No cry was uttered by any one of the victims, nor the slightest resistance offered to their venerable judge and executioner; for such cowardice would, in the estimation of the Indians, have been far more contemptible than the crime of which they had been convicted. Silently they withdrew; nor did they, even by the expression of their countenances, seem to question the justice of their chastisement.

The next step to be pursued, was to prepare for securing Coubitant and Salon the moment they should make their appearance in the camp, and before they could be made aware of the discovery at their treason. For this purpose, very effectual steps were taken; and Jyanough—the faithful and energetic Jyanough—took the command of the band of trusty warriors who were appointed to seize the leaders of the conspiracy, and to bring them into the presence of the Chiefs.

That evening, soon after sunset, the searching party returned; and, no sooner did Jyanough perceive, from the spot where he had posted his men among the rocks and bushes that commanded the pathway, that Coubitant and his fellow-criminal were with them, than he gave the concerted signal, and rushed upon them. In an instant, they were seized by the arms, and dragged forcibly forward to the village. They asked no questions of their captors—for conscience told them that their sin had found them out, and that they were about to expiate their crimes by a death, probably both lingering and agonizing.

Doggedly they walked on, and were led to the spot where Tisquantum and his son-in-law awaited their arrival. This was beneath a spreading tree that grew near the banks of the river, which in that part were rather high and precipitous. The shades of evening were deepening; and the dark visage of Coubitant looked darker than ever, while the lurid light of his deep-set eyes seemed to glow with even unwonted luster from beneath his shaggy and overhanging brows.

The greatest part of the tribe were gathered together in that place, and stood silently around to view the criminals, and to witness their expected fate; for now all were acquainted with their guilt and all who were assembled here were indignant at their treachery against their venerable and beloved Sachem, and their scarcely less respected white Chieftain.

The voice of Tisquantum broke the ominous silence.

Coubitant, he solemnly began, 'you have deceived your Chief. You have spoken to him words of peace, when death was in your heart. Is it not so?

'I would be Chief myself,' replied the savage, in a deep, undaunted voice. 'I was taught to believe that I should succeed you; and a pale-faced stranger has taken my place. I have lived but to obtain vengeance—vengeance that you, Tisquantum, who were bound to wreak it on the slayer of your son, refused to take. A mighty vengeance was in my soul; and to possess it, I would have sacrificed the whole tribe. Now do to me as I would have done to Henrich.' And he glared on his hated rival with the eye of a beast of prey. Tisquantum regarded him calmly, and gravely continued his examination.

'And you have also drawn some of my people into rebel lion, and persuaded them to consent to the murder of their Chief. One of them has already shed his life-blood in punishment of his sin; and the rest will bear the marks of shame to their graves. All this is your work.'

'If more of your people had the courage to join me in resisting the pretensions of the proud stranger, you and Henrich would now have been lying dead at my feet. You would never again have been obeyed as Sachems by the Nausetts. But they loved their slavery—and let them keep it. My soul is free. You may send it forth in agony, if you will: for I am in your power, and I ask no mercy from those to whom I would have shown none. Do your worst. Coubitant's heart is strong; and I shall soon be with the spirits of my fathers, where no white men can enter.

The wrath of Tisquantum was stirred by the taunts and the bold defiance of his prisoner; and he resolved to execute on him a sentence that should strike terror into any others of the tribe who might have harbored thoughts of rebellion.

The death that you intended should be my portion, and that of all my family, shall be your own!' he exclaimed. The torments of fire shall put a stop to your boasting. My children,' he added — turning to the warriors who stood around him — ' I call on you to do justice on this villain. Form a pile of wood here on the river's brink; end when his body is consumed, his ashes shall he cast on the stream, and go to tell, in other lands, how Tisquantum punishes treachery.'

A smile of scorn curled the lip of Coubitant, but he spoke not; and no quivering feature betrayed any inward fear of the approaching agony.

Hear me yet, Coubitant,' resumed the old Chieftain; and, as he spoke, the strokes of his warriors' hatchets among the neighboring trees fell on the victim's ear, but did not seem to move him. 'Hear me yet, and answer me. Was it by your arts that Salon's soul was turned away from his lawful Chief, and filled with thoughts of murder? Was he true to me and mine until you returned to put evil thoughts into his heart? or had pride and jealousy already crept in there, which you have only fostered?'

'Salon hugged his chains till I showed him that they were unworthy of a true-born Indian. The smooth tongue of the pale-face had beguiled him, till I told him that it would lead him to ruin and subjection. Yes: I taught Salon to long for freedom for himself, and freedom for his race. And now he will die for it, as a red man ought to die. Let the same pile consume us both!'

'No!' interrupted Henrich, eagerly. 'His guilt is far less than yours, and mercy may be extended to him. By every law of God and man your life, Coubitant, is forfeited; and justice requires that you should die. But I would desire your death to be speedy, and I would spare you all needless agony. My father,' he continued, addressing Tisquantum, 'let my request be heard in favor of Salon, that he may live to become our trusty friend again; and since Coubitant must die, let it be by the quick stroke of the knife, and not in the lingering horrors of the stake.'

'Cease to urge me, my son,' replied the Chief, in a tone of firm determination, that forbad all hope of success. 'I have said that Coubitant shall die the death he intended for us; and his funeral pile shall light up this spot ere I retire to my lodge. Salon, also, shall die: but, as he was deceived by the greater villain, he shall die a warriors death.'

The Sachem rose from his seat, and took a spear that leaned against the trunk of the tree beside him.

'Now meet the stroke like a man!' he cried; and gathering his somewhat failing strength, he bore with all his force against the naked breast of Salon. The life-blood gushed forth, and he fell a corpse upon the earth.

'Now drive in the stake, and heap the pile!' exclaimed the aged Chieftain in a clear, loud voice of command, as he withdrew the bloody lance, and waved it high above his head. He was excited by the scene he was enacting, and the feelings of his race were aroused within him with a violence that had been long unknown to him. He felt the joy that savage natures feel in revenging themselves on their foes; and he forgot the influence that Henrich's example and precepts of forbearance had so lung exerted over his conduct, though they had not yet succeeded in changing his heart.

'Heap the pile high!' he cried; 'and let the flames bring back the light of day, and show me the death struggles of him who would have slain me, and all I love on earth. Drag the wretch forward, and bind him strongly. The searching flames may yet have power to conquer his calm indifference.'

The lighted brand was ready, and the victim was led to the foot of the pile. A rope was passed around his arms, and the noose was about to be drawn tight, when, quick as lightning, the devoted victim saw that there was yet one chance for life. The river was rolling beneath his feet. Could he but reach it! His arms were snatched from those who held them with a sudden violence, for which they were unprepared; and, with one desperate bound, the prisoner gained the steep bank of the broad dark stream. Another moment, and a heavy plash was heard in the waters.

Darkness was gathering around the scene; and those who looked into the river could distinguish no human form on its surface.

'Fire the pile!' cried Tisquantum; and the flames burst up from the dry crackling wood, and threw a broad sheet of light on the dark stream below.

'He is there!' again shouted the infuriated Chieftain. 'I see the white foam that his rapid strokes leave behind him. Send your arrows after him, my brave warriors, and suffer him not to escape. Ha! will Mahneto let him thus avoid my vengeance?'

The bow-strings twanged, and the arrows flew over the water. Where did they fall? Not on Coubitant's struggling form; for he had heard the Sachem's command, and had dived deeply beneath the surface of the water, and changed his course down the stream. When he rose again, it was in a part of the river that the flames did not illuminate; and those who sought his life saw him no more.

'Surely he was wounded, and has sunk, never to rise again!' exclaimed Henrich. 'His doom has followed him!'

'Mahneto be praised!' cried Tisquantum; 'but I would I had seen him writhing in those flames!' And he turned and left the spot.

Coubitant gained the western shore of the river; and he smiled a strange and ominous smile, as he looked across the waters, and saw the forms of his enemies by the light of that fire which had been intended to consume his quivering flesh, and dismiss from earth his undaunted and cruel spirit.

'I will have vengeance yet!' ha muttered: and then he turned his steps towards the south, and paused not until he had traveled many miles down the river, when he lay down on its margin, and slept as soundly as if no guilt lay on his soul.

CHAPTER XVIII

Out of small beginnings great things have arisen, and as one small
candle may light a thousand. So the light here kindled hath shone on
many.
GOVERNOR BRADFORDS JOURNAL.

Once more we must leave our Indian friends, and return to New
Plymouth, and to comparatively civilized life, with all its cares and anxieties,
from so many of which the wild tenants of the woods are free.

Cares and anxieties had, indeed, continued to be the portion of the
Pilgrim Fathers and their families, though mingled with many blessings.
Their numbers had considerably increased during the years that elapsed
since last we took a view of their condition; and their town bad assumed a
much more comfortable and imposing appearance. Many trading vessels
had also visited the rising colony from the mother-country, and had brought
out to the settlers useful supplies of clothing, and other articles of great
value. Among these, none were more acceptable to the emigrants than the
first specimens of horned cattle, consisting of three cows and a bull, that
reached the settlement about the third year after its establishment. They
were hailed with universal joy by all the inhabitants of New Plymouth, who
seemed to feel as if the presence of such old accustomed objects, brought
back to them a something of home that they had never felt before in the land
of their exile. These precious cattle were a common possession of the whole
colony, and were not divided until the year 1627, when their numbers had
greatly increased, and when a regular division of the houses and lands also
took place.

The trade of the colony had, likewise, been considerably augmented,
both with the Indians and with the English, whose fishing vessels frequented
the coast, and were the means of their carrying on a constant intercourse
and traffic with their friends at home. One of these vessels brought out
to the emigrants the sad intelligence of the death of their beloved pastor,
John Robinson—he who had been honored and respected by every Puritan
community, whether in Europe or America, and for whose arrival the

Pilgrims had looked, with anxious hope, ever since the day of their sorrowful parting in Holland. 'Surely' — as a friend of Bradford's wrote to him from Leyden — our pastor would never have gone from hence, if prayers, tears or means of aid could have saved him.' The consternation of the settlers was great indeed. Year after year they had gone on, expecting and waiting for his coming to resume his official duties among them; and, therefore, they had never taken any measures to provide themselves with regular pastors, who might preach the gospel to them three times every Lord's day, according to their custom in Europe and also administer to them the sacrament, which, previous to their exile, all the grown-up members of the community had habitually received every Sunday.

The death of their spiritual leader and counselor had destroyed all their hopes of being again united to him on earth; and the blow fell heavily on all, and cast a gloom over the settlement that was not soon dispersed; but still the Pilgrims did not immediately proceed to choose another minister. The belief that the divine service could receive no part of its sanctity from either time, place, or person, but only from the Holy Spirit of God, which hallows it — was then, as it is now, a leading feature of the Independent and Presbyterian churches of America, and, therefore, the Puritans of New Plymouth did not feel it a necessity — although they deemed it a *privilege* — to enjoy the spiritual ministrations of ordained clergymen.

Hitherto the venerable Brewster, with the occasional aid of Bradford, Winslow, and a few others distinguished for piety and eloquence, had delivered the customary addresses and prayers, and had performed the rite of baptism. At length, in the year 1628, Allerton, the assistant of Bradford, after he had been on a mission to England, brought back with him a young preacher of the name of Rogers, who very shortly gave such evident signs of insanity, that the settlers were obliged to send him back to his native land, at a considerable expense and trouble.

In the meantime, the number of settlers on other parts of the coast of New England had augmented to a great extent; and in Salem alone there were four ministers who had come out with the English emigrants, of whom only two could find adequate employment. One of the others, therefore, named Ralph Smith, who was a man of much piety, and judged orthodox by the Puritans, went to Plymouth, and offered himself as pastor to the inhabitants. He was chosen by the people to be their spiritual leader, and became the first regularly-appointed preacher who officiated among these, the earliest settlers in New England.

Two or three small vessels were, about this time, built by the men of Plymouth for their own use, and proved of great service to them, as their connection with other colonies of Europeans on the American coast became more extensive and profitable. A friendly intercourse with the Dutch settlers at the mouth of the great river Hudson had also lately been established, to the great satisfaction of the Plymouthers, and to the mutual advantage and comfort of both parties. It was commenced by the men of Holland soon after their formal settlement near the Hudson, where they erected a village, and a fortress called Fort Amsterdam. From thence they addressed a courteous letter to their old connections, the English exiles from Leyden; and invited them to an occasional barter of their respective goods and productions, and also offered them their services in any other way that could be useful.

Governor Bradford—who still by annual election retained his important office—returned an equally friendly reply to these overtures: and at the same time tendered his own and his people's grateful acknowledgements of all the kindness and hospitality that they had received during their residence in Holland, in years gone by. The following year they were surprised and gratified by a visit from De Brazier, the Secretary of the Dutch colony, who anchored at Manomet, a place twenty miles to the south of New Plymouth, and from thence sent to request the Pilgrims to send a boat for him. His ship was well stocked with such wares as were likely to be acceptable to the English; and, according to the custom of the times, he was attended by several gaily dressed trumpeters, and a numerous retinue of servants. The new pinnace, which had recently been built at Manomet, was immediately dispatched for the welcome visitors, and he was hospitably entertained by his new friends for three days; after which the Governor, attended by Rodolph and some others, returned with him to his vessel, to make their purchases, and to give in exchange for their European goods, such furs, and skins, and tobacco, as they had been able to collect in their general storehouse on 'the Burying Hill.'

From this period, an active trade was carried on between the two settlements, which proved highly advantageous to both—the Dutch supplying the men of Plymouth with sugar, linen, and other stuffs, in return for their skins, timber, and tobacco.

During all this time, an almost perfect peace was maintained with the neighboring Indian tribes; and the friendship that had so early been established between the English settlers and the Wampanoges became more confirmed and strengthened. All external matters now wore a far more prosperous aspect than they had hitherto done; and the Pilgrims felt that they had both the means and the leisure to add to the comforts of their social and domestic life. Some years previously, a small portion of land had been assigned to each family for its own particular use: but the possession of this land had not been made hereditary; and although the fact of its being appropriated to one household had considerably increased the zeal and industry of the cultivators, yet they still desired that feeling of inalienable property which so greatly adds to the value of every possession.

To gratify this natural desire, the Governor and his council had deemed it advisable to depart so far from the terms of the original treaty as to allot to each colonist an acre of land, as near the town as possible, in order that, if any danger threatened, they might be able to unite speedily for the general defense. This arrangement gave much satisfaction to the settlers; but in the year 1627 they were placed in a still more comfortable and independent position. They were, by their charter, lords of all the neighboring land for a circle of more than one hundred miles. That portion of their territory, therefore, which was most contiguous to the town, was divided into portions of twenty acres, five long on the side next the coast, and four broad; and to each citizen one of these portions was assigned, with the liberty of purchasing another for his wife, and also one for every child who resided with him. To every six of these pieces were allotted a cow, two goats, and a few pigs; so that each settler became possessed of a little farm of his own, and a small herd of cattle to stock it with: and peace and plenty at length seemed to smile on the hardy and long- enduring settlers.

Meanwhile, the colony of Massachusetts, which had been founded in the year 1624, increased rapidly. It was first planted at Nantasket, a deserted village of the Indians, at the entrance of the Bay of Massachusetts, where the Plymouth settlers had previously erected a few houses, for the convenience of carrying on their trade with the neighboring tribes. Another settlement had been formed, two years later, at Naumkeak, a tongue of land of remarkable fertility, where also a deserted Indian village was found, which formed the commencement of the town afterwards called Salem; and which had become — at the period we have now arrived at in our story — a place of some importance. It was founded by a man of much zeal end enthusiasm, of the name of Endicott; who was one of the original possessors of the patent granted to several gentlemen of Dorsetshire, for the land in Massachusetts Bay, extending from the Merrimak to the Charles River, from north to south; but stretching to an indefinite distance westward, even over the unexplored regions between the boisterous Atlantic, and the Silent Sea, as the Pacific has been very aptly and beautifully designated.

Endicott had been invested, by the society to which he belonged in England, with the government of the whole district of Massachusetts; and he soon found himself called on to exercise his authority for the suppression of the disturbances excited by the settlers of Quincy. This place was inhabited by a set of low and immoral men, one of whom, named Thomas Morton, had come over in the wild and dissolute train sent out by Weston several years previously. He was a man of some talent, but of very contemptible character: and had attached himself to the retinue of Captain Wollaston and his companions, who first settled at Quincy, and gave it the name of Mount Wollaston. He afterwards, with his friends, removed to Virginia, leaving some of his servants and an overseer to manage the plantation during his absence. But, no sooner was Morton relieved of the presence of those who had hitherto kept him in some restraint, than he roused the servants to a complete mutiny, which ended in their driving the overseer from the plantation, and indulging in every kind of excess. They even had the boldness and the dishonesty to sell the land which had been left in their charge by the lawful possessors, to the Indians; and to obtain fresh estates, which they claimed as their own. And, having thus established a sort of lawless independence, they passed their time in drinking and wild revelry. On the first of May, they erected a may-pole, in old-English fashion; but, not contented with celebrating that day of spring-time and flowers with innocent pastimes, they hung the pole with verses of an immoral and impious character, and, inviting the ignorant heathen to share in their festivities, they abandoned themselves to drunkenness and profligacy.

The horror and indignation of the severe Puritans of New Plymouth at this outbreak of licentiousness, was great indeed. In their eyes almost every amusement was looked upon as a sin; and the most innocent village dance round a maypole was regarded as nearly allied to the heathenish games in honor of the Goddess Flora. The conduct, therefore, of the disorderly settlers of Quincy filled them with shame and grief; and they felt humbled, as well as indignant, when they reflected on the discredit which such proceedings must necessarily bring on the Christian profession, and the British name. Nor was this all: it was not merely discredit that they had to fear. The insane and profligate conduct of Morton threatened to bring on them eventually, as well as on all the emigrants, evils of a more personal kind. For, when Morton and his wild associates found their means of self-gratification again running short, they had the folly to part with arms and ammunition to the Indians, and to teach them how to use them; thus giving them the power of not only resisting the authority of the English, but also of effectually attacking them whenever any subjects of dispute should arise between them and the pale-faced invaders.

Most joyfully the natives took advantage of this impolitic weakness; and so eagerly did they purchase the coveted firearms of their rivals, that Morton sent to England for a fresh supply of the dangerous merchandise. Such conduct was quite sufficient to arouse the fears and the vigilance of every other colony of New England; and the chief inhabitants of the various plantations agreed to request the interference of their brethren of New Plymouth, as being the oldest and most powerful settlement, in order to bring the offenders to their senses. Bradford willingly listened to their petition; for he desired nothing more earnestly than to have an opportunity of openly manifesting to his countrymen, and to the Indians, how greatly opposed he and his people were to the proceedings of Morton's gang. He had also a very sufficient pretext for such interference, as he could bring forward the positive command of his sovereign, that no arms of any kind should be given or sold to the natives.

He resolved, however, before he had recourse to harsher measures, to try and bring Morton and his wild crew to a better mode of life, by friendly and persuasive messages. But these only excited the contempt and derision of the ruffian; and the doughty warrior, Miles Standish, was therefore dispatched, with a band of his veteran followers, to seize on the desperadoes. They came upon them when they were in the midst of their drunken revelry, and, after a fierce struggle, succeeded in making them all prisoners, and conveying them safely to Plymouth. From thence Morton was sent, by the first opportunity, to England, to be tried by the High Council, who, however, did not take any active measures against him or his followers. Many of the latter escaped, and continued their disorderly life, until they were checked by the vigorous proceedings of Endicott, who severely reprimanded them, and cut down the may-pole which had given rise to so much offence, and he named the hill on which the notorious plantation was situated, 'Mount Dagon,' in memory of the profane doings of its inhabitants.

The coast of Massachusetts Bay was now studded with plantations, and with rising towns and villages. The stream of emigration continued to increase; and the wealth and prosperity of the colonies in general kept pace with the addition to their numbers, and with their extended trade with foreign colonies and with the mother-country. Boston had become a place of some note, and seemed to be regarded as the seat of commerce for the Massachusetts district, as well as the center of the civil government. Most of the families of the neighboring plantations, especially of Charlestown, removed to Boston; and ere long it was deemed expedient to found a regular church there, and the building of a house of God was commenced. Winthrop, the governor, also exerted himself in the erection of a fortress, to repel the dreaded attacks of the Indians; but he soon perceived that this was a needless precaution, for all the neighboring tribes readily offered their friendship, and even their submission; and, as the strength of the colony daily increased, he found that he had less and less to fear from the Indians. The Sagamore of Sawgus, in the vicinity of Boston, remained the steady friend of the English until his death; and Chickatabot, Sachem of Neponset, one of the neighboring Chiefs of the Massachusetts, frequently visited the rising town of Boston. On one of these occasions he excited the mirth of the

Governor and his suite, by requesting to be allowed to purchase his fall-dress coat, to which he had taken a great fancy.

To this strange and original request, the Governor courteously replied that it was not the custom of the English Sagamores to dispose of their raiment in that manner; but he consoled the disappointed Chieftain by sending for his tailor, and ordering him to measure Chickatabot for a full suit. This treasure the Sachem carried away with him three days afterwards, to astonish the eyes of his subjects in his native wilds; and his loyalty towards the English was greatly strengthened by so handsome and judicious a present.

Cundincus, also, the Chief of the powerful and much dreaded Narragansetts, sent his son with a friendly greeting to the new settlers of Boston; and, in the following year, his nephew and co-ruler, Miantonomo, came on a visit to the Governor. He was for some days an inmate of Winthrop's house; and it is recorded that he not only conducted himself with the greatest decorum, but that be also sat patiently to listen to a sermon of an hour and a half's duration, of which, of course, he scarcely comprehended one word.

Governor Winthrop followed the good example that had already been set by both Carver and Bradford at New Plymouth, in regard to all dealings with the natives. He always maintained their rights with the most strict and impartial justice; and if any Englishman committed an injury against the property of an Indian, he compelled him to replace it—in some cases even to twice the value of the article in question.

The new settlers had always been on very friendly terms with the elder colony of Plymouth; and visits were frequently exchanged between the Governors and others of the inhabitants, which, though performed with much difficulty and even danger, were a source of mutual pleasure to the two bands of British emigrants. If the men of Plymouth regarded with some feeling of jealous anxiety the growing power and greatness of their rival, it was but natural. Nevertheless, no differences of any importance arose between the colonies on the subject of civil superiority. It was on spiritual matters that they sometimes disagreed; and on these points the Plymouthers watched the newcomers with suspicious sensitiveness, and resolved to maintain their dearly- purchased based rights to religious freedom, against any pretensions that might be made by the church of Boston.

This latter community was frequently subject to divisions and disputes, on those points of faith and discipline that each party regarded as all-important, but on the carrying out of which they could not agree; and a certain spirit of intolerance had already begun to show itself among them, which, in later times, ripened into actual cruelty and persecution.

The first instance of any display of this unchristian spirit with which our narrative is concerned, was the treatment of a young clergyman, named Roger Williams, who came over to New England several years after the emigration of the Pilgrim Fathers, when the renewed oppression of the Puritan ministers, by the English bishops, drove many of their number to seek a refuge in America. In the same year also arrived John Elliott, a man whose name is deservedly remembered and respected in New England, as standing conspicuous for zeal and virtue. So great and so successful were his labors among the native heathen, and so eminent were his piety and his self-denying charity, that he has been well named the *'Prince of Missionaries'* and 'the Great Apostle of the Indians.'

The arrival of these holy and zealous — though somewhat eccentric — men, and of several others equally resolved to maintain the freedom of their religious views and practices, tended greatly to strengthen and establish the emigrants; and also added considerably to their comfort, as every settlement became provided with regular and authorized ministers of the gospel, and could enjoy all those religious privileges from which they had been so long debarred. But it must also be confessed that it became the source of much dissension and party feeling, and led to that display of bigotry and intolerance that eventually disgraced the Christian profession of the men of Massachusetts.[*]

[Footnote: The cruel fate of Mary Dyer, the Quaker, who was condemned to death by Governor Endicott, at Boston, is a lamentable instance of the narrow-minded and cruel policy of the rulers of that community. She was banished from the state, but 'felt a call' to return and rebuke the austerity of the men of Boston, and reprove them for their spiritual pride. She was accompanied by two friends, William Robinson and Marmaduke Stevenson, and all three were seized, imprisoned, and, after a summary trial, were sent to the gallows. The two men were executed; but at the moment when Mary Dyer was standing, calm and resigned, with the rope around her neck, expecting to be launched into eternity, a reprieve arrived, and the victim was released. But it was only for a little time. She was again banished; and again returned, as if to seek her fate. A second trial took place, and she was again condemned. Her husband, who knew not of her return to Boston until it was too late, appeared before the magistrates, and pleaded with all the eloquence of affection and anguish. But he wept and prayed in vain. His young and lovely wife was led to the scaffold, where she met her fate with a pious and even cheerful resignation; but her blood has left a dark stain on the history of the Church of Boston, that no time will ever efface. This dreadful event occurred about forty years after that period of which we are now treating.]

Roger Williams was a man comparatively unknown in his own country, but he was destined to exercise considerable influence in the land of his adoption, by his peculiar views of religious freedom which went far beyond those of the generality of his fellow Puritans. He desired to extend to others that liberty of conscience which he claimed as his own privilege, and for the attainment of which he had become a wanderer and an exile. But he soon found that many of his countrymen had forgotten in America the principles of spiritual freedom, for which they had so nobly contended in England, and were ready to employ against those who differed from them, the same 'carnal weapons' that had already driven them from their mother-country. His sufferings were indeed light, in comparison of those which were afterwards inflicted on the miserable Quakers by the government of Massachusetts; but still they were hard for flesh and blood to bear, and galling to a free spirit to receive from those who boasted of their own love of freedom.

Roger Williams was not more than thirty-two years of age when he arrived in New England. He had boldly separated himself from all communion with the high church of his native country; and, before he would attach himself to the Church of Boston, he demanded from its members a similar declaration of independence. The fathers of the colony were, however, by no means prepared to take so decided a step, which would lay them open to the attacks of the English hierarchy; and although a few years afterwards, when they could do it with less risk of punishment, they abjured all connection with the Church of England, yet they dared not at present give any countenance to such individual boldness as that which Williams had manifested. His uncompromising principles were, however, in unison with those of the Church of Salem; and he was invited by that community to be their teacher, as an assistant to their pastor, Skelton, whose health was then declining. The rulers of Boston were extremely indignant at this act of independence on the part of the Salemers; and they addressed to them a remonstrance, desiring them to take no such steps without the concurrence of the government of the state of Massachusetts. But the men of Salem did not withdraw their invitation, which was accepted by Roger Williams; and in a short time his piety, his eloquence, and the kind courtesy of his manners, gained for him the esteem and affection of the whole community.

He was not, however, permitted to remain in peace in his new home. The suspicion and ill-will of the Boston government followed him to Salem, and so greatly embittered his life, and interrupted his labors, that he found it expedient to withdraw to Plymouth, where he found employment as assistant to the regular pastor, Ralph Smith. His preaching caused great excitement in New Plymouth, from the fervor of his eloquence, and the freedom of his opinions, which aroused the sympathy of many of the Pilgrim Fathers. Governor Bradford was much interested by the young and enthusiastic minister; and he described him in his journal as 'a man full of the fear of God, and of zeal, but very unsettled in judgement.' Certainly, his opinions were peculiar, and his spirit bold and defying, to a degree that rather shocked and astonished the sober, severe, and exclusive men of Plymouth; but his sincere piety caused him to be respected, even by those who shrank from going such lengths as he did; and his engaging manners won the affection of all who were admitted to his intimacy.

One cause of the anger of the rulers of Boston against this energetic young man was an essay which he wrote and addressed to the Governor of Plymouth, in which he stated his conviction that 'the King of England had no right whatever to give away these lands on which they had settled; but that they belonged exclusively to the natives, and must be bought in by auction from them.' No one who entertains a sense of justice will now be disposed to object to this opinion; but it gave great offence to the government of Boston, and he was summoned before the general court, to answer to Governor Winthrop for having promulgated such notions. He did not, however, attempt to defend them, but good-humoredly declared that they were privately addressed to Bradford, who, with tin chief men of Plymouth, agreed with him in all the material points of his essay, and he offend to burn it if it had given offence at Boston. The subject was then dropped, and Williams returned to Plymouth, where he continued to reside for a considerable time.

During that period, he not only gained many friends among the inhabitants, but he also, by a constant intercourse with the Wampanoges and other neighboring tribes, obtained a considerable knowledge of their language and manners, and secured their veneration and love. This, as we shall have occasion to observe, proved afterwards of the greatest advantage to him.

But his own restless spirit was not satisfied with quietly discharging the duties of his office, and enjoying the society of his own countrymen and their Indian allies. Again he drew upon himself the wrath of the Boston Church, by openly stating his conviction that no civil government had a right to punish any individual for a breach of the Sabbath, or for any offence against either of the four commandments, or the first table. He maintained that these points should be left to the conscience alone; or, in the case of those who had agreed to a church covenant, to the authorities of the church.

The civil magistrates he considered as only empowered to punish such violations of the law as interfered with the public peace. This unheard-of heresy against the principles by which the Bostoners were governed, was received with amazement and indignation: and, although they could not take any immediate measures to testify their displeasure, and to punish the offender, yet he thenceforth became the object of hatred and suspicion to the rulers, and they only waited for a fitting opportunity of openly manifesting it.

Williams was aware of the feeling entertained towards him by the government of Massachusetts, but he was not thereby deterred from expressing his opinions in New Plymouth; and so great was his attachment to the people of Salem, who had first afforded him a home, that he would again have ventured thither, had he not been detained by his new friends. They were both numerous and sincere: and, among them, none were more attached to him than the Maitland family, who agreed with him in most of his religious and political opinions, and valued his society on account of his unaffected piety, and the various powers and accomplishments of his mind. Possibly, it was the attraction that Roger Williams found in this family that caused him so long to turn a deaf ear to the repeated solicitations of his old friends at Salem, that he would again take up his abode among them. Certainly, it was not fear of the rulers of Boston that kept his undaunted spirit in a district over which they had no authority; neither was it altogether the harmony that subsisted between his views and those of the hospitable Plymouthers. On many points they agreed, but not on all; and those who differed from him feared that his continued residence among them might excite a party spirit, and mar that peace which had hitherto reigned in their community.

Still Roger Williams did continue to dwell at New Plymouth; and still his visits to the house of Maitland became more and more frequent.[*]

[Footnote: A few liberties are taken with the private life of this interesting character, in order to connect him more closely with the events of the narrative. But all the incidents which can be regarded as important are strictly historical, although the date and order of them may be slightly altered.]

CHAPTER XIX

My child, my child, thou leav'st me!—I shall hear
The gentle voice no more that blest mine ear
With its first utterance I shall miss the sound
Of thy light step, amidst the flowers around;
And thy soft breathing hymn at twilight's close;
And thy good night, at parting for repose!
——Yet blessings with thee go!
Love guard thee, gentlest! and the exile's woe
From thy young heart be far!' HEMANS.

At the period when Roger Williams was induced to seek a home among the Pilgrim Fathers of New Plymouth, Edith Maitland had attained to womanhood. She was not beautiful, strictly speaking, but she was possessed of that 'something than beauty dearer,'—that nameless and indescribable charm that is sometimes seen to surround a person whose form and features would not satisfy the critical eye of an artist. It was Edith's character which looked out from her clear hazel eye, and won the interest and the affection of all who knew her. Gentle and affectionate in disposition, but at the same time, firm, enduring, and fall of energy, she combined the characteristic qualities of both her parents, and added to them an originality all her own. Her education, in the common acceptation of the term, had necessarily been both desultory and imperfect; and yet, under its influence, the mind and character of Edith had strengthened and matured in no common degree. The very circumstances by which she was surrounded had educated her; and sorrow—deep, abiding sorrow, for the loss of both her much-loved brothers—had taught her to look on life in a different point of view, and with different expectations from those with which it is usually regarded by the young. Her mother had watched her opening mind and disposition with much care and anxiety: but she had not sought to check its interesting peculiarity, or to control the wild exuberance of thought and feeling that were occasionally manifested by her intelligent and engaging child. As she grew older, she became more and more the companion of Helen, who studied her character attentively: and, if we be allowed such a figure of speech, wisely endeavored to train it in a right direction, rather than to prune it to any conventional form. Thus a perfect confidence was established, and ever subsisted between the mother and daughter; and the natural thoughtfulness of spirit, and energy of purpose, that belonged to Edith, were unchecked, and she was allowed to possess an individuality of character that is, unhappily, too often repressed and destroyed in these present days of high civilization and uniformity of education.

The courteous manners which both Helen and her husband had acquired in early life—when they dwelt in comparative affluence in England—were inherited by their daughter in full measure; and her whole manner and conduct were marked by a refinement and elegance that seemed little in keeping with the life of extreme simplicity, and even of hardship, that she had experienced from her early childhood. While her brothers were spared to her, she was their constant companion and playfellow; and except when her mother required her attendance, either as her pupil or her assistant in domestic occupations, she spent the greatest part of the day in rambling with them on the sea-shore, or through the adjacent woods, or else in the active and tasteful cultivation of their garden. And when successive calamities deprived her of these cherished objects of her early affection, she still continued to wander to the spots where they had played and conversed together, under the guardianship of the faithful Fingal; and, with no companion but the powerful and sagacious animal, she was even permitted to ramble through the woods as far as the Wampanoge village, and divert her sorrowful thoughts in the society of Apannow, and her lively little son Nepea.

But after the sad day when Edith wept on the lifeless body of her favorite Fingal, and saw him laid in the grave that was dug for him beneath the great tulip-tree, she seemed to concentrate her affections on the bower that Henrich had erected, and the plants that he and Ludovico had transplanted from the forest to cover its trellised walls, and to decorate the garden that surrounded it. Many of these were again removed, and planted on Fingal's grave; and there—on a seat that her brother had constructedwould Edith sit, hour after hour, either buried in contemplations of the past and the future, or else devouring with avidity the few books that her parents possessed, or that she could procure from their friends and neighbors. She formed no intimacy with any of her own young countrywomen. They were too unlike herself—they had generally known no sorrow: or, if it had fallen on them, its strokes had not made a like impression on their characters; and Edith could find no consolation or pleasure in their society. So she lived alone with her own spirit, and indulged her own high aspirations; and none but Helen was the confidant of any of her thoughts and imaginings. Many of them she kept within her own breast, for she felt that it would distress her mother to know how little charm remained to her in life, and how often she looked up into the blue depths of heaven, and wished that she had 'the wings of a dove, and could flee away' from this cold world, 'and be at rest' where Henrich and Ludovico dwelt.

And yet Edith was not unhappy. As she grew up, and became a more equal and rational companion to her parents, the cares and business of life necessarily occupied more of her time and thoughts, and gave her less leisure for solitary meditation; and her daily increasing sense of the duties and responsibilities of a Christian, led her to regard as selfishness that indulgence of her own thoughts and feelings in which she had so much delighted. She was therefore cheerful, and even gay, at home; but she desired no pleasures beyond those that her home afforded, and that were perfectly consistent with the self denying views and principles of her Puritan fellow-countrymen.

In all the doctrines of her sect; Edith was thoroughly well-informed; and to all those that were really scriptural, she gave a sincere and heart-felt assent. But the stern severity of Puritan principles and Puritan bigotry found no response in her gentle nature, and the narrow- minded intolerance of the Boston Church aroused both her contempt and indignation. She was, therefore, quite prepared to regard with interest and favor the free-minded young minister who had made himself obnoxious to their laws end customs, and had sought a refuge among the more liberal and kindly Pilgrims of New Plymouth.

The acquaintance of Roger Williams was soon made by the Maitlands; and, once begun, it quickly ripened into intimacy and friendship. In Rodolph he found a sound and able adviser; in Helen, a kind friend and a well-informed companion; but in Edith he found a kindred spirit to his own—one who could understand and sympathize in his yearnings for freedom of thought and action, and in his strong sense of the injustice of his oppressors. In all their tastes and pursuits they were, likewise, as well agreed as in their religious and social opinions. Edith's passionate love of natural beauty was fully shared by the young refugee; and many an hour passed swiftly away while he instructed his quick and willing scholar in the mysteries of sketching, in which pleasant art he was himself a proficient. Edith loved music also, and frequently accompanied her own rich voice with the simple notes of the mandolin, while she sang the old songs of her fatherland.

Hitherto, her mother had been her only instructor in this most refined and refining of all human pleasures; but now she found an able and very ready teacher in Roger Williams: and it was a matter of astonishment to her father when he observed the rapid progress she made both in the science and the practice of music, from the time the interesting stranger undertook to give her lessons. His deep, manly voice harmonized perfectly with her sweet tones; and they often brought tears to the eyes of Helen, and called forth a sigh from the breast of Rodolph, as they sang together some ancient English ballad, or united their voices in the chants and anthems that were dear to the hearts of the exiles, and recalled days of youth and happiness long passed away, and never to return.

Edith's bower was the usual scene of these domestic concerts; and there the long, sweet summer evenings glided away in happiness, that the 'queen of that bower ' — as Henrich had named her — had never known since the last evening that she spent there with her brother. She began to wonder why she had hitherto associated none but melancholy ideas with the lovely spot; and to find that it was possible to feel even gay and light-hearted while surrounded by Henrich's flowers, and looking on Fingal's grave. How strange it seemed — and yet, how pleasant! A new existence seemed opening before Edith's soul; and life no longer appeared a dreary pilgrimage, which duty alone could render interesting. The powers of her mind also received a fresh impulse from the society of the cultivated Englishman, and was drawn out in a manner as agreeable as it was new. Roger had brought from his native land a collection of books, which, though small in number, seemed to Edith a perfect library; and all were offered for her perusal. Several of them were, of course, on controversial and doctrinal subjects; and these she was able to understand and to appreciate: but among these graver and more abstruse treatises, were some of a more attractive nature — some volumes of foreign travel, and ancient legends, and heart-stirring poetry, in which the soul of Edith reveled, as in a garden of new and fragrant flowers.

It was a fresh, and a very rich enjoyment to one who had known so few literary pleasures, to pore over these volumes, and find her own vivid thoughts and wild imaginings set before her in all the captivating colors of poetry and fiction; or to follow the wanderings of travelers through the civilized and enlightened countries of the old continent, and learn from books those manners and customs of refined life, which, in all human probability, it would never be her lot to witness. But this enjoyment was more than doubled when Roger took the book, and — as he often did — read to her and her mother while they sat at their work in Edith's bower in the heat of the day; and if the younger listener did occasionally pause in her occupation, and forget to ply her needle while she looked up at the fine expressive countenance of the reader, she may be pardoned; for the voice and the expression were in such perfect unison, that the one added greatly to the effect of the other.

Perhaps these days of peaceful intercourse, and growing, but unacknowledged, affection, were among the happiest of Edith's checkered life: certain it is that, in after days of trial and difficulty, she looked back upon them as on some green and sunny spot in the varied field of memory.

But they could not last for ever. Days and weeks passed by, and Edith was too happy in the present to occupy herself much about the future. But her parents thought of it for her; and Roger thought of it for her, and for himself. Her graceful manners and appearance had attracted him on his first acquaintance with her, and the favorable impression had been strengthened from day to day, as he acquired a more intimate knowledge of her thoughtful character and amiable temper: and it was not long ere he felt that his future happiness in life depended on her returning those sentiments with which she had inspired him.

Had he been possessed of much vanity, he would not long have entertained any doubt on this interesting point; for Edith was too open and ingenuous, and too little in the habit of disguising her feelings, to pretend an indifference that her heart soon denied. But the very admiration and respect with which she inspired Roger prevented him from 'laying the flattering unction to his soul'; and caused him, for some time, to suppose that the very evident pleasure she felt in his society arose from the solitary life she had hitherto led, and the natural enjoyment of an intelligent mind in conversing with one who could enter into her feelings and tastes, and impart some fresh ideas to give food to her thoughts and imagination.

Helen, however, was not under this misconception with regard to her daughter's feelings, and she felt much anxiety as to the result of her acquaintance with the young clergyman. The remarkable transparency of Edith's character rendered it easy for a parent's eye to discover the deep impression that Roger's fascinating manners, and rare accomplishments, had made both on her fancy and her heart; and it was equally easy to perceive that his affections were entirely gained, and that he was not a man to draw back in this, or any other pursuit in which his feelings were deeply engaged. There was a simple earnestness of manner in every thing that he said or did that irresistibly won both confidence and love; and Helen and her husband entertained not the slightest doubt of the sincerity of his attachment to their child, or of his full intention to offer his hand to her, as soon as he could feel any certainty of its being accepted. Neither did they doubt his power to make her happy; for it was evident that their tastes and dispositions were admirably suited, and their characters marked to a great degree by the same peculiarities. But it was these very peculiarities in which they so well agreed, and which each would probably strengthen and confirm in the other, that gave rise to the anxious thoughts that dwelt in Helen's mind, and which she communicated to Rudolph.

Roger Williams was already a marked man, and an object of suspicion and displeasure to the rising power of Boston. Already he had been compelled to retire before the persecuting spirit of the Boston Church, and to seek shelter in the rival and more charitable colony, where his peculiar opinions were tolerated, even if they were not approved. But the Maitlands knew that his position at New Plymouth did not satisfy the yearnings of his earnest and aspiring soul, and that he felt a strong desire to return to Salem, and minister among those who had been his first friends, and his first congregation. His reason for so bag delaying this measure was very evident; and Edith's parents justly feared that, as soon as the object which now engrossed his whole mind was attained, and he had won their daughter's heart and band, be would take her from her present safe and peaceful home, to share with him the trials and difficulties, and even dangers, which might await him on his return to the state of Massachusetts, where they felt sure he would again proclaim the opinions that had already given so much offence.

This was a reasonable cause for anxiety; but it was not a sufficient ground on which to refuse a connection with such a man as Roger Williams—a man who might, indeed, by his daring freedom of spirit and uncompromising opinions, bring earthly trial on himself and any one whose fate was united to his; but whose lofty piety and steadfast faith must carry with them a spiritual blessing, and gild and cheer the path, however dark and thorny, in which he and his partner should be called to tread.

It was, therefore, with mingled feelings of pain and pleasure that Helen heard from Edith that Roger had, at length, taken courage to declare to her his own feelings, and to ask whether she could return them. Her glowing cheek and glistening eye, as she revealed the interesting fact, would have left her mother in no doubt as to the answer she had returned, even if she had not already guessed her sentiments; and she and Rodolph could but give their consent to her wishes, and ask a blessing on her choice. The joy and gratitude of Roger knew no bounds. Now he felt that life lay all bright and clear before him, and that no outward trials could have power to cloud his path, so long as Edith walked by his side, to divide his sorrows and double his joys.

He employed all his eloquence to persuade Rodolph and Helen to consent to his speedy marriage; for, now that his object in lingering at Plymouth was attained, all his love for his flock at Salem, and his desire once more to dwell among them, returned with added force. He was impatient to resume his spiritual duties where first he had commenced them in New England; and he was eager, also, to present Edith as his bride to the friends who had once so kindly received him, and who now so pressingly invited him to return.

The aspect of affairs in the State of Massachusetts was then peaceable, and no demonstration of enmity towards Roger had lately been made by the Boston rulers; so that Rodolph and Helen had no well-grounded pretext for delaying their daughter's marriage, and her removal to Salem with her husband. The letter of invitation to Roger Williams from that community, also contained such alarming accounts of the rapidly declining health of their pastor, Skelton, that the necessity for the presence of his intended successor could not be denied. With some reluctance the Maitlands, therefore, agreed to an early day for the performance of the simple ceremony that would unite their beloved and only remaining child to one whom they loved and respected, but whose fiery zeal inspired them with doubt and anxiety.

No sooner was the happy day fixed, than Roger hastened to dispatch a trusty messenger to Roxburgh, with a letter to his valued friend and brother minister, Elliot—who was appointed preacher in that town—to entreat him to be present at his marriage, and to honor the ceremony by giving the customary address at its conclusion.

Much to his satisfaction—and that of all the Maitland family—this request was acceded to, and the 'Prince of Missionaries' arrived at New Plymouth, accompanied also by his bride. He was betrothed when he left England, but circumstances had then prevented his intended wife from accompanying him. But as soon as he was settled at Roxburgh, she followed him to the land of his exile, and became his faithful and devoted companion through a long and toilsome life, and his able and efficient helpmate in all his difficulties.

The chief object of this excellent man, in leaving his own country, was not so much to escape the persecution that then awaited the ministers of his sect, as to attempt the conversion of the native heathen. For this pious and disinterested purpose, he abandoned home and kindred, and all that was dear to him, and, at the age of twenty-seven, entered that land of distant promise, to the evangelization of which he had resolved to devote all the powers of his life, and the faculties of his energetic mind. So abstemious and self-denying was he, that his mode of life resembled that of a hermit; and, at the same time, so liberal was he in relieving the wants of others— whether his own countrymen or the red Indians—that, if his wife had not been a careful and clever manager, they must often have been reduced to absolute want. There is an anecdote recorded of him, so characteristic of the self-forgetting spirit of the 'Great Apostle of the Indians,' that it ought not to be omitted here, where we are endeavoring to give a faithful picture of the manners and the principles of the Pilgrim Fathers, and their immediate followers.

The society in England, under whose auspices he had emigrated, allowed him a salary of £50 a year, a great portion of which, as well as of his small private resources, was always dedicated to charitable purposes. It was his custom, when he received his quarterly payment from the treasurer of the colony, to give away a considerable part of it before he reached his home, so that *Dame* Elliot—as she was called—only received a very small sum, inadequate to the necessary expenses of her frugal housekeeping. The paymaster knew the good man's peculiarities, and was aware of the domestic embarrassments that his too-liberal bounty often occasioned. He therefore tied the money up in a handkerchief with so many knots, that he was sure the pastor could never untie them; and gave it to him, saying in jest, 'Now really, reverend sir, you must this time give it all to your worthy spouse. Elliot smiled, and departed: but, before he reached his dwelling, he remembered an afflicted family who stood in need of his assistance and consolation; and, on going to visit them, he found them overwhelmed with unexpected distress. He immediately attempted to open his handkerchief, but all his efforts were unavailing to loosen the complicated knots. 'Well, well,' he said, at last, 'I see it is the will of the Lord that you should have the whole. And, giving them all his wealth, he returned home penniless.

Dame Elliot never showed any displeasure at these improvident acts of her husband. She admired and respected his pious motives, and his beautiful spirit of self-denial: and she only strove the more to limit her expenses, and to make their home cheerful and comfortable with the scanty means she possessed, while she willingly conformed to the life of extreme simplicity which he felt it right to adopt. More than one dish was never allowed to appear on his table, and water was his only beverage. If wine was offered him at the house of a friend, he courteously declined, but never blamed in others the indulgence which he denied to himself. He used to say, 'Wine is a precious, noble thing, and we should thank the Lord for it; but to suit me aright, water should rather be there.'

Such were the Christian pair who came to attend the wedding of Edith and Roger; and to offer their congratulations on the event, and their prayers that it might tend to the present and the eternal happiness of their valued friend and his interesting bride. It could not be otherwise than that Dame Elliot and Edith should form a speedy and a lasting friendship. There was a similarity of feeling, and a difference of character, that rendered them peculiarly agreeable to each other; and made them mutually rejoice in the prospect of future intercourse which the strong regard that subsisted between Elliot and Williams, and the nearness of Salem to Roxburgh, promised to afford them. The young matron was of a much more calm and subdued temperament than her new friend. Her early life and education had been very different from Edith's; and the man on whom she had fixed her affections, and the mode of life to which her marriage had conducted her, had alike tended to promote a quiet composure, and steady regulation of mind, rather than to arouse the enthusiastic feelings and the lively fancies that distinguished Edith's character, and which had proved so irresistible a charm to the fervid soul of Williams. But each of the young women was well adapted to the lot which Providence had assigned them; and each proved a blessing, and a support through life, to their respective partners.

But little preparation was required for the Puritan nuptials that were now about to be celebrated: and little gaiety or display was manifested on the occasion. According to the custom of the sect, the marriage ceremony was performed by Bradford, as the chief civil magistrate, and the personal friend of the family. At that period, marriage was regarded as a mere civil act; and either the magistrate of the place, or a commissary appointed for the purpose, was alone required by law to officiate. If a clergyman chanced to be present, he was generally requested to offer up a prayer, or even to deliver a suitable discourse to the, parties; but this was a matter of choice, and not of necessity, and had no share in the validity of the ceremony. Even the wedding ring had already begun to be regarded by the Plymouthers as a relic of Popish corruption and superstition, and was, in many cases, dispensed with, and some time afterwards formally forbidden. But on this occasion it was retained, at the wish of both Edith and her mother; who were accustomed to regard it as a beautiful, and almost a sacred, symbol of the purity and the duration of the holy tie of marriage.

On the appointed day, the civil rite was duly and solemnly performed by the Governor, in the presence of a few chosen friends, among whom none felt more interest in the future welfare of the young bride than the venerable William Brewster. Although he was not a regular minister, he was invited by Rodolph and Helen to offer up a prayer for the temporal and eternal happiness of their beloved child, and fervently and eloquently the old man complied with their request: and tears of affection and anxiety glistened in his eyes as he concluded his prayer, and added his own heartfelt blessing to that which he had asked from Heaven.

Elliot then delivered a powerful and impressive address to the young married couple, on their social and domestic, as well as their spiritual duties; and a simple, but well-arranged repast at Rodolph's house completed the ceremonies of the day.

It was about this time that the marriage of Henrich and Oriana was celebrated in the distant wilderness, where all the outward circumstances were so different, and where no prescribed forms could be observed, to render the simple ceremony legal or impressive. And, yet, surely it was as sacred and as binding to those who then plighted their faith to each other as if it had been performed with all the rites of civilized life. The vows of Henrich and his Christian bride were made in the presence of that God who instituted marriage, and hollowed it; and they were sanctified by the 'prayer of faith, which rises as freely, and as acceptably, from the wilderness as from the stately cathedral. Had Edith and her much-loved brother known that their earthly fate was thus being decided so nearly at the same period, how would the supplications which they offered for themselves have been mingled with prayers for the happiness of one another!

A brief sojourn in her much-loved home was allowed to Edith after her marriage; and then she gladly, but tearfully, left her parents, to share the fortunes of him who would be more to her than father, or mother, or brother, or sister, could be. The pinnace that belonged to the colony was appointed by the Governor to convey Roger and his bride to Massachusetts Bay, and land them as near as possible to their new home in Salem; and thus Edith was spared the fatigue and difficulty of a long and toilsome journey through the woods and the wilderness by land. She was kindly and joyfully welcomed by her husband's friends and admirers, who were already disposed to regard her with favor, and who soon learnt both to love and respect her for her own many amiable and estimable qualities.

CHAPTER XX

'She was a woman of a steadfast mind,
Tender and deep in her excess of love.'

The life of peace and tranquillity which Roger and his young bride enjoyed in their new home, was not long permitted to be their happy lot. The apprehensions that had been felt by Edith's anxious parents, were but too soon realized; and, notwithstanding all the good advice that he received at Plymouth, and all his own sincere resolutions to avoid, if possible, all future disputes with the elders or the Boston Church, Roger Williams again became the object of their persecuting intolerance.

The fact of his being again invited to Salem to assist the pastor, was regarded as extremely offensive to the government of Boston: but when Shelton died very shortly after Roger's arrival, and he was elected to be the regular minister of the congregation, it was looked upon as a sinful defiance of lawful authority, and one which demanded exemplary punishment. An opportunity for this exercise of power soon occurred. The township of Salem lain claim to a certain disputed piece of land, and addressed a petition to the government of Massachusetts, in which they demanded to be put in possession of it. But in consequence of the recent act of the community with regard to Roger Williams's election, the claim was unjustly rejected. The Salemers then, by the advice of their pastor, wrote to all the other churches in the Bay, and requested them to unite in a remonstrance to the government. This act was in perfect accordance with the spirit of the puritanical principles, which distinctly separated the church from the state; and it ought not, therefore, to have given offence to any one. But their practice differed greatly from their theory; and the feeling against Williams was so strong that all the churches — the elders of which were opposed to his opinions — now took part with the government of Boston against him.

This treatment so irritated the warm feelings of Williams, and so keenly wounded his sense of justice and love of liberty, that he required the Church of Salem to renounce all connection with the other congregations; and even went so far as to refuse all intercourse with his own church until this separation was agreed to. But strongly as the Salemers were attached to their pastor, they could not consent to so decisive a measure as he demanded; and, being vexed and dispirited by the general disapprobation which their conduct had excited in the rest of the colony, the greatest part of the congregation fell away from him.

This desertion grieved the heart of the zealous minister but it did not discourage him, or subdue his determined spirit. He began to hold spiritual meetings at his own house, which were attended by those members of the church who fully concurred in his views, and who considered that he had been treated with injustice. This proceeding naturally aroused a strong party spirit in the town, and even threatened to produce a permanent division in the church, as the followers of Williams held themselves entirely aloof from the rest of the congregation.

Deeply did Edith lament this unhappy state of affairs. Her devotion to her noble-minded husband, and the natural tendency of her own mind, led her to sympathize entirely in his opinions and feelings; and her strong sense of right and wrong caused her to condemn the injustice of the government, and the weak, truckling spirit of the sister-churches. But her judgement was more calm and dispassionate than that of Roger, and her temper far less excitable. She therefore saw the impropriety, as well as the danger, of, causing a schism in the church; and she used all her powerful influence to induce her husband to give up these irregular assemblies; and, without compromising his own opinions, to endeavor to ward off the enmity of the men of Boston.

She earnestly besought him again to leave the Congregation of Salem — the greater portion of which had already deserted him and his cause — and to return to Plymouth, where a safe and a happy home might yet be afforded to them, and where no persecution for conscience' sake, need be feared. But all her arguments and her persuasions were alike ineffectual. On this one point she found her Roger firm and inflexible — for on this point he felt that his honor and his conscience were both concerned; and, even for Edith's sake; he could not act contrary to their dictates. He knew that danger hung over his head; and, though he would not shrink from it himself, he besought her to seek a temporary refuge with her parents, and remain at Plymouth until the threatened storm had blown over. But it was now Ediths turn to show herself firm and decided; and so clearly did Roger perceive that separation would be to her a far greater trial than any other that could befall her in his company, that he forbore to urge a measure that it wrung his own heart to propose.

At length the boding storm began to break over his head. For all his supposed offences he was again summoned before the General Assembly at Boston; and, in fear and anxiety, Edith saw him depart. She knew full well that he would never renounce, or even soften down, his opinions, through any fear of man; and she did not, for a moment, desire that he should thus lower himself in her estimation and his own. But she also knew the bitterness of the enmity felt towards him by the authorities at Boston, and she could not repress her apprehensions of its consequences.

As she anticipated, Roger refused to acknowledge himself guilty of an offence against the church or state; nor would he even yield one point of his religious or political opinions, during a long disputation with the celebrated pastor Hooker. He was, therefore, declared contumacious by the government: and, with the assent of all the assembled clergy, except his friend Elliot, he was banished from the territory of Massachusetts.

Six weeks were allowed him by the General Assembly to make his preparations, and remove beyond the boundary of their dominions: but as this term would have brought the time of his banishment to the winter season, when such a journey would have been impracticable, he was afterwards permitted to remain at Salem until the spring.

With great apparent unconcern he returned to his home, where his fond and admiring wife welcomed him with joy, and strengthened his spirit by the cheerful manner in which she received the news of their sentence of banishment. She had felt an undefined dread of something much more hard to bear—of something which might possibly separate her husband from her: but banishment *with him* was only a change of home, and, let their lot be cast where it might, she could be happy. Indeed, she entertained a hope that. Roger would consent to remove to Plymouth, and take up his abode there, which would have, given her extreme satisfaction. But she soon found that this hope could not be accomplished; for her enthusiastic husband had formed a design of founding a church of his own, and of being entirely independent of all government in spiritual matters. In order to carry out this purpose, he daringly continued to hold the obnoxious assemblies in his own house, and to instill his opinions into the minds of the many young and zealous friends who gathered around him. These meetings were even more numerously attended after his return from Boston than they were before he was summoned to the bar of the General Assembly; for persecution and injustice naturally recoil on the perpetrators of it, and the victim of such harsh measures is sure to gain friends and supporters among the warm-hearted and the generous.

A report of these proceedings was carried to Boston, and also a rumor of Williams's supposed plan for founding an independent church and settlement in Narragansett Bay. It was even declared that some of his friends had already gone off to the south, and were seeking, a fitting spot on which to commence building.

This information roused the fears, as well as the wrath, of the government. The eloquence and abilities of Williams were well known to the rulers, and they dreaded the influence that he would inevitably exercise over the neighboring churches, if he established himself and his followers in a district so contiguous to their own. They, therefore, resolved to employ still more harsh and stringent measures than had yet been attempted, in order to put a stop to his disorderly proceedings, and prevent the further dissemination of his opinions. He was, accordingly, once more summoned to the chief town; and, had he obeyed the summons, he was to have been forcibly conveyed on board a vessel then in the harbor, and sent off to England as a rebel and schismatic, unworthy to dwell in the new settlement.

When the summons arrived at Salem, Roger was ill, having caught a fever from some members of his flock on whom he had been attending; and he therefore replied, with truth, that it would endanger his life to attempt the journey to Boston. His serious indisposition had occasioned to Edith much anxiety and alarm; but now she was made to feel how often those events which we regard as misfortunes are really 'blessings in disguise'; and how frequently our merciful and all-seeing Father renders them the means of our preservation from far greater evils. It would be well if the conviction of this blessed truth were constantly present to our minds. How many anxious cares would it disperse or soothe, and how many thanksgivings would it call forth.

Edith felt its truth, and its consolation, as she sat by the side of her husband's couch, and wrote, from his dictation, the reply that saved him from immediate compliance with the dreaded summons. Nothing would have induced Roger to plead illness as an excuse for disobedience unless it had actually existed: and his fearless spirit would probably have led him into the snare that was laid for him. Edith knew this secret danger; for Governor Winthrop, who had seen and admired her on one of his visits to Plymouth, and who now kindly sympathized in her feelings, had sent her a private note by the messenger, in which he warned her of the danger that waited Williams at Boston, and desired her, by some means, to prevent his appearing before the General Assembly. Winthrop highly disapproved of the young minister's bold and independent conduct; but he shrunk from so cruel an act as was resolved on by his council. He did not, however, choose to declare his more lenient judgement; and he adopted the plan of informing Roger's wife of the fate that was designed for him, and leaving it to her judgement and affection to take the proper measures to avert it.

It was not until after the departure of the messenger, that Edith told her husband of Winthrop's kind interference, and showed him his note. The indignation of Williams at such a flagrant disregard of all common justice was so great, that Edith feared it would bring on an accession of the fever. It, however, acted in a perfectly contrary manner. He slept well that night, and the following morning declared his intention of setting off immediately to Boston, and there accusing the General Assembly of their unlawful intention, and daring them to put it into execution.

'I will upbraid them with their injustice, and charge them with their purposed crime!' he exclaimed; and his fine eyes flashed with excitement, that almost made Edith fear that the fever had affected his mind. 'I will appeal to God and man against their lawless cruelty,' he continued; 'and rouse the whole colony to defend my right to liberty of thought and action.'

Oh, Roger!' cried his wife—and she caught his burning hand, and pressed it to her throbbing heart—'cease such wild and desperate words! Would you drive me to distraction, by thus throwing yourself into the power of your bitter and relentless enemies? Who in Boston would stand up to defend your cause? Who could deliver you from the evil intentions of these cruel men? It is true that the Governor has shown himself your friend—I should rather say, my friend—by giving me this secret information; but he would not openly espouse your cause, or resist the will of the Assembly. Why, then, should you spurn from you the means of safety that have been so mercifully afforded, and tempt Providence to leave you to your fate'?

'Edith,' he replied—and the bright flush faded from his cheek, and the fire in his eye died away, and he sank again upon his couch—'Edith, you have subdued my spirit; or perhaps,' he added, smiling up in her face, 'weakness has subdued it. I feel that I have no strength to accomplish what I desire, and to show my persecutors that liberty of thought and feeling is my birthright, and that I will never relinquish the privilege. I must, therefore, submit to the will of One who is wiser and mightier than I am; and believe me, my Edith,' he continued— as he saw the tears falling from her gentle eyes—'believe me, I do to with perfect contentment now. The passion—the sinful passion—that stirred me so mightily just now, is gone; and I feel the goodness of my God in holding me back from the rash act I contemplated, and from rushing upon dangers that I might indeed defy, but could not hope to conquer. I will be calm, my love; and you shall devise some means for my escape. I feel assured that still more violent measures will be adopted by the Assembly to get me into their power; and now that I can quietly reflect on the consequences of such an event, I am aware that they would, probably, be our violent and indefinite separation. I could not bear that, Edith; though I believe that I could bear much to vindicate my honor.'

How changed was Roger's countenance now! All passion—all excitement— was gone; and the natural sweetness of his disposition, and tenderness of his heart, resumed their interrupted influence over his whole manner and expression. Edith thought she had never either admired or loved him so much as at this moment, when he had conquered his impetuous feelings, and yielded his fiery impulse to show a bold resentment of injury, to her influence and persuasions.

Heaven bless you, my own Roger!' she exclaimed, 'and reward your better resolution, by granting us many future years of united happiness. But now we must think of the present, and provide for its emergencies. I see clearly that there is now no safety for you in Salem, and that a speedy flight can alone ensure your liberty. You have made a great sacrifice for my sake; and I will also make one for yours. I will not even ask to fly with you, for I could only be an encumbrance to you at this inclement season of the year, and my presence here may be of use to you. My heart rebels while I say it, Roger; but you must go alone, and use every exertion to reach Plymouth as speedily as possible. When you are safe beneath my father's roof, then will be time enough to think of me. I feel no doubt that Governor Bradford will afford you every assistance in his power; and, probably, will again allow the vessel that brought us here in brighter days, to convey me once more to you and to happiness.'

Edith had tried to speak with steadiness and composure; and, so far, she had succeeded tolerably well. But when she realized to herself the time that must elapse before she could rejoin her husband, and all the dangers and privations that might await him in the interval, her calmness quite gave way, and she burst into tears of uncontrollable agony.

Roger strove to cheer her, and to point to the happy future that he trusted was in store for them—if not on earth, yet assuredly in a better world, where faithful hearts will never know the misery of parting. But it was not until he had knelt with her in prayer, and had humbly asked to meet the coming trial, and to be sanctified by it, that her tears ceased to flow, and a smile of hope and resignation illumined her interesting countenance.

'I must act now, Roger,' she said, in a cheerful voice, as she rose from her knees. 'Our time is short; and I must make such arrangements for your comfort during your journey as are in my power. All other things that are needful to you I will endeavor to send by sea to Plymouth; or, if no opportunity occurs during the winter, you must have patience until I can convey them myself.

Her voice again trembled; and unbidden tears again rose to her eyes. But she sought relief in occupation; and on the day after the morrow, when Roger was to commence his toilsome journey at break of day, his knapsack was ready, and stored with everything that would be most requisite to his comfort.

The moment of parting came; but we will not describe it. It was borne by Edith as a devoted Christian wife can bear anything that is necessary for the safety and welfare of her husband. But when he was gone, and her swimming eyes could no longer see his beloved form, or catch his last signal of farewell, the whole desolation of her own position burst upon her: and Edith was, for a time, bowed down with grief. She felt herself alone in the world, and she shrank from seeking comfort or sympathy from any human being who was then near her. But friends whom she could not then expect to see were near, and the wounded heart found a balm and a consolation beyond its hopes.

The very evening after Roger's departure, Edith's spirit was cheered by the arrival of Elliot and his wife at her now dreary home. O, how she welcomed them! and how deeply they sympathized in her distress and anxiety! They had heard of the last summons that had been sent from the General Assembly; and had hastened to Salem, in spite of the severity of the weather to offer any assistance or counsel that might be needed by either Roger or Edith. They rejoiced, with much thankfulness, when they heard of his having escaped the cruel vengeance of his adversaries; but their minds were filled with fear and anxiety, when they reflected on the many perils that he might encounter on his long journey, and the sufferings from cold, and hunger, and fatigue, that he must endure in his present debilitated state of health. They did not, however, add to Edith's anxiety by telling of their own, but exerted themselves to cheer and rouse her, and lead her to place a perfect trust in the over-ruling care of Him, without whose permission not even a sparrow can fall to the ground.

The wisdom of the plan that Edith had persuaded her husband to adopt was soon but too apparent; for, in a few days, a pinnace arrived at Salem, bringing an officer and attendants, who were commissioned by the General Assembly to seize on the offending pastor, and convey him on board a vessel that was lying at Nantasket, ready for sea. But this cruel and arbitrary intention was happily frustrated. The officer came to the dwelling of Williams, and had the mortification of finding that he had been gone three days; nor could all his threats or persuasions obtain from any of the inmates the least information concerning his flight. He also sought out, and strictly interrogated, several of the inhabitants of Salem, who were known to be the partisans of this persecuted friend of liberty. But, although they were well acquainted with his sudden departure and his destination, and some of the younger men were even preparing to follow him, not one of them betrayed their respected leader.

The officer therefore returned to Boston, to report the ill-success of his errand, which excited much wrath and vexation in the members of the Assembly, but afforded secret satisfaction to the amiable Governor Winthrop, who had unwillingly submitted to the decision of a large majority of the government, and who had kindly exerted himself to rescue from a cruel and unjust fate the man whose only fault consisted in a determination to think for himself.

Meanwhile, the fugitive was pursuing his slow and difficult way through the woods and wilds to the south of Salem. But whither should he direct his steps? Every road out of the district must lead him through the territory of his foes and persecutors; and he dared not show in any of the hamlets or villages, where his person and reputation were well known, lest he should be seized and given up to the magistrates of Boston. He, therefore, traveled chiefly by night, guided by the moon and stars, and lay concealed in some damp covert, or rocky ravine, during the day. The small stock of provisions that Edith had placed in his knapsack was soon expended, and for some days he subsisted on the nuts and berries that still remained on the trees.

At length he felt himself safe from immediate pursuit, and changed his course suddenly to the east. He emerged from the shelter of the woods, and, hurrying across the open plain that skirted the bay, he found himself at the spot which he desired to reach. This was a little cove on the shore, surrounded on the land side by rocks, and only capable of receiving a small boat into its tranquil harbor. As Roger approached the water's edge, and stepped round the last point of rock that concealed the inlet, he made a signal, which, to his great joy, was instantly replied to from within. Day was just dawning over the far horizon, and a dim twilight shone on the smooth and boundless ocean that spread to the east. A few light strokes of an oar fell on Roger's ear, and then he saw the white spray, and the dark form of a boat emerging from the gloomy cavern that was formed by the overhanging rocks. In a moment his hand was grasped in that of a friend, and all his sense of loneliness vanished away.

Seaton entreated him to lose no time in entering the boat, and leaving the inhospitable shores of Massachusetts; and Williams gladly obeyed him. The little shallop, which his friends at Salem had secretly purchased, and sent by one of the most devoted of their number to meet him at the appointed place, was well supplied with provisions and warm clothing, which proved a most seasonable relief to Roger; but the most acceptable part of its contents was a letter from Edith, informing him of the welcome arrival of their friends, the Elliots, at Salem, and of the futile efforts of the men of Boston to make him a prisoner. Edith wrote more cheerfully than she felt; and she spoke of the happy time when they would be reunited, and of her hopes that it was not far distant, assuring him that she was willing—and trusted, ere long, to be able—to follow him to any spot where he might fix his home.

This letter, and the refreshment with which Seaton furnished him, raised his drooping and exhausted spirits; and, at his friend's request, he wrapped himself in the large boat-cloak that his provident wife had sent for him and lay down to enjoy the first calm and undisturbed repose that had been permitted to him since he left his beloved home.

Silently and rapidly the little boat glided over the calm surface of the bay; and, ere long, it was opposite to the harbor of Boston, and might be espied by some of the vessels lying there, Roger still slept the deep sleep of exhaustion and security; but Seaton now required his aid, and reluctantly aroused him to take a second oar, and speed the shallop past the region of danger. Roger sprang to his feet, and seized the oar, and the boat darted forward from the impulse of his now fresh and powerful arm. It passed near several boats belonging to the Bostoners; but the fugitive drew his large Spanish hat over his brows, and hid his well-known form and dress beneath the folds of the ample cloak, and thus escaped detection or observation.

It was his intention to row down the bay as far as New Plymouth, where he designed to visit Edith's parents and apprise them of all that had befallen him; and also endeavor to prevail on Bradford to send a vessel, as soon as the inclemency of the weather had subsided, to bring his wife to her paternal home. He then proposed to go on with Seaton, and any of the Plymouthers who would accompany him, and seek a settlement further to the south, in some part of Narragansett Bay. But this scheme was not permitted to be carried out.

Towards evening, a fresh breeze sprang up from the east; and before sun-set it blew so violently, that Roger and his companion had the greatest difficulty in keeping their little vessel out at sea, and preventing its being dashed on the coral reefs that girt that 'stern and rock-bound coast.' Manfully they wrought at the oars; but their strength was almost exhausted, and no creek or inlet offered them a secure refuge. Still they persevered—for it was a struggle for life! The least remission of their toil would have placed them at the mercy of the wind, and they must have been driven violently against the sunken rocks.

At length, when the light of day was failing them, and they began to give themselves up as lost, the keen eye of Roger espied an opening through the foam-covered reef; and though it was narrow, and evidently dangerous, he and Seaton resolved to make a desperate effort to pass through it, and gain the smooth still waters that they knew must lie between the rock and the shore.

They breathed a fervent and heart-felt prayer for help from above, and then commenced the fearful contest. The moment they turned the prow of their shallop towards the shore, the light and buoyant little vessel darted forward, impelled by both wind and tide, and mounted like a seabird on the rolling waves. The dashing spray fell ever it, almost blinding its crew, and the helm no longer had power to divert its headlong course.

'Now may He who rules the storm have pity on my Edith!' exclaimed Roger, as he saw the fail extent of their peril, and not a fear for himself crossed his steadfast soul. 'May the Lord of the winds and the waves be our guide and protector, or the next minute will be our last!'

He clasped his hands in prayer, and raised his kindling eye to the frowning heavens above him. But his eye of faith could look through those dark clouds, and see a Father's hand of love and mercy governing and controlling the elements: and his spirit was at peace.

'Now God be praised!' cried Seaton, as he drew a long shivering breath; and snatching up both the oars, projected them on each side of the boat to protect it from the rocks that bounded the narrow channel. 'We have entered the passage; and, with Heaven's help, we shall yet be saved.'

They had, indeed, dashed straight into the opening that divided the reef, and through which the waves were rushing at a terrific rate; and their only apparent chance of safety lay in the possibility of guiding the little bark through the channel, without its being impelled against the rugged sides. Williams caught one of the oars from his friend, and both directed their whole strength to this object. There was a brief interval of breathless suspense; and then the boat struck on a hidden coral rock. It was but for a moment — another swelling wave lifted it again, and rolled forward, bearing the little vessel on its summit into the smooth water that lay, like a narrow lake, between the dangerous reef and the flat sandy shore.

But the peril was not yet over. The blow-on the rock, though momentary, had been so violent as to spring a leak in the bottom of the boat; and through this the water gushed up with fearful rapidity, threatening to sink it before the shore could be reached. Again the oars were pulled with the strength of desperation; and again the danger was averted. But Roger Williams and his friend found themselves on a desert and uninhabited coast, with a useless vessel, and no means of proceeding to Plymouth.

Still their lives had been providentially preserved, and they were deeply grateful to the Divine power which had been exerted for their rescue. And faith and courage, and bodily strength were their portion likewise: and they did not despair. They slept long and soundly; and the following morning, having ascertained that the boat was too seriously injured to be repaired by any means at their command, they resolved on abandoning it, and recommenced their journey on foot.

The extreme difficulty of reaching Plymouth by land, and the wide circuit from the course that he wished ultimately to pursue that must be traveled in order to reach the settlement of the Pilgrim Fathers, caused Williams to relinquish that part of his plan, and decide on striking at once into the forest, and pursuing a south-westerly course until he should arrive at Narragansett Bay. This would lead him through the trackless woods, and the dreary wilds, inhabited only by the barbarous and untutored red men. But from them he hoped to meet with that hospitality and succor which was denied him by his fellow- countrymen and fellow-Christians.

CHAPTER XXI

Alas! to see the strength that clings
Round woman in such hours!
A mournful sight,
Though lovely! an o'erflowing of the springs,
The full springs of affection, deep and bright!
And she, because her life is ever twined
With other lives, and by no stormy wind
May thence be shaken; and because the light
Of tenderness is round her, and her eye
Doth weep such passionate tears — therefore,
She thus endures.' HEMANS.

Without any guide, Roger and his faithful friend Seaton wandered through the wilderness. They took from the stranded boat as much of food and other useful articles as they could carry; but the provision did not last long, and before they reached any Indian encampment they were seduced to extreme want and suffering. Their clothes were drenched by the frequent heavy rain, which so completely saturated the ground and the dead branches that lay strewed upon it, as often to preclude all possibility of lighting a fire. Their nights were passed on the damp ground, or beneath any sheltering rock that they could find and once a hollow tree afforded them a refuge from the storm that raged around them, when no other was at hand.

At length, after fourteen weeks of trial and hardship, they reached the village of Packanokick, where dwelt Masasoyt, the aged Sagamore of the Wampanoges. During the time that Williams had resided at Plymouth, he had learnt the language of the natives; and on some of his visits to the village of Mooanam, he had become acquainted with his father, Masasoyt, the chief Sachem of the divided tribe. The regard and respect with which his eloquence and his attractive manners had inspired the younger Chieftain were fully shared by the Sagamore; and both prince and people learnt to love and reverence the man who honored their rights, respected their prejudices, and prayed to his God for their welfare.

His appearance in the village of Masasoyt was hailed with joy, and regarded as a privilege by all the inhabitants. The Sachem received both him and is way-worn companion with kindness and hospitality, and gave them a chamber in his own lodge; which, if not remarkable either for cleanliness or comfort, yet seemed a luxurious abode to men who had passed so many days and nights in the unsheltered depths of the forest.

On the following morning, when food and rest had somewhat restored the exhausted strength of the travelers, Masasoyt invited Williams to a private conference, in which he informed him that a serious quarrel had again arisen between his tribe and that of Cundineus, the Chief of the Narragansetts; and he entreated him to use all his powerful influence with the latter to heal the present dissension, and prevent the dispute from ending in open hostilities. Williams undertook this negotiation with much satisfaction; for peace-making was not only in accordance with his feelings, and with the duty of his profession, but he also desired to secure the favor and protection of the Narragansett Chief, on the borders of whose dominions he designed to fix his future home. He, therefore, made no delay in setting out, with a few Indian attendants, on the proposed expedition and in a few days, returned to Packanokick with the welcome intelligence that the wrath of Cundincus was appeased, and that he had listened favorably to the explanation of his rival Chieftain.

The old Narragansett Chief also was so captivated by the English stranger, and so won by his peculiar eloquence, that we are told that 'the barbarous heart of the old prince loved him like a son to his latest breath'; and his nephew and co-ruler, the young Miantonomo, also regarded him as a friend, and placed in him a perfect confidence.

'Let no one,' thankfully exclaimed Williams in his diary, 'mistrust Providence — these ravens fed me in the wilderness!'

But inactive repose was neither the wish nor the lot of Roger Williams; and he earnestly desired to reach the spot where he proposed to found his new settlement, and prepare a home for his beloved Edith; and from whence, also, he hoped to be able to send a letter to Salem or to Plymouth, which might allay the anxious fears that he well knew she had so long been enduring. Since he had received the letter that Seaton brought him from his high-minded wife, he had not had any opportunity of conveying to her the intelligence of his own safety; or of hearing from her whether her strength and spirits were supported under the protracted trial of absence and anxiety. He knew, also, that ere this time he had reason to believe himself a father; and his heart yearned to be assured of the welfare of his wife and child, and to see them safely lodged beneath the shelter of his own roof. It was a source of extreme consolation to him, under all his feelings of anxiety, to believe that his Edith had been cheered and supported by the presence of Dame Elliot and her excellent husband, who, he felt assured, would not leave her until she could be removed either to Plymouth or to her husband's new abode: and to their kind care, and the protection of his heavenly Father, he was contented to leave her, while he used every effort to procure for her a safe and happy home, in which he could hope, ere long, to welcome her.

He, therefore, lost no time in concluding a bargain with Masasoyt for a piece of land in the district called Seacomb[*], not far from the east arm of Narragansett Bay; and thither he proceeded with Seaton, and commenced building and planting. From this place, he found means to convey intelligence, both to Salem and Plymouth, of the safe termination of his perilous journey, and his intention to fix his settlement on the piece of ground that he had purchased. His messengers returned, after a considerable interval, and brought him a letter from his now joyful wife, which gladdened his heart with the welcome news of her health and safety; and that also of his little daughter Edith. This name, she told him, had been given to the infant in accordance with what she knew to be his wish; and his friend John Elliot—who, with his wife, had resided chiefly at Salem since his departure—had performed the rite of baptism. She further informed him that Governor Bradford, on hearing of her lonely position, had kindly promised to send a vessel for her; and, as the severity of winter had already partially subsided, she was in daily expectation of the arrival of the pinnace, which would carry her back to the happy home of her youth; and then she hoped the time would not be long until she could rejoin her husband, and once more be at peace.

[Footnote: Now Reheboth]

This letter called forth the lively joy and gratitude of Roger, and animated him to fresh zeal and activity in all his proceedings at Seacomb. He was also encouraged greatly by the arrival, at the same time, of five of his most devoted adherents from Salem, who had no sooner learnt from his Indian messenger, of his arrival at the place of his destination, than they determined to accompany the friendly savage on his return to Seacomb, and assist their friend and teacher in all his labors for the formation of an independent settlement.

All this visa cheering and satisfactory; but the trials of this undaunted man were not over yet. His trusty messenger had brought him another dispatch, which he had not yet attended to. He now opened it, and found that it came from the Governor of Plymouth; and contained an earnest injunction to him to abandon Seacomb, which, he informed him; was included in their patent, and to remove to the other side of the river that formed their boundary, where he could be free and independent, like themselves. 'I accepted his wise counsel as a voice from God,' wrote Williams: and he' immediately resolved to be guided by it, and again commence his wanderings.

In a frail Indian canoe, he and his companions rowed up the arm of the sea, now called the river Seacock. They knew not where to land, or where again to pitch their tent in the wilderness; but they were soon guided by the friendly voices of a party of Narragansetts on the opposite shore. These natives had recognized their friend Williams, and now shouted out, in broken English, the welcome words, What cheer?' The sound fell like music on the ears of the desolate exiles; and, in remembrance of the event, the spot of ground where they first landed on the Narragansett territory received the name of *What Cheer?* which it still retains. A spring, called *'Williams's Spring,'* is also shown by the present inhabitants of this district, in proud and grateful memory of the spot where the founder of a future free state first set foot on shore.

The place where the wanderer landed was called by the Indians Maushasuck; and it was made over to him by the generous Cundincus, as a free and absolute possession, and also all the land included between the rivers Pawtucket and Maushasuck.[*] This property he shared equally with his present comrades, and also with some others who shortly after joined him from Salem, and made their whole number amount to thirteen. He did not reserve any advantage to himself, although the land actually belonged to him alone; but divided it into thirteen equal portions, on each of which a rude hut was immediately erected. These were soon improved, and became a rising village, to which Williams gave the name of Providence, in grateful remembrance of the Divine guidance and protection which had brought him at length to 'the haven where he would be.'

[Footnote: Now called the Providence River.]

He and his associates united themselves into a sort of 'town-fellowship,' and independent church; and one of the first rules which they laid down, for their future guidance and government, was that no one should ever suffer, in that settlement, for conscience' sake.

It was summer when the little village began to be built; and, before the land could be cleared and prepared for cultivation, the season was too far advanced to allow any hope of a corn-harvest. The new settlers had, therefore, to endure the same poverty and privation that had been the lot of the earlier planters in New England. They had no means of obtaining any of the comforts of civilized life, except from Boston or Plymouth: and as they possessed no vessel besides an Indian canoe, this was a service of toil and much hazard. Still they did not repine, for liberty was here their precious portion; and hope for the future sustained them through the trials of the present time.

But where was Edith? Where was that true-hearted woman while her husband was thus struggling with difficulties and privations? She was where both inclination and duty had led her—by his side; and smiling at trials that she was permitted to share with him, and to lighten by her presence.

We must here revert to the time before Edith had been blessed by receiving intelligence of her husband from Seacomb, and had so cheerfully replied to the note which he wrote to her on a scrap of paper torn from his pocket book. In order not to interrupt the history of Roger's difficulties and their successful issue, we have not yet narrated the trials that his exemplary wife had endured—and endured with a resolution and fortitude equal to his own.

When the joyful news of Roger's safety reached Edith at Salem, she was slowly recovering from a long and dangerous illness, which anxiety and sorrow had brought on her a few weeks after the birth of her child. Through all her sufferings of mind end body, Dame Elliot had been her nurse and her comforter; and she and her husband had sacrificed their own domestic comfort, and their own humble but cherished home, to lessen the sorrows of their afflicted friend.

All the consolation that human sympathy and affection could afford to Edith, was given by these true Christian friends; and all the spiritual strength that the prayers end exhortations of such a minister as Elliot could impart to a sorrowing spirit, were received, and gratefully appreciated, by the object of his solicitude and care. But when weeks and months had elapsed, and still no tidings came of the beloved wanderer, what hope could be given to the desolate heart of Edith Her friends had themselves given up all hope of Roger's having survived the toils end privations of the journey; and how could they bid his wife cheer up, and look for brighter days, which they believed would never come? A letter which Edith received from her parents, by the captain of a fishing-boat from Plymouth, too clearly proved that Williams had never reached that settlement; and from that day the health and spirits of his wife visibly declined. She did not give way to violent grief; but a settled melancholy dwelt on her pale and lovely countenance, and all the thoughtful abstraction of her early year, which happiness had chased from her features, returned again. No object but her infant seemed to rouse her; and then it was only to tears: but tears were better than that look of deep and speechless sorrow that generally met the anxious gaze of her friends, and made them, at times, apprehensive for her reason. At length her physical powers gave way, and a violent attack of fever brought Edith to the brink of the grave.

During this period both Elliot and his wife devoted themselves, day and night, to the poor sufferer, whose mind wandered continually, and whose deeply-touching lamentations for the beloved one, whom she mourned as dead, brought tears to the eyes of her faithful friends. They had no hope of her recovery, nor could they heartily desire it; for they believed her earthly happiness was wrecked for ever, and they could ask no better fate for her than a speedy reunion with her Roger in a home beyond the grave.

Her child they looked on as their own, and cherished her with almost a parent's love and care; while they resolved to bring her up in those high and holy principles that had been so nobly contended for by her unfortunate father, and so beautifully exemplified in the amiable character of her mother.

The fever ran high, and bore down all the strength—both moral and physical—of its victim. At length, after days and nights of restlessness and delirium, a deep and heavy sleep came on; and Edith lay still and motionless for hours, while her untiring friends sat watching her in silence, and offering up fervent prayers for the soul that seemed to be departing. During this anxious period, a gentle knock was made at the door; and Elliot, on opening it, was presented by Edith's single attendant with the small packet that Roger's Indian messenger had brought for her mistress.

In trembling agitation, the pastor showed the direction—which he knew to be in his friend's handwriting—to his wife: and now, indeed, they lifted up their hearts to the God who heareth prayer, that He would be pleased to recall the precious life that seemed to be fast ebbing away; and to permit His tried and faithful servants again to be united, and enjoy the happiness that yet might be their portion on earth.

Noiselessly Elliot glided from the room—for he feared to awaken the sleeper—and sought the friendly Indian, from whom he learnt the good news of Roger's safety, and all the particulars that the red man could relate concerning him. He then returned to Edith's chamber, and, in a low whisper, communicated all that he had heard to his wife, and consulted with her as to the best method of communicating the startling tidings to Edith, should she ever awake from her present death-like slumber.

They were still engaged in earnest, but scarcely audible, conversation, when Dame Elliot, who did not cease from watching her patient, observed her open her large eyes, and fix them with a look of intelligent inquiry on herself and her husband. She made a sign to him; and he likewise was struck with the evident change in Edith's countenance, and filled with hope that her reason had perfectly returned. This hope was quickly confirmed by the invalid saying in a very low voice, but in a collected manner—

'I have slept very long, and my dreams have been very painful. I dreamt that I was alone in the world, and that an angel came to take my soul where he had gone to dwell. And then—just as I bade farewell to earth—a little form came between me and the angel, and held me back. Where is that little being? Dame Elliot, let me look on her, that my trembling spirit may be stayed. No, Roger; no—I must not ask to follow you yet.'

Edith seemed too weak for tears, or for any strong emotion; but she closed her eyes, and slowly clasped her almost transparent hands upon her breast, and looked so still and colorless, that she might have been taken for a marble monument, but for the dark waving hair that fell upon her pillow, and shaded her snowy neck. Dame Elliot took up the infant from its little wicker cradle, and held it towards Edith, saying gently—

Look up, my Edith, and bless the little being that God has given to call you back to life and happiness.'

'Happiness!' murmured Edith. 'That word has no meaning for me! Duty is my only tie to life.'

But she did look up; and as her eyes were long end fondly fixed on the unconscious features of the child, her own sweet look of gentleness rose into them again, and she raised her feeble arms, as if to take the infant.

'And he will never see her,' she whispered. 'He will never look on his child in this world.'

Elliot thought that hope might now be given without danger; and he took her wasted hand in his, and said—

'Edith, you have had much sorrow, and it has nearly brought you down to the grave. But can you bear to feel the agitation of hope? Can you listen calmly while I tell you that some tidings of your husband have reached us, and that he was certainly alive after the time when you believed him dead?'

He paused, and looked anxiously to see the effect of this sentence; and he was almost awed by the expression of Edith's countenance. It was not agitation—it was not joy—it was not trembling uncertainty. But it was a look of concentrated mental power and endurance, and of speechless inquiry, that seemed to say, 'Now utter my sentence of life or death, and do it quickly!'

Dame Elliot could not bear it. Bursting into tears of deep emotion, she beat down and imprinted a kiss on Edith's cold brow, while she exclaimed, in broken accents—

'Yes! it is true, dearest Edith. You may live—and live, we hope, for happiness as great as has ever been your portion.'

'O, my God!' cried Edith—'this is too much!—too much of joy for one so weak and faithless. But tell me, my friends—tell me all. I can bear it now.'

Gently and gradually Elliot prepared her for the blissful certainty of her husband's safety; and when he found that illness had not greatly weakened her natural strength of mind, and that she could bear the joy that awaited her, he gave her Roger's own letter, and felt assured that the tears she, at length, shed at the sight of his hand-writing, would relieve and calm her over-burdened heart.

In this he judged truly; for, though Edith was greatly exhausted after this strong excitement, yet she passed a tranquil night, and was so much recovered on the following morning as to be able to converse composedly with her kind friends. The fever had passed away; and the sense of restored happiness, joined to youth and a naturally good constitution, had a rapid effect in renovating her strength and spirits, and recalling a faint bloom to her cheek.

Before the Indian set out on his return to Seacomb, she insisted on seeing him, and herself delivering to him a letter to Roger, in which she had carefully avoided all mention of her illness. She made numerous inquiries of him relative to her husband's health and present situation; and charged him to convey her packet safely, and tell his employer that he had seen her and his child well and happy. She could say this with truth; for so rapidly had she recovered, that the inexperienced eye of the Indian could detect no remaining indisposition in the slight and graceful form of the interesting pale-face, or any trace of disease in the bright eye that smiled so kindly upon him.

He departed with the friends of Williams, and earnestly did his wife wish that it had been possible for her to accompany them, and join her husband at once. But this could not be; and she could only endeavor to regain her strength, so as to be able to proceed to Plymouth, as soon as the promised vessel arrived. In due time it came: and bidding her kind and devoted friends an affectionate farewell, Edith and her child embarked, with all the little property that remained to her, and soon found herself once more beneath the peaceful roof of her parents.

Until she arrived at Plymouth, she was not aware of the fresh trial that had befallen her husband, in being compelled to abandon his settlement at Seacomb, and remove into the Narragansett district. This change was distressing to her, as it net only placed the lines of her future habitation at a greater distance from her parents and friends at New Plymouth, but also removed it further from all civilized life, and into a district inhabited by a tribe whom she had learnt to dread from her childhood, as the rivals and foes of the friendly Wampanoges. Still these considerations did not, in any measure, abate her eagerness to fellow Roger, and take her part in all his toils and anxieties. The winter had passed away, and, though far from genial, the weather was more tolerable for travelling; and Edith resolved to set out.

All the arguments and entreaties of Helen and Rodolph to induce her to delay her journey for some months, were ineffectual. Her husband lived; and he was suffering hardship—and could she remain separated from him, now that her own strength had been restored? The only concession she could be persuaded to make, was to wait until some friend from Plymouth was found to accompany her. Gladly would her father have done so; but he was suffering so severely from the ague that so often attacked the settlement in the spring months, as to be perfectly incompetent to attempt the toilsome journey. No vessel could now be procured, and it was on foot that Edith proposed to traverse the wide extent of wilderness that stretched between Plymouth and Roger's place of refuge.

Two faithful and active Indians were appointed by Mooanam to be her guides, and to carry the infant which she would not consent to leave behind her; and, in order that this might be accomplished with greater facility, Apannow provided her with one of the Indian cradles—or, rather, pouches—in which the red squaws so commonly carry their young children on their backs. This was thickly lined with soft and elastic bog-moss, and well adapted to the purpose for which it was designed.

All was prepared, and the impatient Edith only waited for a companion from among her own countrymen, who were all so much occupied at that busy season as to feel little disposed to undertake so long a journey. But she found one at length who was sufficiently interested in her happiness, and that of her husband, to leave his home and his occupations, and offer to be her protector. This was the excellent Edward Winslow, who had been her father's constant friend ever since their first emigration, and who bad also learnt to know and value Roger Williams, during his residence at Plymouth.

With such a companion, Edith felt she had nothing to fear; and her anxious parents committed her to his care with greater confidence than they would have done to that of any other protector. His natural sagacity, his courage, and his knowledge of the Indians and their language, rendered him peculiarly suitable for the enterprise; and his warm friendship for Rodolph and all his family, and the lively powers of his pious and intelligent mind, ensured to Edith both a kind and an agreeable fellow-traveler.

Nevertheless, it was not without many prayers and tears that Helen saw her daughter once more leave her childhood's home, and commence her journey. But Edith's spirits were joyous, and her hopes were high; and her child lay smiling contentedly in its strange nest, which was slung on the shoulders of one of the Indian guides. The other carried a small stock of provisions, and other necessaries, and thus the little party set forth.

We will rot follow them, day by day, in their fatiguing journey; but merely state that its length and difficulty exceeded even the expectations of Edith and her companion; but never damped the persevering courage of the former, or drew from her a complaint, or a wish to return. She only felt that every step, however rough and toilsome, carried her nearer to the object that was dearest to her on earth; and this conviction supported her when otherwise her strength must have failed.

Sometimes an Indian wigwam afforded her rest and shelter; but, frequently, a bed of dry leaves, and a roof of boughs, were the best lodging that Winslow and the Indians could provide for her and her little infant. Happily the weather was calm and mild, and the season sufficiently advanced to enable the Indians to find a quantity of nutritious roots, which, with the meal, or nokake, that they carried with them—or procured from the natives by the way—formed the chief subsistence of the party. Occasionally, their fare was improved by a wild turkey, or wood duck; or, perhaps, a squirrel or hare, that Winslow brought down with his gun; but often the day's journey was performed with no other refreshment than a few spoonsful of dry meal, and a draught of cold water, until something more nourishing could be procured at their place of repose for the right.

Roger Williams was standing one evening on the bank of the river, or rather, arm of the sea, called Seacock, near the spot where he had first landed, and to which he had given the name of 'What Cheer?' He was examining the landing-place, and contriving some means of turning it into a sort of harbor for canoes that belonged to the settlers in his new village, when his attention was attracted to the other side of the river, by hearing his own name loudly called by native voices. He looked to the spot, and saw two Indians plunge into the water, and swim rapidly towards him: and, as they did so, he also observed two other figures emerge from a grove of trees that reached nearly to the eastern brink of the inlet.

The distance was considerable, but Roger's keen eye could discern that one of them was a female form; and, as they approached nearer to the water's edge, and the rays of the evening sun fell brightly upon them, he also saw that the arms of that graceful and familiar form carried an infant.

Surely it is an illusion!' he exclaimed. I have so long pictured to my mind that blessed sight, that at length my fancy seems realized. It cannot be!'

But again his name was called—not now with an Indian accent, but in the manly English tones of Edward Winslow 'Bring down a canoe, Roger!' he shouted across the Water. 'Edith and your child cannot swim this, arm of the sea.'

It was then true! Edith—his beloved wife—was there and only that narrow inlet divided them! The Indians had sprung to the shore, and were waiting his directions, to go in search of a canoe; but for a few moments he did not regard them, so riveted were his eyes, and all his senses, on the opposite shore. But now he remembered that only by means of a boat could he attain that shore; and making a signal of wild joy and welcome to Edith, he hurried up the creek with the Indians, and rapidly unloosed the moorings of his canoe, which lay securely behind a projecting rock. He leaped into it, leaving the natives on the shore, and paddled the canoe swiftly down the creek, to the spot where Edith stood waiting to receive him, trembling with agitation and joy.

When the first burst of emotion, at this, long-desired meeting with his wife and hitherto unknown child, had subsided, Roger warmly welcomed the friend who had so kindly protected them during their long journey, and brought them to the wild spot that was now his only home. He then led them to the canoe, and, with Winslow's assistance, soon rowed them to the other side, and conducted them to his, infant settlement.

The huts were indeed erected, and covered in with shingle roofs; but their appearance promised little of outward comfort to Edith. Yet an inward joy and satisfaction were now permitted to her, which, at one time, she had never hoped to enjoy again on earth; and all externals were as nothing when compared with this. Nevertheless, she exerted herself with all a woman's taste and skill to arrange the simple furniture of the hut, and even to add a something of decoration; and both her husband and Winslow wondered at the improvement which she soon effected in the appearance of the dwelling, and the ingenuity with which she converted the rudest materials into articles of use or ornament.

Her joyous spirits, and active moments, gave a life and animation to the hitherto dreary scene; and Roger felt that he had, indeed, in her a helpmate, who would cheer the loneliest situation, and shed a grace and charm ever poverty itself.

Winslow appreciated all her excellent and amiable qualities very highly also; and yet he lamented the lot of both his friends, who had to endure, in this comparative solitude, all the struggles, and all the hardships, that the Pilgrim Fathers had once encountered, and had now conquered.

But the visit of this, 'great and pious soul,' as Roger described Edward Winslow, very greatly cheered the heart of the exiles. He remained for many weeks in the new settlement; and only left it when the advance of the season warned him that the short Indian summer was drawing to an end. A vessel which arrived at that time from Plymouth, and which brought the wives and families of several of the settlers, afforded him the means of returning by sea, and avoiding the tedious land journey. He departed, with the thanks and blessings of his friends, to convey to Edith's, parents the happy intelligence that she was both well and happy, and that it was evident her cheerful spirit had power to sustain her through every difficulty by which she might be surrounded.

CHAPTER XXII

'Epictetus says: "Every thing hath two handles." The art of taking things by the right handle, or the better side—which charity always doth—would save much of those janglings and heart-burnings that so abound in the world.' ARCHBISHOP LEIGHTON.

For a long period an unbroken peace had subsisted between the English settlers and the native tribes. But this could no longer be maintained, and a succession of petty injuries and mutual misunderstandings brought about a state of hostility that the Pilgrim Fathers had labored—and, generally, with success—to avert.

Their kind and equitable treatment of the Indians had not been, as we have had occasion to show, adopted by the later emigrants, and doubt and suspicion had taken the place of that confidence and respect with which the red men had soon learnt to regard the settlers of New Plymouth.

The recent colony of Connecticut, which was composed of bands of settlers from Plymouth and Massachusetts, and also a few Dutch planters, first came into hostile collision with the natives. The settlers of New Plymouth had entered upon an almost deserted land; those of Massachusetts had ensured to themselves safety by their superior strength; and those among the Narragansetts were protected from injury by the friendly feelings of the neighboring Indians. But the settlement of Connecticut was surrounded by hardy and hostile races, and could only enjoy security so long as the mutual hatred of the native tribes prevented them from uniting against the intruders.

In the extreme west of the Narragansett district, and near the entrance of Long Island Sound, dwelt a powerful division of the Pequodees; of that race of red warriors whose pride and ambition caused them to be both feared and hated by the other tribes in the vicinity. They could bring upwards of seven hundred warriors into the field, and their Chief, Sassacus, had, in common with almost all the great Indian Sagamores, a number of subordinate chiefs, who yielded to him a certain degree of obedience. The Narragansetts were the only tribe that could at all compete in strength with the fierce and haughty Pequodees; and their young Chieftain, Miantonomo, was already regarded by Sassacus as a dangerous rival.

Such was the feeling that existed among the tribes near the settlements of Connecticut, when an event occurred that disturbed the peace of the whole community. Two merchants of Virginia, who had long dwelt in Massachusetts, and who were engaged in trafficking with the Connecticut settlers, were suddenly and treacherously attacked by a party of Pequodees, and, with their attendants, barbarously murdered. And shortly afterwards another trader, named Oldham, met the same fate, being assassinated while he was quietly sleeping in his boat, by some Indians who had, but an hour before, been conversing with him in a friendly manner. This latter murder did not take place actually among the Pequodees, but on a small island belonging to the Narragansetts, called Block Island. But the inhabitants denied all knowledge of its perpetration, and the murderers fled to the Pequodees, by whom they were received and sheltered. A strong suspicion, therefore, lay on them as being guilty of the latter crime, as well as the former.

The government of Massachusetts immediately resolved on punishing the offenders, and a troop of eighty or ninety men were sent off to Block Island, to seek for the murderers. The natives endeavored to oppose their landing; but, after a short contest, they fled, and hid themselves in the woods. For two days the Boston soldiers remained on the island, burning and devastating the villages and fields, end firing at random into the thickets, but without seeing a single being. They then broke up the canoes that lay on the beach, and sailed away to the country of the Pequodees to insist on the guilty individuals being delivered to them and, on this condition, to offer peace. But neither the murderers nor their protectors were to be found. All had fled to the forests and the marshes, whither the English could not follow them, and they merely succeeded in killing and wounding a few stragglers, and burning the huts that came in their way.

This fruitless expedition rendered the Pequodees bolder than ever, and the neighboring towns were harassed by their nightly attacks, and, notwithstanding all their precautions, and the patrols that were set on every side, the savages fell on the whites whenever they were at work in the distant fields. They slew the men with their tomahawks end dragged their wretched wives and daughters away to captivity; and thus, in a short time, thirty of the English settlers had become the victims of their fury. Meanwhile, messengers were sent to Plymouth and Massachusetts, to implore their aid, and the latter state promised two hundred soldiers, and the former forty, which were as many as its small population could afford.

The Pequodees, dreading the power of the English, endeavored to move the Narragansetts—who had from the most distant times been their rivals and enemies—to join them in an offensive and defensive alliance against the white men, whom they represented as a common foe to the Indians, and the future destroyers of their race.

This intended confederation was discovered by Roger Williams, who spent much of his time in visiting the Indian villages and instructing the natives, with all of whom he obtained a remarkable degree of influence. This noble-minded and truly Christian-spirited man immediately seized the opportunity of repaying with benefits the heavy injuries that he had received from the Massachusetts; and, with an admirable magnanimity and self devotion, he set himself to prevent the dangerous alliance.

The government of Massachusetts were well aware that Williams was the only man who could effect this desirable object; and, on hearing from him of the schemes of Sassacus, they immediately requested the former victim of their unjust persecution to employ his influence with the natives for the benefit of his countrymen: and well and zealously be complied with this request. He left his now comfortable home, and all the various employments that occupied his time, and travelled restlessly from place to place, defying the storms and the waves, in a miserable canoe; and meeting, with an undaunted courage, the assembled parties of hostile tribes whom he sought, at his own extreme peril, to bring into alliance with the English. He succeeded in his patriotic object, and, after along doubtful negotiation, he persuaded the Narragansetts to refuse the proffered coalition with the Pequodees. Their young chief, Miantonomo, even went a journey to Boston, where he was received with distinguished marks of honor and respect, and signed a treaty which allied him to the settlers against his own countrymen.

The troops from the river-towns assembled together, and went down the Connecticut to attack the Pequodees in their own land. Their numbers were but small — not exceeding eighty men — as each town furnished a much weaker force than had been promised. But they were joined by a band of the Mohicans, a hardy race inhabiting the valleys of the Connecticut, and who had been alienated from the Pequodees by the oppression and arrogance that had excited the enmity of so many other tribes. The combined forces of the English and Indians were placed under the command of Captain Mason, a brave and intelligent officer who had served in the Netherlands under General Fairfax.

The detachment that was expected from New Plymouth was not ready to march at the time of the troops taking the field. Captain Standish, therefore, did not set out himself; but he allowed such of his brother-soldiers as were ready, to precede him, and take part in the commencement of the campaign. Among these, Rodolph Maitland, who still retained all the fire and energy of his youth, was the foremost; and he led a little band of brave companions to the place of rendezvous. The learned minister Stone—the friend and colleague of Hooker—accompanied the troops from Boston; for a band of Puritanical warriors would have thought themselves but badly provided for without such spiritual aid.

The instructions of the government of Connecticut directed Mason to land in the harbor of Pequod,[*] and thus attack the Indian forces on their own ground. But he found the natural strength of the place so much greater than he expected, and also observed that it was so watchfully guarded by his enemies, that he resolved to pass on to the harbor in Narragansett Bay; and, after having strengthened his forces with the warriors promised by Miantonomo, to attack the Pequodees from thence. A circumstance occurred here that is so characteristic of the time, and of the manners of the Puritans, that it must not be omitted. The officers under Mason were dissatisfied with this alteration in the plan of the campaign, and asserted that the instructions given to the commander ought to be literally followed. It was, therefore, resolved to refer the question to the minister, who was directed 'to bring down by prayer the responsive decision of the Lord.' Stone passed nearly the whole night in prayer and supplication for wisdom to decide the matter, and the next morning declared to the officers that the view taken by their leader was the right one; on which they all submitted without a murmur.

[Footnote: Now Newhaven]

The Indian reinforcements continued to increase. Miantonomo brought two hundred warriors, and other allied tribes joined them on their march, until the number of native auxiliaries amounted to five hundred. In these Mason placed little confidence, and would gladly have awaited the arrival of the forty men from Plymouth, who were already at Providence on their way to join him. But his men were eager to attack the savages, and the Indians taunted him with cowardice for desiring to delay the conflict; and he was forced to advance at once.

The great strength of the Pequodees consisted in two large forts, in one of which the redoubted Chief, Sassacus, himself commanded. The other was situated on the banks of the Mystic, an inconsiderable river that runs parallel to the Connecticut. These Indian forts or castles consisted of wooden palisades, thirty or forty feet high, generally erected on an elevated situation, and enclosing a space sufficiently large to contain a considerable number of wigwams for the aged men—or whiteheads—and the women and children.

These two fortresses were the pride and the confidence of the Pequodees, who believed them to be invulnerable; as, indeed, they had hitherto found them to the assaults of their own countrymen. And the other Indian tribes appeared to hold them in the same estimation; for when they found that it was Mason's intention to march directly to the fort on the Mystic, their courage failed completely. They were only accustomed to the Indian mode of warfare, which consists in secret attacks and cunning stratagems; and the idea of braving the terrible Pequodees in their strongholds, overpowered their resolution. The very warriors who, only the day before, had boasted of their deeds, now were crest-fallen, and cried out, 'Sassacus is a God; he is invincible!' and they deserted in troops, and returned to their own dwellings. Thus the English found themselves deprived of at least a hundred of their Narragansett allies. The rest remained with them, as did also the Mohicans; but their fear of the Pequodees was so great, that Mason could only employ them as a sort of rear-guard.

Meanwhile, these haughty Indians were exulting in their supposed security, and indulging in songs and feasting. They believed that the English were terrified at their strength and reputed numbers, and had fled from the intended place of landing in Pequod harbor in fear, and had abandoned their enterprise altogether. They, therefore, amused themselves with fishing in the bay; and then inviting their allies to join their revels, they passed the night in vaunting of their own great actions, and defying the cowardly whites.

We have seen that their assuming arrogance had aroused the jealousy and hatred of most of the neighboring tribes; but there were still a few who adhered to their cause, and were willing to unite with them against the British intruders. Among those, none were more powerful or more zealous than the Nausetts — that tribe which had so greatly harassed and annoyed the first settlers at Plymouth, and which still retained the same feelings of enmity that had then influenced them. The presence of Henrich among that portion of the tribe that was governed by Tisquantum had, indeed, secured to himself the respect and regard of almost the whole community; but it had not weakened the strong prejudice that they, as well as the main body of their tribe, entertained against his race, or lessened their ardent desire to rid the land of the powerful invaders.

Sassacus was well acquainted with the sentiments of his Nausett allies, and he had lost no time in securing the co-operation of the Sagamore of the tribe, as soon as he knew that the British troops were preparing to attack him, and he had, also, dispatched a swift messenger to meet Tisquantum and his warriors, and entreat them to use all possible expedition to join him in his own fortress, and assist in defending it against his enemies.

With the present position and intended movements of Tisquantum's party, the Pequodee Chief was perfectly conversant; for there was one in his castle who was acquainted with the plans of the Nausetts, and had only left their councils when their camp was pitched on the banks of the great Missouri.

This individual had reasons of his own, besides his wish to strengthen his countrymen against the English, for desiring the presence of Tisquantum's warriors in the approaching contest. He hoped to place Henrich in such a position, that he would have no alternative but either to lead the Nausetts against his own people or to excite their distrust, and even hatred, by refusing to do so. He expected, and wished, that he should adopt the latter course; for he knew that he had himself still many secret adherents in the tribe, who would gladly make this an excuse for withdrawing their allegiance from the white Sachem, and bestowing it on him; and thus, at length, the long-sought object of his restless ambition might he attained. And then—then revenge!—that burning passion of his soul—might quickly be also satiated!

It was now many months since Coubitant had escaped the punishment that was due to his many crimes, and had fled from the wrath of Tisquantum. But he had contrived to keep up an exact knowledge of the movements of the tribe, and even an intercourse with his own treacherous partisans. Often, indeed, as the Nausetts traveled slowly across the wide plain between the Missouri and the Mississippi, that well-known and terrible eye of fire was fixed upon them from the elevated bough of some thick tree, or from the overhanging summit of a neighboring rock; and often at night, when the camp was sunk in the silence of repose, his guilty confederates crept forth to meet him in some retired spot, and form plans for the future.

In this way Coubitant dodged the path of the Nausetts while they traversed the forests and savannas, the lulls and the valleys, that led them at length to the great lake, now so well known as Lake Superior. Here they encamped for a considerable time, in order to construct a sufficient number of canoes to carry the whole party across it and also, by following the chain of lakes and rivers that intersects that part of the great continent, and ends in Lake Ontario, to enable them to land at no very great distance from their own native district.

When the little fleet set out on its long and circuitous voyage, Coubitant actually contrived to be one of the passengers. His partisans secured a canoe to themselves; and, pretending that some of their arrangements were incomplete, they lingered on the shore until the rest of the boats were nearly out of sight. They then summoned their leader from his place of concealment, and, giving him a seat in the canoe, followed at their leisure. Thus he performed the whole of the voyage; and when the tribe landed on the eastern shore of Ontario, and recommenced their wanderings on land, he left their route, and hastened forward to try and contrive some schemes that could further his own views.

The news of the war between the English and his old friends, the Pequodees, soon reached him; and, in an incredibly short time, he arrived in their country, and joined Sassacus in his fortified village. It was he who travelled from thence to the head-quarters of the Nausetts, near Cape Cod, and secured their assistance in the coming conflict; and then returned in time to send a trusty emissary to meet Tisquantum, and deliver to him a courteous message from Sassacus.

This message had the desired effect; for Tisquantum called a council of his braves, and submitted to them the request of their powerful ally, that they would fight with him against the Narragansetts. The emissary was instructed to say nothing of the quarrel with the English; for Coubitant wished to get Henrich into the power of the Pequodees, before he became aware of the service that was to be required of him; and he trusted that no intelligence would reach him in the desolate country through which he and his warriors would have to march.

All the assembled council were unanimous in their decision, that the request of Sassacus should be complied with; and Tisquantum then turned to Henrich, who sat beside him, and said —

'My son! the days are past when I could lead forth my warriors to the battle, and wield my tomahawk with the best and the bravest. I must sit in my tent with the children and the squaws, and tell of the deeds that I once could perform, while my young braves are in the field of fight. You must now be their leader, Henrich; and let them see that, though your skin is fair, you have in your breast an Indian heart.'

'I will, my father,' replied the Young Sachem. 'Your warriors shall be led into the thickest of the battle, even as if your long-lost Tekoa went before them with his glancing spear. Tisquantum shall never have cause to feel shame for the son of his adoption.'

'I know it, my brave Henrich,' said the old Chief, 'I know that the honor of Tisquantum's race is safe in your hands; and that you will fight in defence of my ancient friends and allies, even as I would have fought in the days of my young strength. Come away, now; my warriors must prepare to go with the messenger of the great Sassacus. No time must be lost in giving him the aid he asks; and you, my son, will be ready by to-morrow's dawn to lead them on their way. I cannot go with you, for these feeble limbs are unfit to travel at the speed with which you must cross the forests and the plains; neither could the women and children bear it. We will follow the course that we designed to take, and go to the land of my fathers in the far east; and there we will wait for our victorious warriors.

As Tisquantum said this, he left the hall of council, which consisted of a shadowing maple tree, and led his companion to the hut of boughs, in which Oriana and Mailah sat anxiously awaiting the result of the conference. They did not regret when they heard that their husbands were to hasten to the scene of war, for they were Indian women, and could glory in the deeds of their warriors. But when they were informed that the main body of the tribe was to pursue the intended route towards Paomet,[*] their grief and disappointment were very great.

[Footnote: Cape Cod]

'Must I leave you, Henrich?' exclaimed Oriana. 'Must I know that you are in the battle-field; and wounded perhaps, and wanting my aid, and I far away? Let me go with you! You know that Oriana can bear danger, and fatigue, and hardship; and with you there would be no danger.'

'It cannot be,' replied Henrich, gently but decidedly. 'Your father cannot travel, as we must do, with no respite or repose; and you, my Oriana, could not leave him and our boy. You must go with them to Paomet, my love; and prepare a home for me after the fight is done. The camp of the fierce Pequodees is no place for you.'

Oriana felt that her husband was right; and she said no more. But she did not the less sorrowfully assist him in his preparations for the journey and the battle, or feel less keenly the grief of separation when, at daybreak on the following morning, he and his warriors were ready to set out.

'My son,' said Tisquantum, as he grasped the hand of Henrich, 'I have one request — I would rather say command — to impress upon you before we part. Let it not be known in the camp that you are a pale-face. I know that your good arm will bring glory on yourself and those who follow you; and I would have that glory belong to my own people, among whom you have learned to fight. I ask it also for your own sake; for in the camp of Sassacus there may be some who regard your race with jealousy and hatred, and would not bear to see a pale-face excelling the red men. You may trust my warriors. They look on you as they would have done on my Tekoa. But you may not trust either our Indian friends, or our Indian foes.'

Henrich regarded this precaution as needless; yet, when Oriana joined her entreaties to those of her father, he readily gave the promise required. His costume and accoutrements were strictly native; and constant exposure to the air and sun had burnt his skin almost to a copper color. But his eyes were a deep blue; and his hair, though now dark, had a rich auburn glow upon it, that differed greatly from the jet black locks so universal among the Indians. To hide this, Oriana gathered it up into a knot on the top of his head in native fashion, and covered it with a close black cap. Over this his Sachem's coronet of feathers was placed; and it would have required a very scrutinising and suspicious eye to have detected the disguise. The blue eyes alone gave intimation of an European extraction; and they were so shaded by long black lashes, and had an expression so deep and penetrating, that few could discover of what color they were. The tongue of Hannah, too, had learnt to speak the Indian language with a pure, native accent, that no one could acquire who had not been brought up among the red men; so that there was little fear of his being known for a pale-face, amid the excitement and confusion of the war.

The warriors departed; and Tisquantum's party resumed their journey, though not so joyously as before their separation from those who were going to meet danger, and, perhaps, death.

With unremitting speed, the Nausett braves pursued their way, and reached the land of the Pequodees before the campaign had begun. Sassacus had, as we have seen, taken up his position in one of his boasted forts, and he wanted no reinforcements there; for his presence was regarded by his people as a panoply of strength. He, therefore, sent to desire the Nausett detachment to march to Fort Mystic, and assist the garrison there in defending it against any attack that might he made.

CHAPTER XXIII

'Merciful God! how horrible is night!

There the shout
Of battle, the barbarian yell, the bray
Of dissonant instruments, the clang of arms,
The shriek of agony, the groan of death,
In one wild uproar and continuous din,
Shake the still air; while overhead, the moon,
Regardless of the stir of this low world,
Holds on her heavenly way. MADOC.

Henrich was now called on to perform the part of an Indian leader in an Indian camp. It was no new position to him; for, during his years of wandering with the Nansetts, he had taken an active part in many of the wars that were being waged by the tribes among whom they had sojourned, against their hostile neighbors. He, therefore, was fully conversant with Indian modes of warfare; but he was as unaccustomed as his followers were to the defence of a fortress, or to a pitched battle between assembled forces in an open field.

He had not been long at Fort Mystic ere he found that he was about to be opposed to some of his own countrymen, and the information filled him with grief and dismay. It is true, he had dwelt so long among the Nausett Indians, and all his personal interests were so bound up with theirs, that he felt as if they were indeed his kindred. But still his heart yearned towards his own people and the friends of his childhood, and the idea of being instrumental in shedding the blood of a Briton was utterly repugnant to him. It was now, however, too late to retract. He had pledged his word to Tisquantum that he would lead his warriors bravely against the foes of his allies, and honor forbad him to decline the post of their Sachem and commander. He therefore concealed his scruples and anxieties in his own breast, and resolved to do what he now felt to be his duty. It was with much satisfaction that he learnt, from one of the Indian spies, that the detachment of troops from New Plymouth had been unable to join the forces of their countrymen; for thus he should be spared the trial of being placed in opposition to those with whom, perhaps, he had been brought up in childhood. Towards the other settlers be entertained a far less friendly feeling; as reports of their cruel and unjust conduct towards the natives had, from time to time, reached him during his residence in different parts of the continent.

The Pequodees and their allies treated him with respect and honor, as the representative of their ancient friend Tisquantum; and if his English blood was known to any of them, they made no remarks on the subject. They did not dare to notice what such a man as the Nausett Sachem appeared to be, chose to conceal.

But it is certain that there was one in the fortress of Mystic whose keen eye had penetrated the disguise, and to whom the features of Henrich were so familiar, that he could even read his thoughts in his open and ingenuous countenance. Coubitant was already in the castle before the Nausett detachment arrived; and, while he dexterously contrived to conceal himself from Henrich, he watched him narrowly, and his eye was on him when he first became aware that English soldiers were with the foes with whom he must contend. Then did the savage exult in the painful struggle that he could perceive the news excited in his rival's breast, and he hoped that the white Sachem would find some pretext for leaving the fort, and deserting to his own countrymen. He kept spies continually watching his every movement, with orders to allow him full liberty to escape, but to follow and secure him before his purpose could be effected, and bring him in bonds to receive from Coubitant's own hand the punishment of a coward and a deserter.

But he waited in vain for any such attempt on the part of the young Sachem. Henrich never left the fortress, and employed himself in endeavoring to keep his men from sharing in the revelry and wild security of their countrymen.

In this endeavor he had but little success, and Jyanough alone remained with his friend, and took no part in the noisy songs and dances that followed the feast, and con-tinned almost until midnight.

Then a deep and profound stillness gradually succeeded to the barbarous noises of the wild festival; and long before day-break the exhausted revellers were all buried in a heavy sleep. Even the watch, whose business it was to patrol round the fort, had that night carelessly left their respective stations, and come inside the palisades to light their pipes. Here they found none awake but the Nausett Sachem and his friend, who were slowly walking among the weary and sleeping warriors, attended only by a large and powerful dog. There was another wakeful eye in the fortress, and that was even now fixed on Henrich. Bat he whose dark soul looked forth from that singular eye, was himself concealed from view, and was intently watching the object of his hatred, and hoping that he would now attempt some act of cowardice or treachery.

Henrich and Jyanough approached the guard, who had thus thoughtlessly left their post, and desired them immediately to return to their duty. But while the men remonstrated on the uselessness of so strictly keeping a watch, now that no present attack could be expected, they were startled by the loud and furious barking of Rodolph, who had wandered to the open gate, and thus gave ominous warning of approaching danger. The terrified guard now reached to the gate, accompanied by Henrich and Jyanough, when, to their dismay, they beheld in the faint moonlight a large body of men approaching close to the fort.

They easily discerned that the foremost of the troop were Europeans; and they raised a loud cry of Owannux! Owannux!—Englishmen! Englishmen!—which quickly aroused the sleepers, and brought them towards the gate. In the next minute the fort was thickly hemmed in by the British force, and a second dense ring was formed beyond them by their Indian allies.

The main entrance was soon forced by the swords and muskets of the vigorous assailants; and, though the Pequodees fought with all the fury of despair, they were driven back, and compelled to retreat towards the wigwams. They were closely pursued by their foes; and, at length, threw themselves into the huts, which contained the terrified women and children, and resolved to defend them to the last gasp. While the murderous strife continued, the light of day began to dawn; and soon the full glow of the rising sun revealed the work that had been done in darkness. The ground was strewed with dead and dying Indians; but the band of English warriors was yet unbroken, and was fiercely bearing onward towards the wigwams. Their numbers were small, indeed, when compared with those of their opponents; but the latter had no firearms, and a panic seemed to have struck them from the force and suddenness of the attack. Still they defended the lines of wigwams with desperation, until Mason, with amazing boldness, entered one of them, and, seizing a brand from the hearth, set fire to the roof of reeds. An Indian warrior was in the act of levelling his arrow at him, when an English officer sprang forward, and cut the string of the bent bow with his sword.

This officer caught the eye of Henrich; and, though he knew not why, riveted it by a strange and unaccountable attraction. He was a noble-looking man; and, though his dark hair was slightly tinged with grey, his muscular limbs had apparently lost none of their force, and his spirit none of its courage and energy.

So fixedly was the attention of Henrich fastened on the gallant soldier, that, for a time, he was regardless of the battle that raged around him, and of the fearful conflagration that was spreading along the Indian huts. These were only composed of weed and dry moss and reeds; and the flames quickly caught hold of them, and promised soon to bring the conflict to a dreadful close.

The eye of Henrich was still fixed on that noble English officer; and the instinctive feeling of admiration and respect with which his aspect inspired him, was increased by seeing him, regardless of his own safety, actively engaged in rescuing an Indian woman and her child from a mass of burning ruins.

He had been observed by other eyes also — by eyes that recognised him, and glared with irrepressible fury as they fell on him'. An Indian warrior approached him from behind, while he was unguardedly pursuing his work of mercy; and Henrich saw the savage preparing to strike a deadly blow, that would have cleft the head of the stranger in twain. Could he stand and see the noble Briton thus fall by a secret and unresisted attack? No! every feeling and every instinct of his heart forbad it! One instant his tomahawk flew in a gleaming circle round his head; and the next it fell with crushing force on the right shoulder of the savage, and sank deeply into his chest. It was a timely blow, and saved the white man's life. But it could not save him from a severe wound in the back, where the axe of the Indian fell heavily, as his arm dropped powerlessly by his side — never to be raised again.

Coubitant sank on the ground; and, as he turned to look on his unexpected assailant, his blood-shot eyes met those of Henrich, and glared fiercely, first at him, and then at his intended victim, whose life had been so strangely preserved. They stood side by side, unconscious of the tie that bound them so closely together. Coubitant knew it well; and he felt in this awful moment that Mahneto had, in righteous retribution, sent the son to preserve the father's life from the hand of him who had hated both alike. He hated them still: and, even with his dying breath, he would not reveal the secret that would have united those seemingly hostile warriors in the embrace of deep affection.

Rodolph had not seen the friend whose timely aid had partially averted the deadly blow that had been aimed at him by the savage. But, on turning round, he was astonished to perceive that his foe and his avenger were apparently of the same party. The latter — whose countenance expressed the deepest indignation, and who was raising his bloody hatchet from the prostrate form of the wounded Indian — was evidently not one of the allies of the English; and his dress and ornaments, and air of dignified command, indicated him to be a Chief among his own people. Why, then, had he come to the aid of an enemy?

Rodolph gazed inquiringly at the fine countenance of the young Sachem, which was now bent upon the dying Indian at his feet.

'Coubitant!' he exclaimed in the Nausett tongue, is it, indeed, you whom I have thus slain unknowingly? You have been a bitter and an untiring enemy to me; but it was not for this that I smote thee to the earth. I knew you not. But I saw you aim a cowardly blow at the white chief; and I saved him. I forgive you now for all your hatred, and all your evil designs, which Mahneto has thus recompensed upon your own head.'

'I ask not your forgiveness,' replied the savage in a deep, struggling voice—for the hand of death was on him, and the dark fire of his eye was waning out. 'In death, I hate and defy you! And in death I enjoy a revenge that you know not of.'

He strove to raise his hand in menace, but it fell to the ground; and, with a groan of suppressed agony, he expired.

The fight was raging with unabated violence, and the conflagration had already spread to the farthest end of the fortress. Henrich looked around for his comrades, who were bravely contending with their powerful foes at some distance, and he hastily prepared to join them. But, as he turned away, he courteously waved his hand to Rodolph, and said in the English language, but with an Indian accent,

'Farewell, brave Englishman!'

Rodolph started. That voice had thrilled through his heart when it had spoken a strange language: but now it struck upon him with a sense of familiarity that be could not account for, as the Indian Chief was evidently an utter stranger to him. He returned his parting salutation and 'farewell'; but still he watched his retreating form, and thought he distinctly heard him utter the name 'Rodolph!' as a large dog, which had stood near him during their brief encounter, bounded after him over foe heaps of slain and dying.

'Surely it was my own fancy that conjured up that name,' thought Rodolph. The next moment he found himself compelled again to join the conflict, and, at the head of his little band, to fight his way out of the fortress, which was rapidly becoming a prey to the devouring flames. All the English withdrew outside the palisades, and thickly surrounded the fort; while their Indian allies, who had hitherto kept aloof, now took courage to approach, and form a second circle outside. The most furious despair now took possession of the souls of the devoted Pequodees: and their terrible war-cry was heard resounding high, and mingled with the agonising yells of the women and children, and helpless aged men, who were expiring amid the flames. Many of the warriors climbed the palisades, and leaped down among their foes, hoping to escape; but they were quickly despatched by the muskets and bayonets of the English; or if any had power to break through the first hostile line, they fell beneath the battle-axes of the Mohicans.

Rodolph had received a considerable wound, but it had not entirely disabled him. At the head of his men he passed through the open gate of the fortress, and attempted still to lead and command them. He found, however that his strength was failing, and that he could no longer wield his good broad sword. He therefore stood leaning on it, and watching, with mingled feelings of pity and horror, the progress of the work of destruction.

Presently he saw a side entrance to the fort thrown suddenly open, and the form of the Indian Chief—whose tomahawk had saved his life, and whose voice had awakened such strange feelings—appeared rushing forth. He was attended by another striking looking warrior, and followed by a band of determined natives, who were resolved to escape, or sell their lives dearly.

Rodolph's men, who occupied the position opposite to that gate, raised their muskets to fire on these brave men; but their commander loudly and authoritatively bade them desist.

'Hold! I command you!' he exclaimed. 'Let that noble Chieftain escape, and all his attendants for his sake. He saved my life in the fort; and death to the man who injures him!

He attempted to rush forward to enforce his orders, but pain and loss of blond prevented him from moving; and he would have fallen but for the support of one of his comrades.

Meanwhile, Henrich and Jyanough, and their band of Nausetts, had rushed through the unopposing ranks of the English, and were now contending desperately with the Indian line beyond. The British troops paused, and looked after them; and the sympathy that brave men feel for each other prevented any of them from attempting to pursue or molest them. On the contrary, all now wished them success.

With breathless anxiety Rodolph gazed after them, and watched the towering plumes that adorned the noble head of the Sachem, as he bore onward through the opposing crowd of Indians. He passed, and gained the plain beyond, attended by his followers; and, from the elevated position at which the fort was erected, Rodolph could still watch the little band retiring, until the Indian heroes were hidden from view by a thicket.

So fiercely had the fire seconded the efforts of the English that the whole conflict only lasted one hour. In that brief space of time, between five and six hundred Indians—young and old, men and women— were destroyed by fire and sword; and the small remainder were made prisoners of war by the English, or carried off as prizes by the hostile natives. Only two of the British soldiers were slain, but many were wounded; and the arrows remaining some time in the wounds, and the want of necessary medicine and refreshment, added greatly to their sufferings The medical attendants attached to the expedition, and the provisions, had all been left in the boats, and a march of more than six miles through their enemies' land was necessary, in order to reach them.

Litters were therefore constructed and, in these, the wounded were sent off under the charge of the Mohicans, while the able-bodied men, whose number was reduced to little more than forty, prepared to follow as a rear-guard. The whole party were still near the smoking ruins of the fort, when they were startled by perceiving a large body of armed natives approaching. These were a band of more than three hundred Pequodees, sent by Sassacus to aid the garrison of Fort Mystic. Happily, they did not discover the small number of the English who were in a condition to oppose them, and they turned aside, and avoided a re-encounter. The white men took advantage of this mistake on the part of their enemies, and hastened forward with all the speed that circumstances would allow.

But they had not proceeded far when their ears were assailed by the most discordant yells from the Pequodees. They had reached the scene of devastation; and, when they beheld the ruined fort, and the ground strewn with hundreds of mangled corpses and expiring friends, their fury knew no bounds. They stamped and howled with rage and grief, and madly tore their hair; while they gave vent to their excited feelings in that fearful and peculiar yell, at the sound of which the stoutest hearts might quail. Then, with a wild and desperate effort at revenge, they rushed down the bill in pursuit of their cruel enemies. The rear- guard turned, and met the onset bravely. The savages were received with a shower of bullets, which checked their furious assault; but they hung on the rear of the English, and harassed them during the whole of their retreat. They, however, reached their vessels in safety, and arrived in triumph at Hartford, from which port they had sailed three weeks before.

This discomfiture proved a death-blow to the pride and power of the redoubted Sassacus. Disgusted alike by his arrogance, and by his recent defeat, many of his own warriors deserted him and attached themselves to other tribes; and the Sachem then destroyed his second fortress, end carried off his treasure to the land of the Mohawks, near the river Hudson, and, with his principal Chiefs, joined that warlike race.

Meanwhile, the remainder of the troops from Massachusetts, whom the Government had not thought it necessary to send with Captain Mason, had landed at Saybroke, led by Captain Houghton, and attended by Wilson as their spiritual guide. They arrived just in time to hear of the successful issue of the campaign; and had, therefore, nothing left for them to do, except to join a small band from Connecticut, and keep down or destroy the few Pequodees, or other hostile Indians who still lurked about the district, and kept the settlers in fear and anxiety. These wretched natives were chased into their most secret haunts, where they were barbarously slain; their wigwams were burnt, and their fields desolated. Nor were the English the only foes of the once terrible Pequodees. Their Indian rivals took advantage of their present weak and scattered condition, to wreak upon them the suppressed vengeance of bygone years; and pursued, with ruthless cruelty, those whose very name had once inspired them with awe and dread. And yet — with shame be it said! — the *Christian* leader of the troops of Massachusetts, himself a member of the strict and exclusive Church of Boston, surpassed these savages in cruelty.

On one occasion, he made prisoners of nearly a hundred Pequodees. Of these miserable creatures he sent the wives and children into servitude at Boston, while he caused the men — thirty-seven in number — to be bound hand and foot, and carried in a shallop outside the harbor, where they wore thrown overboard. If this barbarous deed was not committed by the directions of the *Christian* Fathers of Massachusetts, yet they certainly neither disclaimed nor censured it. Indeed, so little were cruelty and oppression, when exercised against the red men, regarded as crimes by many of the settlers, that one of their learned divines, even of the age succeeding the perpetrations of the above appalling event, expressed it as his opinion that Heaven had smiled on the English *hunt;* and added, with horrible and disgusting levity, 'that it was found to be the quickest way *feed the fishes* with the multitude of Indian captives!'

The other tribes who had joined the Pequodees in opposing the conquering white men, were pardoned on their submission; but that devoted race, who fought like heroes to the very last, were extirpated as a nation from the face of the earth. The very name in which they had so long gloried, and which had been a terror to all the neighboring tribes, was not permitted to remain, and to tell where once they had dwelt and reigned unrivalled. The river, which had been called the Pequod, received the appellation of the Thames; and the native township, on the ruins of which an English settlement was founded, was afterwards called New London. Numbers of the women and boys, who were taken captive from tune to time by the British troops, were sold and carried as slaves to Bermuda, and others were divided among the settlers, and condemned — not *nominally to slavery,* for that was forbidden by the laws of New England, but — to *perpetual servitude,* which must, indeed, have been much the same thing to free-born Indian spirits, accustomed to the wild liberty of the forests and the prairies.

Sassacus—the once mighty Chief of this mighty and heroic people—was basely slain by the Mohawks, among whom he had sought fellowship and protection, for the sake of the treasures that be had brought with him from his own lost dominions; and his heart was sent by his murderers as a peace-offering to the government of Connecticut.

Thus ended the war which had been commenced as a necessary measure of self-defence, and in which the pious and high-minded Roger Williams had, at first, taken so active and influential a part. The manner in which it was carried out, and the cruelty that marked so many of its details, were repulsive in the highest degree to his just and benevolent spirit; but where mercy was concerned, his opinion and advice had no influence with the stern men of Boston. The only act which met with his approbation in the conclusion of the campaign, was the assignment of the depopulated lands of the Pequodees to Uncas, the Chief of the Mohicans. As being a conquered territory, the usual laws of war would have annexed it to the territory of the victors. But, in this case, the settlers adhered to their original principle of only obtaining, by purchase from the natives, those tracts of land on which they desired to settle; and a great part of that which was now bestowed on Uncas, was afterwards bought back from him and his inferior Sachems, or obtained by friendly contract, until the English became possessors of the whole district.

At a subsequent period, the Pequodees who had escaped from their desolated land, and joined other tribes, assembled themselves together, and made one final effort at establishing their independence in a distant part of the country. But their power and prosperity were broken for ever. Captain Mason was again sent to subdue this remnant of the tribe; and the destruction that was accomplished on these unhappy exiles spread a fear of the white men through all the Indian race in that part of the continent. From that time the settlers of Connecticut—who had been the original cause of this cruel war—enjoyed an unbroken peace and security for forty years.

CHAPTER XXIV

'The voices of my home! I hear them still!
They have been with me through the stormy night—
The blessed household voices wont to fill
My hearts clear depths with unalloyed delight!
I hear them still unchanged; though some from earth
Are music parted, and the tones of mirth—
Wild silvery tones, that rang through days more bright,
Have died in others—yet to me they come
Singing of boyhood back!—the voices of my home!' HEMANS.

One Sabbath evening, a few months after the events related in the last chapter, and when the short second Indian summer, that so often returns late in the month of September, was at its height, the inhabitants of New Plymouth were assembled at their meeting-house on 'the Burying Hill,' and engaged at their usual devotions. None were left in their dwellings except those whom age or sickness prevented from joining the rest of the congregation, or those who were necessarily detained by the care of young children.

The habitation of Rodolph Maitland was, therefore, deserted by all but Janet, who would gladly have gone that evening to listen to the husband of her young mistress; for Roger Williams was to lead the prayers of the congregation, and to deliver to them the customary address. But Ediths little girl demanded her care; and old Janet took too much pride and pleasure in the interesting child to repine at having the charge of her, even though it prevented her from attending at the meeting-house on the first occasion of Roger's officiating there since his marriage.

Little Edith was just beginning to walk alone, and it was her delight to play in the bright sunny garden, and pluck the gay flowers that still bloomed there in profusion. She was thus engaged, and murmuring a sweet but inarticulate song that her mother had attempted to teach her, when Janet, apprehending no danger, returned for a moment to the house, to perform some domestic duty.

Just then a stranger, followed by a large dog, entered the garden by the wicket gate that led towards the forest, and stood silently gazing around him, without at first observing the happy and occupied child. He was tall and of a commanding appearance; and his costume, which was richly ornamented in the Indian fashion, bespoke him to be a native of high rank. But had any one closely examined his countenance, they would have discovered beneath those long dark lashes, and clearly marked eyebrows, the deep blue eye of the Saxon race, which was also indicated by the rich brown hair, that, now unconcealed, waved across his manly forehead. A keen eye would also have detected on the features of that seeming Indian Sachem an expression of deep thought and strong emotion, that told of old remembrances not yet obliterated, and of feelings that belonged to home and kindred.

Yes! Henrich was, indeed, absorbed in those recollections that were revived in his breast by the sight of objects once so familiar, but which many years had elapsed since last he had looked on. Much was changed: but much was still the same. The rude hut commodious log-house that once stood on that site was now replaced by a substantial and picturesque dwelling in the Elizabethan style of architecture, whose deep bay windows were hung with the sweet single roses that were natives of the woods, and other flowering plants; while wreaths of the well-known Virginian creeper, now glowing in its scarlet hue of autumn, climbed to the summit of the carved gables and pinnacles that ornamented the building, and hung from thence in rich festoons.

On the front of this dwelling the evening sun fell brightly, and its slanting beams likewise partially illuminated the garden with long streaks of light, while other parts were thrown into strong shadow by the trees and shrubs that grew among the flower-beds. One of these—a noble tulip-tree—rose in the centre of the enclosure and stretched its giant arms wide on every side. On this tree the eyes of the wanderer rested long; and then he approached it, and stood looking wistfully towards a bower that was situated near the old tree, and over which the creepers fell in wild luxuriance.

Was it a tear that glittered in that warlike stranger's eye, as a ray from the western sun fell on his face through the thick overhanging foliage? And did those manly limbs tremble as he clasped his hands over his face, and sank on the rustic seat beneath the tulip-tree?

'I cannot enter the house!' he exclaimed, in a low voice. 'I cannot seek those loved ones there where once we dwelt in happiness together; and where, perhaps, none now remain to welcome the wanderer home! O, that some one would appear who might tell me of their fate!'

Henrich spoke to himself in his native tongue. He could not speak a strange language in that old familiar spot; and his voice attracted the notice of the little girl, who was now slowly moving towards him, her hands filled with the spoils of the flower-beds. She stopped, and gazed at the stranger, and then uttered a faint cry of fear that at once roused Henrich from his reverie. His eyes fell on the lovely child, and instantly his memory recalled the features and expression of his brother Ludovico, to whom the little Edith bore a strong resemblance.

With an irresistible impulse he sprang forward, and caught the little girl in his arms, and sought, by caresses, to soothe her fears, and hush her cries of terror. But those cries had caught the watchful ear of Janet; and, with all the speed that she could use, she came running from the house, merely anticipating that her charge had fallen down, or was alarmed at finding herself alone.

What was, then, her terror and amazement at seeing her in the arms of an Indian! One instant she stood rivetted to the spot, not knowing how to act. The next she turned, and again hurried in to the house, from whence she escaped by a back door, and sped breathlessly towards 'the Burying Hill.'

She knew that the service was over — for the last strains of the parting hymn had been borne down by the evening breeze as she left the house — and therefore she would find help and succor from the returning congregation. That deep, melodious sound had been heard by Henrich also; and it had struck a chord in his heart that vibrated almost to agony. The stillness and abstraction of his look, as he listened to the dying cadence, silenced the cries of the little child. She gazed into his upturned eyes; and, possibly, she felt that those eyes had an expression that was neither strange nor terrible — for now she suffered the stranger to seat himself again on the bench beneath the tulip tree, and place her gently on his knee.

Such was the picture that met the eyes of Edith, and her husband, and parents, as they rushed into the garden, followed by the trembling and exhausted Janet.

'My child! my Edith! shrieked the young mother and sprang towards the tree. That name told a long history to the wanderer which his heart had already guessed. The Indian warrior rose, but he did not fly. No! he only met the terrified mother; and as he placed her child in her trembling arms, he folded them both in his own.

In amazement and indignation at this rude action, Roger now caught his arm, and in the Indian tongue, inquired hastily —

'Who are you? and what can cause this freedom?'

I am Henrich Maitland!' exclaimed the stranger; 'and the Lord has brought me back to my home once more.'

Oh, the music — the thrilling, startling music — of those words to the ears and hearts of those who bad so long believed him dead! The surprise and joy were too intense for Helen, and she sank fainting into the arms of her long-lost son: while Rodolph grasped his hand, and exclaimed with deep emotion —

'Now, God be praised! my brave, my blessed son! Surely His mercies are infinite, and His ways past finding out! Now I know why my heart yearned so strangely towards the Indian Chief who saved my life in the

Fort of Mystic; and why his voice had such a thrilling and familiar tone, that spoke of home, and bygone years. Look on me, my Henrich, and say, do you not recognise the English soldier whom your generous interference preserved from a dreadful death?'

The change in Rodolph's dress, and his own overpowering emotions, had hitherto prevented Henrich from discovering that, in the noble-looking man whom he was proud to call his father, he also beheld that gallant British officer whose appearance had so powerfully attracted him in the conflict of Fort Mystic. But when he looked into that fine countenance, he well remembered every feature; and he wondered why he, had not known him, even when they met so unexpectedly in the excitement of the battle.

That was a happy hour; and, in the joy of meeting so many that he loved, Henrich for awhile forgot that any one was missing. But soon be looked around, as if seeking some familiar object, which did not meet his eye. He feared to ask for Ludovico: but his father saw the inquiring look, and guessed its import.

'He is gone!' he said, gently. 'Your brother did not remain with us long after you had left us; and his young spirit is now where we believed that yours had long been dwelling in peace. He would have rejoiced to see this day, dear Henrich; for he, as well as Edith, mourned your loss sincerely. But he is happy now, and we will not regret him. The Lord has restored to us one of our sons in a manner so strange, and under such extraordinary circumstances, that we can hardly realise the blessing. Tell us, Henrich, how this has been brought about.'

The violent agitation occasioned by such a meeting had now somewhat subsided; and the wanderer could calmly relate the story of his adventures, while his mother and sister sat on each side of him, gazing fondly at his much-changed, but still familiar countenance; and the scarcely less interested Janet seated herself on the turf, with little Edith on her knees. Rodolph and Roger Williams also reclined on the ground, and all were impatient for the narrative.

'Our group is not complete,' said Henrich. 'Come hither, Rodolph!' And then, addressing his dog in the Indian language, he made him lie down at his feet.

'Then my ears did not deceive me?' exclaimed Maitland. 'When you left me, Henrich, in the midst of that fearful fray, I thought I heard you pronounce my name; and the sound startled me strangely. Have you, then, called your unconscious companion by your father's name; and in all your wanderings, and your trials, and temptations, has that name been dear to you?'

Heaven only knows *how* dear! replied the Sachem. The remembrance of my parents, and all they taught me in my childhood, has been not only my joy and consolation, but my safeguard also. You will find me very unlearned and ignorant in all worldly knowledge, for I have had no means of keeping up the little I had acquired. But, God be praised! I have been kept from forgetting Him, and the Saviour in whom you taught me to put my trust. Nor have I been quite alone in my faith. One there is of whom I shall have much to tell you in the course of my history, who has been, and is, my spiritual companion and support. I have had many blessings!'

'How truly is it declared, "Not by might, nor by power, but by my Spirit, saith the Lord"!' exclaimed Helen, as she raised her eyes in grateful gratitude to Heaven. Now she and Rodolph felt that they had, *indeed*, recovered their lost son—not for time alone, but for eternity.

Henrich's long and adventurous story was told: and so many were the questions and the comments that it called forth, that long are it was finished the light of day had all departed, and been replaced by the softer rays of the unclouded moon. It was with mingled feelings of disappointment and of gratitude, that Henrich's friends heard of his marriage with an Indian female. But as he described her character, and spoke of her sincere and humble faith, and of all that she had been to him since the first day of his captivity, they became more than reconciled to the alliance, and thanked God who had so mercifully provided their son with such a friend and companion, to cheer his otherwise lonely life. They, and Edith also, felt impatient to become acquainted with this new relative, whom they were already prepared to love; and, as she was now dwelling near Cape Cod with her father and the rest of her tribe, they hoped to do so before the winter set in.

Henrich promised that this hope should be compiled with; but it was a source of sorrow and disappointment to his family, when they heard that he was pledged to the aged Tisquantum never to take his only and beloved child from him as long as he lived. He could not, therefore, at present change his mode of life, or take up his abode at New Plymouth but must return to dwell with his Indian friends, and fill the place of Tisquantum's son and representative, until the old man should be gathered to his fathers.

The days that Henrich passed in the home of his childhood flew rapidly away. All his old friends gathered around him to welcome him on his unexpected return, and to offer their congratulations to his happy parents and sister. The joy of the venerable Brewster at again beholding his young friend and pupil, and at finding him still a sincere and intelligent Christian, was very great; and even among those who had never known him, his adventurous story, and his frank and engaging manners, excited the deepest interest. Between himself and his brother-in-law, Roger Williams, a strong and lasting friendship was established; and when the time arrived for Henrich to return to Paomet, Roger proposed to accompany him, and assist in escorting his wife and child to pay their promised visit to New Plymouth. This offer was gladly accepted; and the English minister and the Indian Chief set out on foot. The journey was comparatively easy to men who had long been accustomed to such toils and difficulties as both Henrich and Roger had, for years, been inured to, and they reached Paomet very quickly.

But sorrow met them there. The first sound that fell on their ears as they approached the village was the Indian dirge for a departing soul. Henrich listened for a moment to catch the exact direction from whence the ominous sound proceeded, and then darted forward with such velocity, that Roger, active as he was, could with difficulty follow him. Henrich hastened towards a large dwelling at the upper end of the village; and entering the low door, he beheld a sight which, though it filled his heart with unaffected grief, was yet, in some sense, a relief to his fears.

It was not for his wife or child that the wail was being made. It was Tisquantum who lay on the bed of death, and who turned his dim and sunken eyes towards him as he passed the threshold. The old man smiled a joyful welcome, and held out his trembling hand to greet him. And Oriana — who was seated on the ground by her father's bedside, in an attitude of deep and silent sorrow — sprang to her feet with a cry of joy, and throwing herself into her husband's arms, burst into a flood of long-suppressed tears.

'You are come at lest,' she exclaimed. 'You are come in time to see my father die, and to receive his blessing. O, Henrich! how I have hoped end preyed for your return. I feared you would be too late; and my beloved father has something to confide to you — I know he has — which will fill your soul with joy. Father,' she continued, in a calmer voice, as she led Henrich to his side, and joined their hands in her own — ' Father, say those blessed words again. Tell your son that you believe and love the Christian's God, and that you desire to die in this faith.'

Henrich was surprised. He had not hoped that Tisquantum had been thus far influenced by what he had seen and heard of the Christian religion, and his joy was equal to his astonishment.

He looked inquiringly at the old Chief's countenance, and pressed his withered hand. At length, in a feeble, but calm and decided voice, Tisquantum spoke.

'My son, it is true. I have observed and listened, but I have held my peace. When you were a boy, you talked to me of the Christian's God, and I smiled in my soul at your ignorance. Then I found that you believed in the Great Mahneto, and I was satisfied. But for years I have studied your character, to find out why, young as you were, I felt for you a respect that I never felt for any human being except my own heroic father. At last, I understood that it was because your religion made you true, and brave, and good, and kept you from committing any of the crimes that I saw others guilty of. If all your nation acted as you have done, Henrich, their coming to this land would have proved a blessing indeed to the red men, and our people would not hate them, and seek to destroy them, as I once sought to do. But enough of this. My strength is failing. Henrich, your example has taught me that your God is holy, and just, and good; it has made me feel the truth of the Christian's religion.'

Tears of humble joy and gratitude glistened in Henrich's eyes at this confession. He knelt beside the dying convert, and bowed his head upon the bed; but his heart was too full to allow him to express his thanksgivings audibly. Oriana was equally affected; but another form knelt beside them, and another deep rich voice arose in prayer, which was uttered fluently in the Indian language, and in which the hearts of all present joined fervently, although the speaker was a stranger to all but Henrich.

It was Roger Williams, who had been an unobserved witness of the foregoing deeply interesting scene, and had listened, with deep and grateful emotion, to the words of the expiring Chief. He now spoke the feelings of all his auditors, and, with his wonted power and eloquence, poured forth a fervent prayer for the aged 'babe in Christ,' and blessed the God of all spirits that it had pleased Him, even 'in the eleventh hour,' to call the heathen Chief into the fold of Christ.

When his prayer was finished, Henrich presented his friend and brother to his father-in-law, and told him that, from his lips, he might bear all that one of the Lord's most zealous and devoted ministers could tell him of holy and eternal things. Gladly the old man availed himself of this opportunity of obtaining instruction, end being prepared for what he now earnestly desired — an admittance by baptism into the once despised religion of the white men.

For this task no man was more fitted than Roger Williams. He well knew how to deal with Indian prejudices, and bow to call forth the affections, by the relation of the simple and touching truths of the gospel. Tisquantum heard with a willing and teachable spirit, and he believed, and was at peace. His life was rapidly ebbing away, and no time was to be lost; for though he rallied a little after the arrival of Henrich and Roger, it was evident that his time on earth could only be counted by hours.

The following morning, therefore, at his own earnest desire, he was baptised by Williams, in the presence of his rejoicing children, and of Jyanough and Mailah, who formed a little congregation of sincere Christians in the midst of an heathen population.

The venerable Chieftain did not long survive his admission into the pale of the visible church of Christ. His strength faded hour by hour; but he was calm and collected to the last. He gave to Henrich all his parting directions for the government of his people, if he still continued to live among them, and to be their Sachem. 'But,' he added, 'I know that your heart is with your own people, and that you desire to return to your former home. I cannot blame you; for I well know the yearning of spirit that draws a man to his kindred, and to his fathers house. And Oriana will go with you, and make your home and your people her own. If this is to be, then let Jyanough be Sachem in your stead. He also is just and upright, and will guide my warriors with courage and wisdom. There is none besides yourself to whom I could so confidently leave them. And now, farewell, my children! May the good God in whom you trust receive my sinful soul for His Son's sake; and may his blessing rest on those who have led me into the truth.'

Tisquantum had been supported in his bed, while he thus took leave of his sorrowing relatives and friends. He now lay down, and never rose again. Neither did he utter many more words; but lay as if engaged in thought and prayer, and occasionally fixed his failing eyes with fond affection on his child and Henrich. At length they gently closed, and the venerable old Chief slept the sleep of death.

Oriana's grief was deep and sincere, for she had loved her father almost passionately; but she did not now 'sorrow as those without hope'; and, ere long, she was calm. The funeral was conducted in the simple manner of the Puritans; and all Tisquantum's warriors stood respectfully and silently round his grave, while Williams addressed them in their own language, and exhorted them to follow the example of their departed Chief, and examine the faith of the Christians, and embrace it to the salvation of their souls.

Not long after the death of Tisquantum, and before the severity of winter prevented the journey being practicable, Henrich and his wife took leave of the Nausetts, and of their Christian friends, Jyanough and Mailah; and, accompanied by Roger Williams, and two or three Indian attendants who desired to follow their fortunes, took their way towards New Plymouth. Their departure from Paomet was much regretted, for they were greatly beloved by the red men. But the promotion of Jyanough to the Chieftainship gave general satisfaction; and there were even some who thought it was more consistent with their dignity and independence, to be governed by one of their own race, rather than by a pale-face, let his personal qualities he ever so estimable.

Henrich's heart beat high when he again arrived at his father's dwelling, and presented his wife and child to his parents and his sister. He cast searching glances at their countenances, to read their feelings at thus greeting an *Indian* as their near relative; but he saw no expression that could give him pain. On the contrary, the native grace and beauty of Oriana, and the gentle refinement of her manner, evidently struck them with surprise and pleasure, and made upon them all a most favorable impression. Nor did a further acquaintance lessen this kindly feeling. It was impossible to know Oriana, and not to love her; and she was soon regarded as a daughter and a sister by all her husband's relatives; while the young Ludovico was cherished and caressed by all the household, and by none more than by his little cousin Edith.

The Maitlands were now a happy family; and when, in the ensuing spring, their daughter and her husband again left them to return to their distant home at Providence, they felt they had still a daughter left to them in the Indian wife of their beloved Henrich. This long-lost son did not again leave them, except to pay occasional visits with Oriana to their Nausett friends. But he fixed his permanent home at Plymouth, where his knowledge of the Indian language and manners, and the influence he continued to possess among the Nausetts and other neighboring tribes, enabled him frequently to render important services both to his own countrymen, and the red natives. His own merits, likewise, won for him the love and respect of the settlers of New Plymouth, who appreciated the unaffected devotion, and the simple truthfulness, of his character; and felt that such men as Rodolph Maitland and his son added glory to the history of 'the Pilgrim Fathers.'